WHEELING AND DEALING

An Ethnography of an
Upper-Level Drug Dealing
and Smuggling Community

Second Edition

PATRICIA A. ADLER

COLUMBIA UNIVERSITY PRESS
NEW YORK

Columbia University Press
New York   Chichester, West Sussex
Copyright © 1993 Columbia University Press

Library of Congress Cataloging in Publication Data

Adler, Patricia A.
Wheeling and dealing.—2nd ed.

Bibliography: p.
Includes index.
1. Narcotics, Control of.   2. Smuggling.   3. Marijuana.
4. Cocaine.   I. Title.
HV5801.A282   1993   364.1'77   85-2644
ISBN 0-231-08132-4 (alk. paper)
ISBN 0-231-08133-2 (pa.)

Casebound editions of Columbia University Press books are Smyth-sewn and printed on
permanent and durable acid-free paper.

Printed in the United States of America

c 10 9 8 7 6 5 4 3 2 1
p 10 9 8 7 6 5 4 3 2 1

TO PETE
My Partner in
Work, Love, and Life

CONTENTS

PREFACE TO THE
SECOND EDITION

In the 1970s I had the good fortune to befriend a group of people engaged in a rather risky, and illegal, occupation. Along with my husband, Peter Adler, I became friends with our next-door neighbor, gaining access through him to a whole community of upper-level marijuana and cocaine dealers and smugglers. This book describes what I found in this hidden drug subculture, from the easy money, to the casual sex, the vast drug consumption, the big deals, the hopes, the dreams, and the nightmares. People have found this book of interest, partly, because of its descriptions and analyses of this rarely seen world, bringing with it answers to questions about recruitment, community, lifestyle, motivation, relations to law enforcement, and retirement. These traffickers embodied an ironic paradox, as they were caught in the contradiction of trying to work rationally in order to live hedonistically and irrationally. *Wheeling and Dealing*'s contribution to the field of sociology also derives from its theoretical explanation of this deviant behavior as based on a search for thrill-seeking, emotionality, spontaneity, and other expressive concerns. This portrayal of a subculture of hedonism fit well within a national culture that glorifies mergers and acquisitions, lifestyles of the rich and famous, and the entrepreneurial spirit fostered by a deregulated business climate.

Over the last ten years significant changes have rocked our national climate, affecting cultural attitudes toward the lifestyle, business practices, and product associated with my subjects. The "me" orientation of the 1980s has been replaced with a call to public service, the barons of Wall Street have fallen, and a new sobriety has arisen. Trends in the 1970s to decriminalize drugs have given way to new social meanings and social movements fostering a political and behavioral conservatism. Yesterday's "head" is today's substance abuser, yesterday's "stud" is today's disease carrier, yesterday's "Marlboro Man" is today's polluter. Recriminalization movements have sprung up in several of the eleven states where possession of small amounts of marijuana had once been reduced to the status of a traffic offense. These trends are all part of a moral agenda condemning and evoking greater governmental control over pleasure-seeking behavior.

Social attitudes and meanings within drug subcultures have shifted as well. Southwest County smugglers used to be able to rationalize their behavior by analogizing it to the bootleggers of the 1920s. This technique was moderately successful when their product was socially acceptable to a sizable segment of the population. But "expert" medical and criminological testimony has been evoked in the campaign to shift social attitudes, bringing a new wave of puritanism to American society. Public attitudes no longer consider drugs either a vehicle for self-expansion or the personal prerogative of the user. Rather, they are viewed as malevolent, the first step toward the destruction of society's moral, economic, and social order. Even drug traffickers now have to contend among themselves with the fact that their product is highly stigmatized and socially disapproved.

Within this changed social context, a reexamination of the dealing and smuggling scene seemed valuable. For this purpose I returned to Southwest County to see if I could find any of my former subjects. I was able to speak to, trace the whereabouts of, or find out some information about thirteen people I had known, none of whom were still actively dealing. Yet their current activities shed further light on the types of career paths these people followed, the consequences they experienced from years spent in drug trafficking, and their varying ability to become reintegrated into society.

For this revised edition I have added two new chapters. In chapter 9 I report the findings of my follow-up study of my former subjects and assess the affects on their lives of ten or more years out of the mainstream, ensconced in the drug community and the fast life. Readers may be particularly interested to know where they are now and what means of earning a living they have pursued. I discuss this, along with some comments on the factors that affected their reintegration back into conventional society and the legitimate economy. These reintegrations should be seen, I argue, as a continuance of the deviant career, as they are substantially influenced by the individuals' past activities and represent the more comprehensive transition out of deviance.

In chapter 10 I offer a comprehensive review of the recent literature on drug trafficking in America, from both the lower to the upper levels, including both part- and full-time modes of operation. Based on both my and others' research, I believe that the basic forms of dealing and smuggling described in this book, along with the subculture and lifestyle associated with its subjects, remain a fairly valid depiction of drug trafficking. Changes have occurred, from the greater incursion of international elements into the drug trade, to shifts in the kinds of drugs currently popular (which has also affected the transformation of public attitudes toward drug use). Yet a core of American entrepreneurs remain actively involved in drug trafficking, and embrace the lifestyle, motivations, organizational forms, and careers described in this book. Chapter 10 also contains a specific discussion of shifts in drug usage patterns over the ten years since the first edition, and a review of the history of drug legislation and enforcement in America from 1965 to 1990. I lay this out against changes in the social organization of drug trafficking over that same time period. This comparison enables readers to see the intricate patterns in the relationship between law enforcement, market dynamics, and the character and form of both international and domestic drug trafficking. I argue that our national drug policy has had several unanticipated consequences, fostering developments that our government precisely sought to prevent.

I hope that readers will continue to find this work both informative and topical, and that the added material enhances a broader understanding of the political, social, and historical context surrounding both this and other forms of drug trafficking in America.

ACKNOWLEDGMENTS

Nearly ten years have passed from the original inception of this project to its final completion. Certainly, when something takes as much time and energy out of one's life as this has of mine, it could not be done alone. In the last decade I have been aided and encouraged by numerous people who stood behind me to make sure that I did, indeed, finish. Most critically, I want to thank my respondents, who sometimes took great risks in order to help me.

The support of my teacher, mentor, friend, and colleague, Jack Douglas, was instrumental in each phase of the research and writing. Jack was there when I first had the idea to make this subculture an object of sociological analysis. Through his close personal contact, joint involvement, and guidance during my early years in the setting, he developed my instinct and appreciation for investigative participant observation as both a science and an art form. He then pushed me, cajoled me, and backed me at times when the research became either too dangerous, too confusing, or too troublesome to continue. But most important, the tremendous impact that his own life's work has had on me guides everything I have done and will continue to do in sociology. Fred Davis, another member of the sociology faculty at the University of California, San Diego, served as a stalwart supporter, certain of my abilities and confident in my ambitions. He never questioned whether I would finish, as others did, but provided unerring impetus and prodding to make sure that I forged ahead. Cesar Graña allowed me to pursue a topic that others found strange, worthless, or petty. He permitted me the latitude to explore this scene as I thought best. I also received intellectual, emotional, and material support from other members of the UCSD community, especially Renee Anspach, Rae Blumberg, Ginny Forrest-Madison, and Jacqueline Wiseman.

Throughout my years in sociology, I have been blessed with knowing a number of people whose friendships prove to be the most im-

xiv   ACKNOWLEDGMENTS

portant reason why I remain so excited about my work and the discipline in general. Scholars such as John Johnson, Peter Manning,
Marvin Scott, and Lou Zurcher have delighted and inspired me with
the vitality of their human contact as well as their creative sociological
enterprise. Others, such as that small group of existential sociologists,
David Altheide, Andy Fontana, Joe Kotarba, Paul Rasmussen, and
Carol Warren, share with me the joy of searching for people's feelings
and subjective understandings. I have also been profoundly moved or
influenced along the way theoretically and/or personally by Marvin
Cummins, Murray Davis, Gary Fine, Ruth Horowitz, John Irwin, Carl
Klockars, Stan Lyman, David Pittman, Craig Reinarman, Marsha
Rosenbaum, David Snow, Malcolm Spector, and Dan Waldorf. Friends,
such as Jim Morgan, Heidi Glow, and John Gundersen, who are not
sociologists but have a great understanding of the human condition,
helped lend a different kind of "optic" to the final analysis.

   In completing this project, I have had the good fortune of being
surrounded by a vibrant group of people in the Department of Sociology at the University of Tulsa. Jean Blocker, Jean Burfoot, Douglas
Eckberg, Barry Kinsey, and Burke Rochford remind me often of how
we, as a discipline, can continue to be creative. Their enthusiasm for
sociology has been infectious and has kept me going. I want to especially thank Tom Staley, Provost of the University of Tulsa, a colleague and a friend, who acted on blind faith in giving me financial
and emotional support. Kelly Peterson helped to coordinate administrative tasks in the final stages of the project.

   There have been several people from the publishing community who
have been noteworthy for their interest and fellowship throughout this
project. Herb Johnson of JAI Press, John Tryneski of the University
of Chicago Press, and John Moore and Maureen MacGrogan of Columbia University Press showed faith in me even before the manu-
script was fully developed. Frank Graham of Mayfield Publishing enlightened me with his knowledge, insights, and humor. A debt of
friendship and gratitude also belongs to Mitch Allen, formerly of Sage
Publications, whose call to the arts is sociology's great loss.

   My parents and in-laws gave me the confidence in myself, the quest
for learning, the unconditional love, and the financial assistance that I

needed to achieve this goal. I hope that I will always be the kind of person that will make them proud.

My children, Jori and Brye, filled my life with more joy, happiness, purpose, and love than I ever thought possible. They taught me about human nature, creative development, and the existential self, bringing out brute instincts I never knew I had and making my life complete.

Finally, my husband, Peter, truly a co-author of this work, has been my steady companion for fourteen years, sharing every aspect of my personal and professional life. He has been more than a loving, sensitive, liberated, nurturant husband; he has been my true other half. To him I respectfully and lovingly dedicate this book.

Earlier versions of chapters 4 and 7 and parts of chapter 8 appeared as, respectively: Patricia A. Adler and Peter Adler, "Relationships Between Dealers: The Social Organization of Illicit Drug Transactions," *Sociology and Social Research*, vol. 67, no. 3, copyright © 1983 *Sociology and Social Research;* idem, "Shifts and Oscillations in Deviant Careers: The Case of Upper-Level Drug Dealers and Smugglers," *Social Problems*, vol. 31, no. 2, copyright © 1983 The Society for the Study of Social Problems Inc.; and idem, "Criminal Commitment Among Drug Dealers," *Deviant Behavior*, vol. 3, no. 2, copyright © 1982 Hemisphere Publishing Corporation. I am grateful to the publishers and copyright holders for permission to reprint this material.

INTRODUCTION

This is a study of a community of drug dealers and smugglers and the social scene they inhabit. These operators constitute the drug world's upper echelons, as they import and distribute tons of marijuana and dozens of kilos of cocaine at a time. In part, the extremely illegal nature of their trafficking activities makes these individuals cluster together for both business and social relations, forming a deviant subculture which reflects common norms and values. This subculture provides guidelines for their dealing and smuggling, outlining members' rules, roles, and reputations. Their social life is deviant as well, as evidenced by their abundant drug consumption, extravagant spending, uninhibited sexual mores, and focus on immediate gratification. They are the jet-setters of the drug world, living the fast life, pursuing the whim of the moment.

Previous portrayals of drug trafficking have been able to penetrate only low and middle levels of the drug trade.[1] While some of these were very good, providing insight into the nature of these levels of dealers and dealing, they could only make extrapolations to top-level drug trafficking. The present study fills this void by describing and analyzing an elite upper-level dealing and smuggling scene.

The methods I used to study this group were direct and personal. With my husband as a research partner, I spent six years in the field (from 1974 to 1980) engaged in daily participant observation with members of this dealing and smuggling community. Although I did not deal, myself, I participated in many of their activities, partying with them, attending social gatherings, traveling with them, and watching them plan and execute their business activities. I thus came to know members of this subculture, and formed close friendships with several of them. In addition to observing and conversing casually with these dealers and smugglers, I conducted in-depth, taped interviews, and cross-checked my observations and their accounts against further sources of data whenever possible. After leaving the field, I continued to conduct follow-up interviews during periodic visits to the community until 1983.

In the following pages I draw upon these data to address some of the problems and issues which have been raised by the literature on drug dealing and on deviant behavior generally. My approach follows an existential-sociology perspective, which suggests that researchers focus on the subjective understanding of how people live, feel, think, and act. While most theories of human behavior view people's feelings as dependent on their rational thoughts and actions, existential sociology analyzes behavior as being motivated by underlying "brute" feelings, drives, and emotions. These stem from our "brute beings," that core of feeling and perception which constitutes our innermost selves. Feelings, then, are relatively independent of and dominant over norms, values, and cognition, although these commonly run into and pervade each other (Douglas and Johnson 1977; Kotarba and Fontana 1984).

In this study I present an ethnographic description and analysis of a deviant social scene and the illicit activities of its members. Through it I offer insights into the nature of drug trafficking specifically, deviant occupations more generally, and, ultimately, hedonism as a motivation for deviance. I begin with a detailed presentation of how the dealers and smugglers I studied live and work. I locate their trafficking within a sociohistorical context, showing how it has been affected by trends and developments both within this country and abroad. I analyze the structure and character of their overlapping business and social affiliations, within the drug world and in conventional society. This is not an arena dominated by a criminal syndicate but an illicit market populated by individuals and small groups of wheeler-dealers who operate competitively and entrepreneurially. I therefore set forth a framework for understanding "disorganized" criminals (Reuter 1983) in terms of their allegiances, mutual trust, and business organization. I trace their careers in this deviant occupation, examining where they come from, their patterns of behavior and mobility within the field, and what eventually happens to them. I then discuss the interplay and conflict between their dangerous, yet exciting, deviant work, and their pleasure-seeking, decadent behavior. This contrast serves as a critical nexus to my analysis. While these dealers and smugglers are businesslike in their occupational orientation, profit motivation, and rationally organized work behavior, they are fundamentally committed to drug trafficking because of the uninhibited lifestyle it permits them to lead. They therefore act rationally for the ultimate end of living irrationally. This, then, is a study of a subculture of hedonism whose members have revolted against conventional society's rationalism and repression in order to indulge the impulses of their brute beings.

I now introduce, in more detail, the place where the dealing and smuggling occurred, the people engaged in drug trafficking, and the range of products they handled.

THE SETTING: SOUTHWEST COUNTY

Located within the sunbelt of the southwestern United States, Southwest County was composed, in part, of a handful of informal beach towns that dotted the Pacific Ocean. Physically, the terrain was semiarid, with pockets of verdant cultivation along the coastal strip where the population was most concentrated. As one drove along the old highway connecting this string of towns, one passed an assortment of small shops (health food markets, surf shops, used clothing stores, head shops) and restaurants that catered to the area's predominantly youthful clientele. Quiet and laid back, these communities housed little commerce or industry, being known instead as tourist, farming, and surfing areas.

Occupationally, fewer people here were employed in conventional work settings than in most other communities. Some people, drawn to the area because of its physical beauty and temperate climate, lived off inherited wealth and did not work at all. Another segment of the population lived in the style of surf bums, working construction, waiting tables, and roving between assorted odd jobs. Others escaped traditional nine-to-five jobs by selling real estate, operating small, independent businesses, providing services (housecleaning, photography, catering, child care, etc.), or pursuing a variety of legitimate entrepreneurial "hustles."

The local surf subculture pervaded the area, creating an ambience that was centered around outdoor living, natural food, good health, physical narcissism, relaxed good vibes, and a general lack of future-orientation. Here, the quest for youth prevailed, and individuals of all ages thought and acted with an intentional freedom and exuberance.

This area was further divided into homogeneous pockets of people who clustered together along racial, age, and economic lines, living in relative separation from each other. Southwest County dealers and smugglers carved out their niche in "Grass City" (a small village of approximately 7,000 people) and the two smaller towns on either side of it. Grass City was peaceful during the daylight hours, as shoppers, beachgoers, and surfers pursued their activities. At night, though, the nightclubs, bars, and restaurants were enlivened by drug traffickers and their entourages. Spending ran high, helping to keep the local community afloat financially.

Several features of Southwest County, and particularly Grass City, combined to make this area attractive to the upper-level dealing and smuggling set. First, its proximity to the Pacific Ocean and the Mexican border placed it at a strategic advantage for the wholesale drug business. It functioned as a point of entry along both land and water frontiers. Second, the local surf subculture provided a compatible social climate for drug traffickers, as dealers and smugglers shared many norms with this drug-using, present-centered group. The drug world and surf subcultures thus had a degree of sympathy toward and reciprocal influence over each other. Third, Southwest County was an unincorporated area, policed by the county sheriff's department. This law enforcement agency was responsible for a large territory and did not have the daily familiarity with individuals and groups operating under its jurisdiction that a local city police force might have had.

THE PEOPLE

The exact size of Southwest County's upper-level dealing and smuggling community was impossible to estimate. People tended to be very secretive, hiding their identity and actions from outsiders. They also varied their involvement with dealing, frequently dropping out and reentering the scene. During the course of my six years of participant observation research with members of this group, I was able to observe closely 65 dealers and smugglers, conducting intensive, taped interviews with 24 of them (see chapter 1). In addition, I observed and interacted with numerous other drug world members, including dealers' "old ladies" (girl friends and wives), friends, and family members, who constituted the dealers' and smugglers' social group.

At these upper levels, Southwest County's drug crowd was quite homogeneous. Participants were predominantly white, came from middle-class family backgrounds, and had a low degree of prior criminality. The dealers' and smugglers' social world contained both men and women, but most of the serious business was conducted by the men, who surrounded themselves with beautiful but flighty "dope chicks." While all of the smugglers I studied were men, about one-tenth of the drug dealers in my sample were women.[2] This primarily included dealers' ex–old ladies who had learned the business from their former mates, and women who had dealt or begun dealing jointly with their spouses. Members of this dealing and smuggling community ranged from 25 to 40 years old. This was an older group than that described by most other studies of drug dealing (Carey 1968; Lieb and Olson 1976; Mouledoux 1972), which, as with much academic research, focus on student and university-related populations. My sample included people who had progressed beyond the low levels of trafficking commonly found among these younger populations, and had moved up to the larger quantities where the opportunities for profit were greater. In addition, many of those I observed were recruited into the drug world, by their peers, at a later age, thus bypassing the lower levels entirely. My subjects' experiences in traveling around the country to buy and sell drugs at the upper levels suggested that this age range was predominant among the people who dealt at this level.

EVOLUTION OF THE PRODUCT

During the course of this study, I witnessed the effects of major changes in the types of drugs used and trafficked. When I first began to observe the scene in 1974, "commercial" (low potency) Mexican marijuana was the dominant commodity handled. Its use was popular throughout the United States, and it could be easily obtained just across the border in great bulk and very cheaply. Better-quality marijuana from Colombia or Jamaica was occasionally seen (more commonly on the East Coast) but rarely handled by Southwest County importers.

Their close proximity to the Mexican border allowed many local drug traffickers to develop supply connections in Mexico. American-grown marijuana was a rare commodity. It was cultivated by people only for their own use, but was hardly worth the bother, since Mexican marijuana could be purchased so cheaply. With their connections to the Mexican marijuana growers and their border location, Southwest County smugglers imported tons of commercial marijuana weekly and filtered it through the area to distribution networks all over the country. The period from the mid-1960s to the mid-1970s was the most lucrative era in the commercial marijuana business, attracting many drug traffickers to the county and sustaining them in a lavish lifestyle. While commercial marijuana was their source of sustenance, few dealers actually smoked it themselves, preferring the more potent forms grown in Central America and Hawaii.

Another commodity they imported from Mexico during this era was low-grade (5 mgs.) amphetamine tablets knows as "whites," or "white crosses." These were manufactured and pressed in small Mexican factories and imported by the thousands in hundred-lot bottles. Southwest County traffickers, for the most part, did not use these pills, but passed them along, untouched, to distributors.

Lastly, Southwest County smugglers imported cocaine from South America. During the late sixties cocaine had not yet reached widespread popularity, but it was used heavily by the dealing and smuggling crowd. Rather than injecting it intravenously, as hard drug users did, they snorted it from spoons or through straws. Cocaine was considered a more esoteric drug, at that time, so it was not highly in demand. Thus, unlike marijuana, which was handled almost strictly for profit, Southwest County dealers and smugglers trafficked in cocaine to obtain a supply for their own consumption.

The transformation in this scene was, in part, brought about by government intervention in the early 1970s. Beginning in late 1969 and continuing through the seventies, the Mexican and American governments instituted a series of cooperative programs designed to combat drug smuggling. Operation Intercept and its successor Operation Cooperation involved more stringent vehicle inspections at the border checkpoints, increased radar surveillance and airport regulation of air smuggling, and a field defoliating program aimed at detecting and destroying opium poppy and marijuana crops (Gooberman 1974; McNicoll 1983). The first two measures actually proved beneficial to Southwest County operators. Many amateur dealers who had imported drugs on a small- or middle-level scale were put out of business. These individuals were then forced to buy from Southwest County traffickers, whose sophisticated technique and organization were unchecked by the enforcement efforts. The defoliating measures, though, had a devastating effect. Beginning with the benzyldiethyl amino benzoate and concluding with the paraquat sprayings, many of the Mexican marijuana fields were eradicated completely and never recovered. Mexican marijuana growers were, at least temporarily, out of business.

Southwest County smugglers, who had bought from them nearly exclusively, were temporarily at a loss. Some switched to importing high-quality marijuana from Hawaii, but they could never purchase enough to satisfy their customers' demands. Some looked to local growers, who were developing sophisticated cultivation techniques, to keep them supplied. With its temperate climate and fertile soil, Southwest County was ideally suited to marijuana production. Cultivation of high-potency marijuana developed into a flourishing local industry, with thousands of pounds per year being grown in indoor greenhouses and remote outdoor areas. One source has estimated that by 1980 the California marijuana crop accounted for about 7 percent of total domestic consumption (Lang 1981).

This did not fill the void, however. Southwest County smugglers therefore ventured farther south, seeking to buy marijuana in Colombia (whose marijuana production had dramatically increased when the Mexicans were driven out of business). The smugglers did fairly well for a year or two, purchasing marijuana in Colombia and transporting it back to the United States. Just as they finally began to reconstruct their marijuana smuggling operations, adjusting to the longer distances, higher prices, and better-quality product, American smugglers were pushed out of this trade. In their stead, Colombian traffickers, who had developed a series of major family-based criminal syndicates, arose. Unlike the cottage-type industries of the Mexican growers and brokers, Colombians dominated local production, local law enforcement, local governments, and the international marijuana trade as well.

By 1975–76 the Mexican marijuana growers had resumed cultivation, albeit on a smaller scale than before. When they did, many farmers switched to growing the more potent grades of marijuana, which had become popular with consumers. This offered them the advantages of more revenue per acre and the ability to hide their smaller fields from law enforcement more easily. With their Mexican connections back in business, many Southwest County smugglers resumed importing Mexican marijuana. The overall results of this period of flux and transition were threefold: (1) commercial marijuana faded from the scene and was replaced by high-potency, quality marijuana (usually called by a brand name, such as Acapulco Gold, Panama Red, Maui Zowie, Mexican sinsemilla); (2) smuggling enterprises were no longer directed toward importing tons of Mexican marijuana at a time but were divided among several different supply areas, usually handling smaller quantities; and (3) many smugglers quit the marijuana market altogether and switched over to cocaine. The importation of low-grade amphetamines also decreased at around the same time.

Cocaine burst upon the American drug scene in the mid- to late 1970s, soaring to popularity as the favorite item among the jet set, the entertainment crowd, highly paid athletes, young executives, and many others. As an intoxicating substance it offered several advantages over marijuana. First, it produced a warm and sociable high, characterized by feelings of friendship and euphoria. Second, it could be snorted quickly and without odor, making it handier and more discreet. Third, when snorted in moderation, it appeared to have few harmful physical consequences. Fourth, it was much less bulky, enabling people to carry it inconspicuously. For Southwest County dealers and smugglers, this last feature was especially appealing because it greatly simplified their transportation problems. In addition, they were already fairly well connected to South America cocaine brokers, having handled cocaine for some time. Thus, when the domestic demand for cocaine skyrocketed, many Southwest County commercial marijuana dealers and smugglers switched to trafficking in cocaine, making it the dominant commodity handled when I left the scene in 1980. Over a six-year period I thus observed the transformation of Southwest County from a major wholesale marijuana market into a distribution center for the cocaine trade.

OVERVIEW

Deviant scenes, such as the one I studied, often appear disorganized to the uninitiated outsider. In the following chapters I examine the internal logic of the drug world as I saw it, experienced it, and learned of it through my respondents' accounts. One of the dangers I have struggled with, however, is the temptation to make too much rational sense out of this irrational world. In trying to set up a logical order for the presentation of my data, I have at times caught myself imposing a structure on the data which did not necessarily exist. The drug world was an organized yet intricate arena, influenced by a variety of diverse and often conflicting factors.

Here I have introduced the people, setting, and basic types of activities inherent in this social world. In chapter 1 I describe how I discovered this deviant scene and decided to study it. I discuss the progression of the research, my membership role in the dealers' and smugglers' social world, and some of the difficulties involved in trying to do participant observation on a secretive community engaged in highly illegal behavior.

In chapters 2 and 3 I outline the basic *modus operandi* for, respectively, smuggling and dealing in Southwest County. I address the types of connections needed for international buying and selling, the organization and technical expertise required for importing drugs by land, sea, and air, factors influencing drug pricing, and the kinds of activities associated with upper-level dealing. I present a hierarchy of the levels of operators I found in the commercial marijuana and cocaine trafficking trades, from major smugglers to low-level consumer-dealers.

In chapter 4 I examine the social organization of the community. Members of the drug world were bound together into deviant peer associations by their overlapping business and social relationships. I examine the character and intensity of these relationships, from the daily contact of partnerships to the relative distance of people known only by reputation. I then relate dealers' and smugglers' social organization to the structure of the illicit drug market, comparing it to monopolistic and competitive market models.

Within the drug community, dealers and smugglers were also bound together by their shared, deviant lifestyle. In chapter 5 I outline the major dimensions of this fast life with its glamor, excitement, and decadence. I discuss some character traits common to upper-level dealers and smugglers, and relate these to the dealing lifestyle. This chapter highlights the motivational role of hedonism and materialism.

In chapter 6 I consider sociological correlates of success and failure. I introduce a prestige hierarchy, based on dealers' and smugglers' reputations within the drug world, and discuss its relationship to the hierarchy of dealing levels presented in chapter 4. I discuss three dimensions of drug trafficking which can foster success and failure, depending on individuals' dealing styles and their adherence to the community's informal norms and conventions. This, in turn, influences their ranking on the prestige hierarchy and their ability to attract desirable associates as connections. The prestige hierarchy thus represents both the structural dimension of success and failure and the means of informal, voluntary regulation in this competitive illicit market.

In chapter 7 I examine the career progressions of Southwest County dealers and smugglers. I show how individuals enter and climb to the top levels of this occupation (as distinct from recruitment and upward mobility at the lower and middle levels). Once they are established, however, the character of their experience changes, and they change with it. A career pattern of oscillations then emerges, as dealers and smugglers alternately quit and reenter the occupation, illustrating the difficulties inherent in leaving this form of deviance.

In chapter 8 I draw generic conclusions about the nature, behavior, and social organization of these dealers and smugglers. I begin by presenting three perspectives on drug trafficking: the organizational, the occupational, and the hedonistic. I evaluate their role in influencing dealers' and smugglers' motivation and commitment to this scene. I then frame the drug world's subculture of hedonism by discussing its relation to the larger society's rationalism and repression. I conclude by discussing why people quit conventional society to become upper-level drug traffickers.

CHAPTER ONE

RESEARCHING DEALERS AND SMUGGLERS

I strongly believe that investigative field research (Douglas 1976), with emphasis on direct personal observation, interaction, and experience, is the only way to acquire accurate knowledge about deviant behavior. Investigative techniques are especially necessary for studying groups such as drug dealers and smugglers because the highly illegal nature of their occupation makes them secretive, deceitful, mistrustful, and paranoid. To insulate themselves from the straight world, they construct multiple false fronts, offer lies and misinformation, and withdraw into their group. In fact, detailed, scientific information about upper-level drug dealers and smugglers is lacking precisely because of the difficulty sociological researchers have had in penetrating into their midst. As a result, the only way I could possibly get close enough to these individuals to discover what they were doing and to understand their world from their perspectives (Blumer 1969) was to take a membership role in the setting. While my different values and goals precluded my becoming converted to complete membership in the subculture, and my fears prevented my ever becoming "actively" involved in their trafficking activities, I was able to assume a "peripheral" membership role (Adler and Adler, forthcoming). I became a member of the dealers' and smugglers' social world and participated in their daily activities on that basis. In this chapter, I discuss how I gained access to this group, established research relations with members, and how personally involved I became in their activities.

Getting In. When I moved to Southwest County in the summer of 1974, I had no idea that I would soon be swept up in a subculture of vast drug trafficking and unending partying, mixed with occasional cloak-and-dagger subterfuge. I had moved to California with my husband,

Peter, to attend graduate school in sociology. We rented a condo-
minium townhouse near the beach and started taking classes in the
fall. We had always felt that socializing exclusively with academicians
left us nowhere to escape from our work, so we tried to meet people
in the nearby community. One of the first friends we made was our
closest neighbor, a fellow in his late twenties with a tall, hulking frame
and gentle expression. Dave, as he introduced himself, was always
dressed rather casually, if not sloppily, in T-shirts and jeans. He spent
most of his time hanging out or walking on the beach with a variety
of friends who visited his house, and taking care of his two young boys,
who lived alternately with him and his estranged wife. He also went
out of town a lot. We started spending much of our free time over at
his house, talking, playing board games late into the night, and smoking marijuana together. We were glad to find someone from whom we
could buy marijuana in this new place, since we did not know too
many people. He also began treating us to a fairly regular supply of
cocaine, which was a thrill because this was a drug we could rarely
afford on our student budgets. We noticed right away, however, that
there was something unusual about his use and knowledge of drugs:
while he always had a plentiful supply and was fairly expert about
marijuana and cocaine, when we tried to buy a small bag of marijuana
from him he had little idea of the going price. This incongruity piqued
our curiosity and raised suspicion. We wondered if he might be dealing in larger quantities. Keeping our suspicions to ourselves, we began
observing Dave's activities a little more closely. Most of his friends
were in their late twenties and early thirties and, judging by their lifestyles and automobiles, rather wealthy. They came and left his house
at all hours, occasionally extending their parties through the night and
the next day into the following night. Yet throughout this time we
never saw Dave or any of his friends engage in any activity that resembled a legitimate job. In most places this might have evoked community suspicion, but few of the people we encountered in Southwest
County seemed to hold traditionally structured jobs. Dave, in fact,
had no visible means of financial support. When we asked him what
he did for a living, he said something vague about being a real estate
speculator, and we let it go at that. We never voiced our suspicions
directly since he chose not to broach the subject with us.

We did discuss the subject with our mentor, Jack Douglas, however. He was excited by the prospect that we might be living among
a group of big dealers, and urged us to follow our instincts and develop leads into the group. He knew that the local area was rife with
drug trafficking, since he had begun a life history case study of two
drug dealers with another graduate student several years previously.
That earlier study was aborted when the graduate student quit school,
but Jack still had many hours of taped interviews he had conducted
with them, as well as an interview that he had done with an under-
graduate student who had known the two dealers independently, to
serve as a cross-check on their accounts. He therefore encouraged us
to become friendlier with Dave and his friends. We decided that if
anything did develop out of our observations of Dave, it might make
a nice paper for a field methods class or independent study.

Our interests and background made us well suited to study drug
dealing. First, we had already done research in the field of drugs. As
undergraduates at Washington University we had participated in a na-
tionally funded project on urban heroin use (see Cummins et al. 1972).
Our role in the study involved using fieldwork techniques to investigate the extent of heroin use and distribution in St. Louis. In talking
with heroin users, dealers, and rehabilitation personnel, we acquired
a base of knowledge about the drug world and the subculture of drug
trafficking. Second, we had a generally open view toward soft drug
use, considering moderate consumption of marijuana and cocaine to
be generally nondeviant. This outlook was partially etched by our 1960s-
formed attitudes, as we had first been introduced to drug use in an
environment of communal friendship, sharing, and counterculture
ideology. It also partially reflected the widespread acceptance ac-
corded to marijuana and cocaine use in the surrounding local culture.
Third, our age (mid-twenties at the start of the study) and general appearance gave us compatibility with most of the people we were observing.

We thus watched Dave and continued to develop our friendship with
him. We also watched his friends and got to know a few of his more
regular visitors. We continued to build friendly relations by doing, quite
naturally, what Becker (1963), Polsky (1969), and Douglas (1972) had
advocated for the early stages of field research: we gave them a chance

to know us and form judgments about our trustworthiness by jointly pursuing those interests and activities which we had in common.

Then one day something happened which forced a breakthrough in the research. Dave had two guys visiting him from out of town and, after snorting quite a bit of cocaine, they turned their conversation to a trip they had just made from Mexico, where they piloted a load of marijuana back across the border in a small plane. Dave made a few efforts to shift the conversation to another subject, telling them to "button their lips," but they apparently thought that he was joking. They thought that anybody as close to Dave as we seemed to be undoubtedly knew the nature of his business. They made further allusions to his involvement in the operation and discussed the outcome of the sale. We could feel the wave of tension and awkwardness from Dave when this conversation began, as he looked toward us to see if we understood the implications of what was being said, but then he just shrugged it off as done. Later, after the two guys left, he discussed with us what happened. He admitted to us that he was a member of a smuggling crew and a major marijuana dealer on the side. He said that he knew he could trust us, but that it was his practice to say as little as possible to outsiders about his activities. This inadvertent slip, and Dave's subsequent opening up, were highly significant in forging our entry into Southwest County's drug world. From then on he was open in discussing the nature of his dealing and smuggling activities with us.

He was, it turned out, a member of a smuggling crew that was importing a ton of marijuana weekly and 40 kilos of cocaine every few months. During that first winter and spring, we observed Dave at work and also got to know the other members of his crew, including Ben, the smuggler himself. Ben was also very tall and broad shouldered, but his long black hair, now flecked with gray, bespoke his earlier membership in the hippie subculture. A large physical stature, we observed, was common to most of the male participants involved in this drug community. The women also had a unifying physical trait: they were extremely attractive and stylishly dressed. This included Dave's ex-wife, Jean, with whom he reconciled during the spring. We therefore became friendly with Jean and through her met a number of women ("dope chicks") who hung around the dealers and smugglers. As we continued to gain the friendship of Dave and Jean's associates we were progressively admitted into their inner circle and apprised of each person's dealing or smuggling role.

Once we realized the scope of Ben's and his associates' activities, we saw the enormous research potential in studying them. This scene was different from any analysis of drug trafficking that we had read in the sociological literature because of the amounts they were dealing and the fact that they were importing it themselves. We decided that, if it was at all possible, we would capitalize on this situation, to "opportunistically" (Riemer 1977) take advantage of our prior expertise and of the knowledge, entree, and rapport we had already developed with several key people in this setting. We therefore discussed the idea of doing a study of the general subculture with Dave and several of his closest friends (now becoming our friends). We assured them of the anonymity, confidentiality, and innocuousness of our work. They were happy to reciprocate our friendship by being of help to our professional careers. In fact, they basked in the subsequent attention we gave their lives.

We began by turning first Dave, then others, into key informants and collecting their life histories in detail. We conducted a series of taped, depth interviews with an unstructured, open-ended format. We questioned them about such topics as their backgrounds, their recruitment into the occupation, the stages of their dealing careers, their relations with others, their motivations, their lifestyle, and their general impressions about the community as a whole.

We continued to do taped interviews with key informants for the next six years until 1980, when we moved away from the area. After that, we occasionally did follow-up interviews when we returned for vacation visits. These later interviews focused on recording the continuing unfolding of events and included detailed probing into specific conceptual areas, such as dealing networks, types of dealers, secrecy, trust, paranoia, reputation, the law, occupational mobility, and occupational stratification. The number of taped interviews we did with each key informant varied, ranging between 10 and 30 hours of discussion.

Our relationship with Dave and the others thus took on an added dimension—the research relationship. As Douglas (1976), Henslin

(1972), and Wax (1952) have noted, research relationships involve some form of mutual exchange. In our case, we offered everything that friendship could entail. We did routine favors for them in the course of our everyday lives, offered them insights and advice about their lives from the perspective of our more respectable position, wrote letters on their behalf to the authorities when they got in trouble, testified as character witnesses at their non-drug-related trials, and loaned them money when they were down and out. When Dave was arrested and brought to trial for check-kiting, we helped Jean organize his defense and raise the money to pay his fines. We spelled her in taking care of the children so that she could work on his behalf. When he was eventually sent to the state prison we maintained close ties with her and discussed our mutual efforts to buoy Dave up and secure his release. We also visited him in jail. During Dave's incarceration, however, Jean was courted by an old boyfriend and gave up her reconciliation with Dave. This proved to be another significant turning point in our research because, desperate for money, Jean looked up Dave's old dealing connections and went into the business herself. She did not stay with these marijuana dealers and smugglers for long, but soon moved into the cocaine business. Over the next several years her experiences in the world of cocaine dealing brought us into contact with a different group of people. While these people knew Dave and his associates (this was very common in the Southwest County dealing and smuggling community), they did not deal with them directly. We were thus able to gain access to a much wider and more diverse range of subjects than we would have had she not branched out on her own.

Dave's eventual release from prison three months later brought our involvement in the research to an even deeper level. He was broke and had nowhere to go. When he showed up on our doorstep, we took him in. We offered to let him stay with us until he was back on his feet again and could afford a place of his own. He lived with us for seven months, intimately sharing his daily experiences with us. During this time we witnessed, firsthand, his transformation from a scared ex-con who would never break the law again to a hard-working legitimate employee who only dealt to get money for his children's Christmas presents, to a full-time dealer with no pretensions at legitimate work. Both his process of changing attitudes and the community's gradual reacceptance of him proved very revealing.

We socialized with Dave, Jean, and other members of Southwest County's dealing and smuggling community on a near-daily basis, especially during the first four years of the research (before we had a child). We worked in their legitimate businesses, vacationed together, attended their weddings, and cared for their children. Throughout their relationship with us, several participants became co-opted to the researcher's perspective[1] and actively sought out instances of behavior which filled holes in the conceptualizations we were developing. Dave, for one, became so intrigued by our conceptual dilemmas that he undertook a "natural experiment" entirely on his own, offering an unlimited supply of drugs to a lower-level dealer to see if he could work up to higher levels of dealing, and what factors would enhance or impinge upon his upward mobility.

In addition to helping us directly through their own experiences, our key informants aided us in widening our circle of contacts. For instance, they let us know when someone in whom we might be interested was planning on dropping by, vouching for our trustworthiness and reliability as friends who could be included in business conversations. Several times we were even awakened in the night by phone calls informing us that someone had dropped by for a visit, should we want to "casually" drop over too. We rubbed the sleep from our eyes, dressed, and walked or drove over, feeling like sleuths out of a television series. We thus were able to snowball, through the active efforts of our key informants,[2] into an expanded study population. This was supplemented by our own efforts to cast a research net and befriend other dealers, moving from contact to contact slowly and carefully through the domino effect.

The Covert Role. The highly illegal nature of dealing in illicit drugs and dealers' and smugglers' general level of suspicion made the adoption of an overt research role highly sensitive and problematic. In discussing this issue with our key informants, they all agreed that we should be extremely discreet (for both our sakes and theirs). We carefully approached new individuals before we admitted that we were studying them. With many of these people, then, we took a covert posture in the research setting. As nonparticipants in the business activities which bound members together into the group, it was difficult to become fully accepted as peers. We therefore tried to establish some sort of peripheral, social membership in the general crowd, where we could be accepted as "wise" (Goffman 1963) individuals and granted a courtesy membership. This seemed an attainable goal, since we had begun our involvement by forming such relationships with our key informants. By being introduced to others in this wise rather than overt role, we were able to interact with people who would otherwise have shied away from us. Adopting a courtesy membership caused us to bear a courtesy stigma,[3] however, and we suffered since we, at times, had to disguise the nature of our research from both lay outsiders and academicians.

In our overt posture we showed interest in dealers' and smugglers' activities, encouraged them to talk about themselves (within limits, so as to avoid acting like narcs), and ran home to write field notes. This role offered us the advantage of gaining access to unapproachable people while avoiding researcher effects, but it prevented us from asking some necessary, probing questions and from tape recording conversations.[4] We therefore sought, at all times, to build toward a conversion to the overt role. We did this by working to develop their trust.

Developing Trust. Like achieving entrée, the process of developing trust with members of unorganized deviant groups can be slow and difficult. In the absence of a formal structure separating members from outsiders, each individual must form his or her own judgment about whether new persons can be admitted to their confidence. No gatekeeper existed to smooth our path to being trusted, although our key informants acted in this role whenever they could by providing introductions and references. In addition, the unorganized nature of this group meant that we met people at different times and were constantly at different levels in our developing relationships with them. We were thus trusted more by some people than by others, in part because of their greater familiarity with us. But as Douglas (1976) has noted, just because someone knew us or even liked us did not automatically guarantee that they would trust us.

We actively tried to cultivate the trust of our respondents by tying them to us with favors. Small things, like offering the use of our phone, were followed with bigger favors, like offering the use of our car, and finally really meaningful favors, like offering the use of our home. Here we often trod a thin line, trying to ensure our personal safety while putting ourselves in enough of a risk position, along with our research subjects, so that they would trust us. While we were able to build a "web of trust" (Douglas 1976) with some members, we found that trust, in large part, was not a simple status to attain in the drug world. Johnson (1975) has pointed out that trust is not a one-time phenomenon, but an ongoing developmental process. From my experiences in this research I would add that it cannot be simply assumed to be a one-way process either, for it can be diminished, withdrawn, reinstated to varying degrees, and re-questioned at any point. Carey (1972) and Douglas (1972) have remarked on this waxing and waning process, but it was especially pronounced for us because our subjects used large amounts of cocaine over an extended period of time. This tended to make them alternately warm and cold to us. We thus lived through a series of ups and downs with the people we were trying to cultivate as research informants.

The Overt Role. After this initial covert phase, we began to feel that some new people trusted us. We tried to intuitively feel when the time was right to approach them and go overt. We used two means of approaching people to inform them that we were involved in a study of dealing and smuggling: direct and indirect. In some cases our key informants approached their friends or connections and, after vouching for our absolute trustworthiness, convinced these associates to talk to us. In other instances, we approached people directly, asking for their help with our project. We worked our way through a progression with these secondary contacts, first discussing the dealing scene overtly and later moving to taped life history interviews. Some people reacted well to us, but others responded skittishly, making appointments to do taped interviews only to break them as the day drew near, and going through fluctuating stages of being honest with us or putting up fronts about their dealing activities. This varied, for some, with their degree of active involvement in the business. During the times when they had quit dealing, they would tell us about their present and past activities, but when they became actively involved again, they would hide it from us.

This progression of covert to overt roles generated a number of tactical difficulties. The first was the problem of *coming on too fast* and blowing it. Early in the research we had a dealer's old lady (we thought) all set up for the direct approach. We knew many dealers in common and had discussed many things tangential to dealing with her without actually mentioning the subject. When we asked her to do a taped interview of her bohemian lifestyle, she agreed without hesitation. When the interview began, though, and she found out why we were interested in her, she balked, gave us a lot of incoherent jumble, and ended the session as quickly as possible. Even though she lived only three houses away we never saw her again. We tried to move more slowly after that.

A second problem involved simultaneously *juggling our overt and covert roles* with different people. This created the danger of getting our cover blown with people who did not know about our research (Henslin 1972). It was very confusing to separate the people who knew about our study from those who did not, especially in the minds of our informants. They would make occasional veiled references in front of people, especially when loosened by intoxicants, that made us extremely uncomfortable. We also frequently worried that our snooping would someday be mistaken for police tactics. Fortunately, this never happened.

Cross-Checking. The hidden and conflictual nature of the drug dealing world made me feel the need for extreme certainty about the reliability of my data. I therefore based all my conclusions on independent sources and accounts that we carefully verified. First, we tested information against our own common sense and general knowledge of the scene. We adopted a hard-nosed attitude of suspicion, assuming people were up to more than they would originally admit. We kept our attention especially riveted on "reformed" dealers and smugglers who were living better than they could outwardly afford, and were thereby able to penetrate their public fronts.

Second, we checked out information against a variety of reliable sources. Our own observations of the scene formed a primary reliable source, since we were involved with many of the principals on a daily basis and knew exactly what they were doing. Having Dave live with us was a particular advantage because we could contrast his statements to us with what we could clearly see was happening. Even after he moved out, we knew him so well that we could generally tell when he was lying to us or, more commonly, fooling himself with optimistic dreams. We also observed other dealers' and smugglers' evasions and misperceptions about themselves and their activities. These usually occurred when they broke their own rules by selling to people they did not know, or when they comingled other people's money with their own. We also cross-checked our data against independent, alternative accounts. We were lucky, for this purpose, that Jean got reinvolved in the drug world. By interviewing her, we gained additional insight into Dave's past, his early dealing and smuggling activities, and his ongoing involvement from another person's perspective. Jean (and her connections) also talked to us about Dave's associates, thereby helping us to validate or disprove their statements. We even used this pincer effect to verify information about people we had never directly interviewed. This occurred, for instance, with the tapes that Jack Douglas gave us from his earlier study. After doing our first round of taped interviews with Dave, we discovered that he knew the dealers Jack had interviewed. We were excited by the prospect of finding out what had happened to these people and if their earlier stories checked out. We therefore sent Dave to do some investigative work. Through some mutual friends he got back in touch with them and found out what they had been doing for the past several years.

Finally, wherever possible, we checked out accounts against hard facts: newspaper and magazine reports; arrest records; material possessions; and visible evidence. Throughout the research, we used all these cross-checking measures to evaluate the veracity of new information and to prod our respondents to be more accurate (by abandoning both their lies and their self-deceptions).[5]

After about four years of near-daily participant observation, we began to diminish our involvement in the research. This occurred gradually, as first pregnancy and then a child hindered our ability to follow the scene as intensely and spontaneously as we had before. In addition, after having a child, we were less willing to incur as many risks as we had before; we no longer felt free to make decisions based solely on our own welfare. We thus pulled back from what many have referred to as the "difficult hours and dangerous situations" inevitably present in field research on deviants (see Becker 1963; Carey 1972; Douglas 1972). We did, however, actively maintain close ties with research informants (those with whom we had gone overt), seeing them regularly and periodically doing follow-up interviews.

PROBLEMS AND ISSUES

Reflecting on the research process, I have isolated a number of issues which I believe merit additional discussion. These are rooted in experiences which have the potential for greater generic applicability.

The first is the *effect of drugs on the data-gathering process*. Carey (1972) has elaborated on some of the problems he encountered when trying to interview respondents who used amphetamines, while Wax (1952, 1957) has mentioned the difficulty of trying to record field notes while drinking sake. I found that marijuana and cocaine had nearly opposite effects from each other. The latter helped the interview process, while the former hindered it. Our attempts to interview respondents who were stoned on marijuana were unproductive for a number of reasons. The primary obstacle was the effects of the drug. Often, people became confused, sleepy, or involved in eating to varying degrees. This distracted them from our purpose. At times, people even simulated overreactions to marijuana to hide behind the drug's supposed disorienting influence and thereby avoid divulging information. Cocaine, in contrast, proved to be a research aid. The drug's warming and sociable influence opened people up, diminished their inhibitions, and generally increased their enthusiasm for both the interview experience and us.

A second problem I encountered involved *assuming risks while doing research*. As I noted earlier, dangerous situations are often generic to research on deviant behavior. We were most afraid of the people we studied. As Carey (1972), Henslin (1972), and Whyte (1955) have stated, members of deviant groups can become hostile toward a researcher if they think that they are being treated wrongfully. This could have happened at any time from a simple occurrence, such as a misunderstanding, or from something more serious, such as our covert posture being exposed. Because of the inordinate amount of drugs they consumed, drug dealers and smugglers were particularly volatile, capable of becoming malicious toward each other or us with little warning. They were also likely to behave erratically owing to the great risks they faced from the police and other dealers. These factors made them moody, and they vacillated between trusting us and being suspicious of us.

At various times we also had to protect our research tapes. We encountered several threats to our collection of taped interviews from people who had granted us these interviews. This made us anxious, since we had taken great pains to acquire these tapes and felt strongly about maintaining confidences entrusted to us by our informants. When threatened, we became extremely frightened and shifted the tapes between different hiding places. We even ventured forth one rainy night with our tapes packed in a suitcase to meet a person who was uninvolved in the research at a secret rendezvous so that he could guard the tapes for us.

We were fearful, lastly, of the police. We often worried about local police or drug agents discovering the nature of our study and confiscating or subpoenaing our tapes and field notes. Sociologists have no privileged relationship with their subjects that would enable us legally to withhold evidence from the authorities should they subpoena it.[6] For this reason we studiously avoided any publicity about the research, even holding back on publishing articles in scholarly journals until we were nearly ready to move out of the setting. The closest we came to being publicly exposed as drug researchers came when a former sociology graduate student (turned dealer, we had heard from inside sources) was arrested at the scene of a cocaine deal. His lawyer wanted us to testify about the dangers of doing drug-related research, since he was using his research status as his defense. Fortunately, the crisis was averted when his lawyer succeeded in suppressing evidence and had the case dismissed before the trial was to have begun. Had we been exposed, however, our respondents would have acquired guilt by association through their friendship with us.

Our fear of the police went beyond our concern for protecting our research subjects, however. We risked the danger of arrest ourselves through our own violations of the law. Many sociologists (Becker 1963; Carey 1972; Polsky 1969; Whyte 1955) have remarked that field researchers studying deviance must inevitably break the law in order to acquire valid participant observation data. This occurs in its most innocuous form from having "guilty knowledge": information about crimes that are committed. Being aware of major dealing and smuggling operations made us an accessory to their commission, since we failed to notify the police. We broke the law, secondly, through our "guilty observations," by being present at the scene of a crime and witnessing its occurrence (see also Carey 1972). We knew it was possible to get caught in a bust involving others, yet buying and selling was so pervasive that to leave every time it occurred would have been unnatural and highly suspicious. Sometimes drug transactions even occurred in our home, especially when Dave was living there, but we finally had to put a stop to that because we could not handle the anxiety. Lastly, we broke the law through our "guilty actions," by taking part in illegal behavior ourselves. Although we never dealt drugs (we were too scared to be seriously tempted), we consumed drugs and possessed them in small quantities. Quite frankly, it would have been impossible for a nonuser to have gained access to this group to gather the data presented here. This was the minimum involvement necessary to obtain even the courtesy membership we achieved. Some kind of illegal action was also found to be a necessary or helpful component of the research by Becker (1963), Carey (1972), Johnson (1975), Polsky (1969), and Whyte (1955).

Another methodological issue arose from the *cultural clash between our research subjects and ourselves*. While other sociologists have alluded to these kinds of differences (Humphreys 1970, Whyte 1955), few have discussed how the research relationships affected them. Relationships with research subjects are unique because they involve a bond of intimacy between persons who might not ordinarily associate together, or who might otherwise be no more than casual friends. When fieldworkers undertake a major project, they commit themselves to maintaining a long-term relationship with the people they study. However, as researchers try to get depth involvement, they are apt to come across fundamental differences in character, values, and attitudes between their subjects and themselves. In our case, we were most strongly confronted by differences in present versus future orientations, a desire for risk versus security, and feelings of spontaneity versus self-discipline. These differences often caused us great frustration. We repeatedly saw dealers act irrationally, setting themselves up for failure. We wrestled with our desire to point out their patterns of foolhardy behavior and offer advice, feeling competing pulls between our detached, observer role which advised us not to influence the natural setting, and our involved, participant role which called for us to offer friendly help whenever possible.[7]

Each time these differences struck us anew, we gained deeper insights into our core, existential selves. We suspended our own taken-for-granted feelings and were able to reflect on our culturally formed attitudes, character, and life choices from the perspective of the other. When comparing how we might act in situations faced by our respondents, we realized where our deepest priorities lay. These revelations had the effect of changing our self-conceptions: whereas we, at one time, had thought of ourselves as what Rosenbaum (1981) has called "the hippest of non-addicts" (in this case nondealers), we were suddenly faced with being the straightest members of the crowd. Not only did we not deal, but we had a stable, long-lasting marriage and family life, and needed the security of a reliable monthly paycheck. Self-insights thus emerged as one of the unexpected outcomes of field research with members of a different cultural group.

The final issue I will discuss involved the various *ethical problems* which arose during this research. Many fieldworkers have encountered ethical dilemmas or pangs of guilt during the course of their research experiences (Carey 1972; Douglas 1976; Humphreys 1970; Johnson 1975; Klockars 1977, 1979; Rochford 1985). The researchers' role in the field makes this necessary because they can never fully align themselves with their subjects while maintaining their identity and personal commitment to the scientific community. Ethical dilemmas, then, are directly related to the amount of deception researchers use in gathering the data, and the degree to which they have accepted such acts as necessary and therefore neutralized them.

Throughout the research, we suffered from the burden of intimacies and confidences. Guarding secrets which had been told to us during taped interviews was not always easy or pleasant. Dealers occasionally revealed things about themselves or others that we had to pretend not to know when interacting with their close associates. This sometimes meant that we had to lie or build elaborate stories to cover for some people. Their fronts therefore became our fronts, and we had to weave our own web of deception to guard their performances. This became especially disturbing during the writing of the research report, as I was torn by conflicts between using details to enrich the data and glossing over description to guard confidences.[8]

Using the covert research role generated feelings of guilt, despite the fact that our key informants deemed it necessary, and thereby condoned it. Their own covert experiences were far more deeply entrenched than ours, being a part of their daily existence with non–drug world members. Despite the universal presence of covert behavior throughout the setting, we still felt a sense of betrayal every time we ran home to write research notes on observations we had made under the guise of innocent participants.

We also felt guilty about our efforts to manipulate people. While these were neither massive nor grave manipulations, they involved courting people to procure information about them. Our aggressively friendly postures were based on hidden ulterior motives: we did favors for people with the clear expectation that they could only pay us back with research assistance. Manipulation bothered us in two ways: immediately after it was done, and over the long run. At first, we felt awkward, phony, almost ashamed of ourselves, although we believed our rationalization that the end justified the means. Over the long run, though, our feelings were different. When friendship became intermingled with research goals, we feared that people would later look back on our actions and feel we were exploiting their friendship merely for the sake of our research project.

The last problem we encountered involved our feelings of whoring for data. At times, we felt that we were being exploited by others, that we were putting more into the relationship than they, that they were taking us for granted or using us. We felt that some people used a double standard in their relationship with us: they were allowed to lie to us, borrow money and not repay it, and take advantage of us, but we were at all times expected to behave honorably. This was undoubtedly an outgrowth of our initial research strategy where we did favors for people and expected little in return. But at times this led to our feeling bad. It made us feel like we were selling ourselves, our sincerity, and usually our true friendship, and not getting treated right in return.

CONCLUSIONS

The aggressive research strategy I employed was vital to this study. I could not just walk up to strangers and start hanging out with them as Liebow (1967) did, or be sponsored to a member of this group by a social service or reform organization as Whyte (1955) was, and expect to be accepted, let alone welcomed. Perhaps such a strategy might have worked with a group that had nothing to hide, but I doubt it. Our modern, pluralistic society is so filled with diverse subcultures whose interests compete or conflict with each other that each subculture has a set of knowledge which is reserved exclusively for insiders. In order to survive and prosper, they do not ordinarily show this side to just anyone. To obtain the kind of depth insight and information I needed, I had to become like the members in certain ways. They dealt only with people they knew and trusted, so I had to become known and trusted before I could reveal my true self and my research interests. Confronted with secrecy, danger, hidden alliances, misrepresentations, and unpredictable changes of intent, I had to use a delicate combination of overt and covert roles. Throughout, my deliberate cultivation of the norm of reciprocal exchange enabled me to trade my friendship for their knowledge, rather than waiting for the highly unlikely event that information would be delivered into my lap. I thus actively built a web of research contacts, used them to obtain highly sensitive data, and carefully checked them out to ensure validity.

Throughout this endeavor I profited greatly from the efforts of my husband, Peter, who served as an equal partner in this team field research project. It would have been impossible for me to examine this social world as an unattached female and not fall prey to sex role stereotyping which excluded women from business dealings. As a couple, our different genders allowed us to relate in different ways to both men and women (see Warren and Rasmussen 1977). We also protected each other when we entered the homes of dangerous characters, buoyed each others' initiative and courage, and kept the conversation going when one of us faltered. Conceptually, we helped each other keep a detached and analytical eye on the setting, provided multiperspectival insights, and corroborated, clarified, or (most revealingly) contradicted each other's observations and conclusions.

Finally, I feel strongly that to ensure accuracy, research on deviant groups must be conducted in the settings where it naturally occurs. As Polsky (1969:115–16) has forcefully asserted:

This means—there is no getting away from it—the study of career criminals *au natural*, in the field, the study of such criminals as they normally go about their work and play, the study of "uncaught" criminals and the study of others who in the past have been caught but are not caught at the time you study them. . . . Obviously we can no longer afford the convenient fiction that in studying criminals in their natural habitat, we would discover nothing really important that could not be discovered from criminals behind bars.

By studying criminals in their natural habitat I was able to see them in the full variability and complexity of their surrounding subculture, rather than within the artifical environment of a prison. I was thus able to learn about otherwise inaccessible dimensions of their lives, observing and analyzing firsthand the nature of their social organization, social stratification, lifestyle, and motivation.

CHAPTER TWO

SMUGGLING

Smuggling drugs, or illegally transporting them across international borders, was the first and most critical function of Southwest County drug traffickers. Nearly all other drug-related activities depended on this primary one, for it provided the supply of drugs which could then be sold and resold among various individual dealers. I will consider the basic *modus operandi* that was used by Southwest County smugglers when I first encountered this group.

ORIGIN AT GROWERS

Marijuana, or *Cannabis sativa*, grows under both wild and cultivated conditions in the warm, moist climates of the equatorial region. Although it is abundant in Africa and Southeast Asia, most of the marijuana imported into the United States comes from Colombia, Jamaica, or Mexico (McNicoll 1983). As noted, Southwest County smugglers traditionally obtained their marijuana in Mexico because of their proximity to the Mexican border.

Within Mexico, marijuana grew heartily all over the remote hills and farm areas.[1] The best, most potent strains were cultivated in the high altitudes and where the rainfall was plentiful. Centrally located Mexican regions such as Michoacan, Oaxaca, and Guadalajara were known for their good product, as were the mountainous terrains of the Caribbean and Central American countries. In this temperate climate there were three harvests yearly, the first and major one coming in October. In the commercial marijuana industry, three cuttings were made for each harvest period. After the tops and seeds were chopped off by the harvesting machines, the middle part of the plant with both leaf and some stems was cut, and then finally, the bottoms, which contained the stalks (although these were discarded). Next, a machine harvested the plants and threw them onto conveyor belts where they were cut and chopped by mechanical knives. Then, the loose marijuana was shot into a machine that sprayed it with a sticky, syrupy substance. This made the marijuana clump together in brick form when it was pressed, and gave it a resiny quality.[2] Mechanically papering the bricks completed the packaging process. A small factory like this was commonly shared by a few growers in a region.

In contrast, the production of high-potency, quality marijuana was much less mechanized. Here, growers paid attention to enhancing both the appearance and the intoxicating power of the ultimate product. High-altitude sites were carefully selected and weather conditions controlled, when possible. A sweep was made through the field during the early growing days to remove the far less potent male plants. By leaving only the female plants to grow, the farmers hoped to ensure that fertilization was prevented so that seeds never formed. This elevated the marijuana's THC (tetrahydrocannabinol, the active ingredient), as the THC level continues to rise until seeds form or the plant is picked. "Sinsemilla" (literally, "seedless," in Spanish, but now increasingly synonymous with any quality strain of marijuana) was thus far more intoxicating than the commercial seeded variety. In order to increase the potency and value of their product, growers of quality marijuana also harvested the crop manually (without the aid of harvesting machines), cutting the plants by hand so that only the "buds" (tops) were left intact. These were the most valuable portion of the plant and were sold separately from the "shake," or lower leaves. After being dried and cured by hanging from racks in, alternately, drying sheds and the sun for ten days, the marijuana was ready to be packaged and shipped.

Mexican growers, especially the peasants commonly responsible for growing commercial marijuana, had little to do with their product's sale and distribution. This was handled by "brokers" who specialized in creating the necessary organization and making arrangements for selling the merchandise to smugglers. One broker ordinarily handled a valley or hillside full of growers, often being related to one or more of the growers within this region. The broker offered special services to his growers, providing them with their harvesting equipment, packaging factory, and curing and drying locations.

As the primary supply connections for Southwest County marijuana smugglers, Mexican brokers were powerful individuals. They had the discretion over whether to sell their commodity to a smuggler, how much to charge him per kilo, and whether to demand cash on delivery or to "front" (extend credit on) the merchandise. Southwest County smugglers thus worked to establish the best possible relationship with their foreign brokers, courting them in an ostentatious manner. One smuggler described a visit with his broker:

When I go down to Mexico I always pick up the tab for all the partying that goes on down there. Your brokers, growers, and their families all party together, and I play the part of the big American honcho who has lots of money. If a grower comes up and introduces me to his cousin Jose I am expected to say, "Hi, how are you Jose, here's $300, go out and buy your old lady something." It doesn't really matter to the Mexicans if you have a lot of money or not; all it goes by is how much you spend. You can be the richest guy in the world and have to pay cash for your grass if you don't act flashy. Or, you can throw it around and get it fronted to you every time. I usually end up dropping about $5,000 every time I go down there for a weekend.

These Mexican growing, packaging, and distributing enterprises were thus characterized by a moderate degree of criminal organization, more than individualized or Mom and Pop operations, but much less than integrated syndicate operations.

Cocaine originated further south than the prime growing territory for marijuana. It came from the rugged highlands of South America, most especially from Bolivia and Peru, with secondary growing areas existing in northern Chile, southern Colombia, and Equador.[3] Two main varieties were common: Bolivian or Peruvian "flake," and Colombian "rock." Cocaine (cocaine hydrochloride) was derived from the leaves of the coca bush *(Erythroxylon coca)*, a rugged plant that required little complex cultivation. Growing coca required intensive labor during certain periods, though, as water had to be hauled up the hills by hand during dry spells, and the harvesting was done manually. Long chewed by the native Indian tribes of South America to reduce hunger and fatigue (by allowing the blood to absorb more oxygen from the thin air at high altitudes), and in religious ceremonies, a certain amount of coca cultivation was legally permitted. Quantities grown greatly exceeded this amount, however, aided in part by reputedly large-scale corruption among local police, narcotics officers, military personnel, Customs Court judges, and politicians.

From its original form as leaves on a bush, cocaine underwent a three-step refining procedure before it was completely transformed into the white crystalline powder used for snorting. In dozens of small, clandestine laboratories ("kitchens") scattered throughout Colombia and Brazil, the leaves were soaked into a moist paste (called *pasta* by the natives) and then dried into a beige powdery substance called "base." Base, the stage before the finished product, could be smoked by sprinkling it onto joints or by burning it inside a glass tubular pipe with a bubble at the bottom. Finally, the base was refined into cocaine and packed inside airtight, clear plastic containers so that it did not become overly moist and melt. The process did not require a great deal of technical sophistication or equipment. In order to achieve the desired chemical changes in the substance, a kitchen chief merely had to know which ingredients to add at the appropriate times, what to do to the mixture, and how long to wait before moving on to the next step. Several strong men were needed to lift the heavy plastic vats of wet solution and pour the contents into other containers, combining and mixing them. The solution was heated at one point (by the sun), squeezed at another, merely left to sit and chemically stew at other points, and poured out onto huge cloth sheets and left to dry outside in the sun at the end of each step. When the final step was completed, the cocaine was bundled up into new sheets, the old sheets were scraped, and the kitchen crew emerged from their week-long stay in some remote jungle ready to deliver the product for packaging. From the time the coca leaves were wrapped into bales for sale to their eventual processing and export, a large number of workers (many of them local Indian men and women) served as "cooks" (laboratory technicians) and "mules" (transporters) to refine and ship the drug.

A BRIEF HISTORY OF IMPORTATION

In the early 1960s, buying marijuana in Mexico and bringing it across the border were relatively easy. Throughout the Southwest, marijuana users were crossing the border and scoring "lids" (a bag containing approximately one ounce of marijuana) or joints on the streets. The protocol was simple: a low-level Mexican seller would approach people and inquire if they were interested in making a purchase. Once they acquired the marijuana, individuals usually transported it back into the United States on their persons. Many women carried small amounts concealed in their bras, underwear, or personal belongings. Another method for bringing marijuana across was to smuggle it in suitcases in cars and commercial airplanes. "Border dodging" or border jumping by foot and air was also common and fairly simple. It was not necessary to take many precautions because marijuana smoking was not yet widespread and vigilance was minimal.

However, as marijuana use came to be seen as a national problem, the political climate changed. Operations Intercept and Cooperation, described in the introduction, clamped down on the flow of drugs across the Mexican-American border. Customs searches became more thorough, unmanned border areas were increasingly fenced and patrolled, and a general air of heightened suspicion ensued. Marijuana smuggling was forced to evolve in response to these law enforcement efforts.

Small Mom and Pop operators, from adventurous youths to amateur groups, who used to account for a large percentage of the illegal border crossings (see Carey 1968), were increasingly driven out of business. In their stead more professional groups flourished: people who could rise to the new sophistication demanded by the law enforcement challenge and who could afford the technology and equipment capable of avoiding detection. Thus, in the 1970s, marijuana smuggling took on a modified version of the form other large-scale drug smuggling (i.e., heroin) had traditionally displayed: the double-funnel effect (see Goode 1970; Preble and Casey 1969). This pattern was characterized by an abundance of people involved at the points of origin (growing and packaging) and disbursement (distribution and consumption), but by relatively few at the delicate and dangerous point of importation.[4]

GROUND-LEVEL SMUGGLING

As noted, the casual joint-smuggling days of the early sixties began to disappear with the first rise in professionalism of the mid-sixties. Fewer people carried marijuana on their bodies; instead, smugglers used elaborately designed vehicles to hide the illegal contraband. Custom-

made vans with "stash buckets" (false bottoms or interiors) could hold
many kilos of marijuana. These had to be made by artisans in the know
who charged an extra fee for the service. As one early smuggler stated:

We had a special custom-made smuggler-camper built in around 1965. We
worked for a week on the design we wanted. It cost us like—the guy that
built it knew what we were using it for and we had to pay him $1,000 extra—
the whole rig was worth about $12,000 for a new truck, a new 12-foot camper
and everything.

Originally, these vehicles were limited to 40-kilo shipments, but as
the art became more refined, vans, trucks, and buses were outfitted to
carry 200–250 kilo-bricks per trip.

A number of smugglers in these earlier days conducted the entire
operation themselves: they went down to Mexico, they obtained the
drugs, they drove them across the border, and they sold them in the
United States. For a relatively small additional expense, though, drivers could be contracted to do the dirty work, reducing the danger for
the smuggler. Hence, a crew system began to evolve where a smuggler employed other people to work for him, while he assumed responsibility for their protection.

The smuggler's job eventually became specialized to setting up arrangements with the Mexican broker and planning the coordination of
the vans with the merchandise for the loading. Generally the deal would
be preplanned; when the driver arrived at the indicated spot the marijuana would be waiting. Some importers, however, were more casual. They went to Mexico with the drivers, negotiated the deal there,
and had the broker send for the marijuana from Central Mexico. A
typical arrangement of the late 1960s and early 1970s began with a
charge of $50 per brick for the broker. Figuring on $10 payment per
piece (kilo) to the driver and a resale value of $140 each, the ground-
level smuggler could realize up to $16,000 net per trip for a maximum
load, before miscellaneous expenses, if all went well.

Proceeding north, the border checkpoint had to be crossed. Getting
through safely, without being pulled into the secondary inspection
station, was, of course, the ideal. Stash buckets worked successfully
until this trick became so widespread that every Volkswagen bus became suspect. One smuggler described how he saw the first sign of
trouble:

My friend that had the other Volkswagen bus, he was doing his own thing and he came across the border and they pulled him into the inspection area, and he had two bolts in his pocket, so they tore the whole bus down 'til they found where the bolts went. They found out that Volkswagens had a stash bucket and it closed up everything for Volkswagen buses from then on.

Ground-vehicle smuggling did not end in the late 1960s, but according to smugglers, customs agents first began to make a lot of arrests at that time. The Customs Department also started cracking down on illicit activities by their employees. Agents were rotated in a nonsystematic way so that scams (schemes) could not be planned. A smuggler described this historical changeover:

It's really a bummer now. They have the guards assigned on a rotating basis so that if you want to plan anything you don't know what time or what station they'll be at. One friend of mine made arrangements to bribe a guard and he went and got on the end of the guy's line. By the time he was halfway up to the front they changed the agents around and there was nothing he could do about it.

For people wishing to import cocaine, the process was slightly different. First, relations with a foreign supplier had to be established. This was usually more difficult than acquiring a marijuana connection because the cocaine-producing countries were much farther from Southwest County. Potential smugglers had to journey south alone and secure their source of supply before a run could be planned. Cocaine connections were not formed casually, but were usually acquired by referrals, since the brokers of Colombia, Peru, and Bolivia were secretive, highly organized, and violent. Some American smugglers therefore bought the names and contact points of their connections from others for a flat fee or a commission on each load. The cocaine market was not closed, however; in many ways it was still open for newcomers to break into and rise to the top rapidly. One coke smuggler described how he fortuitously obtained a connection:

I was going to take a drive up to Cactus City one day and I figured some company for the road would be nice. So I picked up two guys a couple of exits down the road. One of them got in the car and he said, "Hey, Frank, don't you remember me? We used to do business together with Lou a couple of years ago. This here's my friend Bob." Well, we started talking about what we were doing and after awhile I mentioned I was planning a trip to South

America to look into setting up some coke connections. Bob spoke right up and said he knew some guys there who would sell to me and that if I called him later he'd give me all the info. So that's how I got turned on to these heavy guys in Bogota. Kind of an accident, really.

After arriving in South America and contacting their connections, smugglers could select from several alternatives: they could purchase the cocaine and transport it back to the United States themselves; they could purchase the cocaine and arrange for someone else (a mule) to bring it across the border; or they could make arrangements for their agent to return at a future date to purchase and transport the drug. Their decisions varied according to their degree of experience, wealth, distribution capacity, and professionalism.

Because of the great distance between Southwest County and Colombia, smuggling large quantities of cocaine via the ground was never a popular mode. There were too many international borders to cross, and the length of the trip made it vulnerable to serendipitous mishaps. Ground-level cocaine importation thus fell mainly to those fairly amateur smugglers who operated during the 1960s. Yet because cocaine was denser and easier to conceal than marijuana, ground-level smuggling continued to account for some percentage of cocaine importation throughout the entire period I observed the scene.

AIR SMUGGLING

Although airplanes had long been used as a means for transporting a variety of illegal substances into the country, drugs included, the border blockades of the late sixties and early seventies added new popularity to this smuggling mode. By that time flying technology had evolved enormously, and the bulky, World War II surplus bomber planes (that could hold enormous loads) were being replaced by smaller, more powerful planes that could land and take off from remote, makeshift airstrips. Replacing propeller models with jets also gave smuggling pilots a quick thrust capacity which enabled them to elude both ground and air trackers.

In response to the continually modernizing technology of Customs, the FBI, and the DEA (Drug Enforcement Administration), smugglers introduced a range of new techniques. For instance, some individuals switched the kinds of aircraft they used so that their operations did not become known or predictable; they varied their takeoff and landing sites; they shifted between daytime and night flying; and they employed various means to "jump" the border. Some smugglers preferred their pilots to "fly on the deck," skimming the ground to avoid radar detection. Others would send two or three airplanes to fly across together—one full, the others empty—and then have them split off into different directions to confuse and lose the "Feds." Another tack was to fly two planes piggyback, one right above the other, so they came across on the same radar blip. Then the empty one would fly to the airport while the loaded one went to the arranged meeting place.

Landing and unloading techniques varied too, with some crews using ground-to-air radio transmission, others using walkie-talkies, and some maintaining complete silence. In the last case, pilots and ground personnel used a variety of signals to indicate that it was safe to make the drop-off, from flashing their headlights, to burping the engine, to lighting colored flares. Most pilots landed the plane and helped unload the cargo onto specially equipped desert trucks or vans. These vehicles were capable of driving long distances (they were often outfitted with extra gasoline tanks), carrying heavy loads, and keeping hoisted off the ground. The planes then took off again and returned to their hangers.

Pickup trucks transported the drugs away from the landing strip, usually within fifteen minutes of the plane's touchdown. They often signaled to the point man, located a short distance away from the landing area, that everything had proceeded as planned. On its way to its destination each vehicle passed another lookout who observed its progress, checked for police tails, and called the smuggler to let him know the truck had passed the checkpoint on time. The driver then continued toward the ultimate destination, usually stopping a short distance away to call and make sure it was safe to arrive.

Most of the time the intended destination was the smuggler's "stash house," a place maintained for the express purpose of storing large quantities of drugs (especially marijuana). At each stash house a person was employed to live on the premises, to receive and weigh the goods as they came in, and to be in telephone touch with the smuggler. Smugglers never went to their stash houses when these were "holding" (filled with drugs). Occasionally, for an especially big customer, smugglers might bypass the delivery to their stash house and send one truckful directly to the customer's preferred location. This only occurred for presold loads.

Within a day after the drugs' arrival, customers started arriving at the stash house to pick up their goods. The stash house man supervised this distribution, usually conducted inside a locked garage. As a security precaution he staggered the customers' arrivals and departures to ensure their privacy. Once the drugs were removed, the smuggler was called so that the money could be exchanged. Hotel rooms were the usual setting for these financial matters.

During the early and middle 1970s, when commercial marijuana was in its heyday, Southwest County smugglers might have done one load each week during the October to April prime season. One such operation broke down as follows: the gross profit for the sale of 1,000 kilo bricks was $140,000; out of this the smuggler paid $10,000 to the pilot, $500–$1,000 for the plane rental (or for buying and servicing his own), $1,000 for renting or servicing two vans, $12,000 for four drivers, $3,000 for the stash house operator, and another $10,000 for miscellaneous transportation expenses. If the marijuana was purchased in southern Mexico it cost around $35 per brick. The higher price of $60–$70 a brick was charged in northern Mexico. Many smugglers thought that this extra transportation surcharge was well worth the price, since it meant that their planes would not have to stop to refuel and face the extra risks of mechanical difficulty or arrest. In either circumstances such a one-ton run yielded between $35,000 and $70,000 net profit (before entertainment, personal consumption, and other miscellaneous costs).

The airborne importation of cocaine has followed a very different history from marijuana. Its compact volume has enabled smugglers to cross the border with it concealed on their persons or among their possessions more easily. Rather than having to obtain private planes and border jump, importers could transport it aboard regular commercial airlines and smuggle it through the airport Customs checkpoints. Favored hiding places included specially designed suitcase compartments, hollowed out bootheels, or, most often, the body of a female compatriot. It was thus common to use women or family groups as the actual mules, since smugglers felt that they were less suspicious-looking to customs agents. One smuggler described how he set up an operation:

> I knew this down-and-out couple who would do just about anything stupid for money, and they kept asking me if they could do a coke run for me. When I finally said yes, I sent them down ahead of me with some spending money for their trip. I arrived, scored the coke, packaged it, and gave it to them. Then I went home. They stayed a while longer and then came back themselves. Fay stuck the whole plastic baggie up her cunt, and with their kids and all they never were questioned. They got a free trip and $3,000 out of it. Not bad.

Using the commercial airline route imposed certain restrictions on the quantity which could be transported, however. Whether the cocaine was hidden on one's body or among one's possessions, it was hard to import more than a kilo at a time (body smuggling was even more limiting). A typical cocaine run by commercial airline in the early 1970s involved a purchase price of $5,000 for a kilo of almost pure South American cocaine. Importing expenses for plane fare, living expenses en route, and courier salary averaged around $4,000. The cocaine was then sold for $10,000 a pound. Net profit for a trouble-free trip ran from $11,000 to $31,000 (depending on whether "cuts" [adulterants] were added) minus miscellaneous expenses.

With the border crackdowns in the early seventies and the move to private aircraft by marijuana smugglers, cocaine smugglers slowly began to move into private air transportation as well. This mode of importation became especially popular with the rise in cocaine consumption in the middle and late seventies. Commercial airline smuggling could not get the product into the country fast enough, or in large enough quantities. Some marijuana smugglers began to include cocaine in with their loads, while those trafficking exclusively in cocaine adopted the technology of their marijuana colleagues and organized their own airborne runs. Major Southwest County cocaine smugglers usually brought in between 10 and 40 kilos of cocaine per trip, depending on their capital base, their source of supply, and their distribution network.

One group of three smugglers, who usually brought across 30 kilos of cocaine every four to six weeks (when they were working), ran a fairly simple operation. A pilot was hired for the run (they had a couple of regulars whom they tried to use as much as possible), and an airplane located. This group did not own a plane, so they either tried to find a pilot who owned his own aircraft or rented a plane (they often held the pilot responsible for this task). A copilot was also hired to fly shotgun for security reasons (although sometimes this role was performed by one of the smugglers). This latter individual's job included handling the money, helping with the drug purchase, and carrying a weapon to prevent rip-offs. On the day of the run the copilot was given the money. The plane took off, stopped for refueling at a clandestine airstrip en route (prearranged by the smugglers), and landed in South America. The two men met their contact at a hotel, exchanged the money for the goods, and returned to the plane. On some occasions one of the smugglers was already down there maintaining relations with the supplier. In these cases, he took care of acquiring the cocaine. The pilot and copilot then left South America and headed toward the United States, stopping again at a different makeshift airstrip to refuel.

Because thirty kilos of cocaine was compact enough to fit into two large suitcases, a remote landing to remove the contraband before arrival at the airport was not planned. Instead, the pilot flew to the nearest international airport and tried to lose whatever trackers were still observing him by blending in with the general air traffic. He then left the major airport, flew to a small airport, and landed. After unloading the suitcases into a car he washed off the plane, filed his fraudulent flight plan, and checked the aircraft into the hanger.

The copilot did not wait while this was happening, but left directly with the suitcases and drove toward his appointed meeting place with the smugglers. It was common for him to stop on the way for a cup of coffee or food to make sure that he was not being followed and to call the smugglers to inform them of his estimated arrival time. Once he arrived with the drugs (usually at an expensive hotel), the smugglers weighed it, sampled it liberally, divided it among themselves, and packaged it in plastic bags in the anticipated resale quantities (kilograms and multikilograms). Sometimes cutting occurred at this point, although most of the time they did not want to be bothered with anything other than just selling it. Each partner then left with his share of the cocaine and prepared to contact his customers.

The financing on a deal of this sort broke down as follows: $10,000 per kilogram was paid for the cocaine in South America; $30,000 went to pay the pilot; the copilot received $15,000; $2,000 was allotted for the rental of the plane, and the kilos sold in the United States for $65,000 each (these prices as of the late 1970s). This left a profit of around $1 million for the whole partnership (to be split evenly), before the miscellaneous costs were deducted.

While expenses like drug costs, employee salaries, and equipment rentals were clear-cut and calculable, smugglers incurred a host of other costs which were much harder to figure. Most individuals had little or no idea how much they were actually earning because keeping track of these expenses was extremely difficult. Maintaining a written record of the money they spent was both out of character for drug smugglers and, from a legal standpoint, highly dangerous.

Incalculable, or miscellaneous, costs could be divided into two categories: regular and sporadic. Sporadic costs included the occasional trips to Central or South America to spread goodwill among foreign suppliers, legal costs (including attorneys, bail bondsmen, and fines), product and capital losses from fronts which were never repaid, "burns" (receiving inferior quality merchandise), "busts" (arrests), and rip-offs. These costs were an expected part of doing business, yet were not calculated into the routine figures of each run. They tended to be major ones, however, and could bankrupt a financially unsteady partnership or individual operation.

Regular miscellaneous costs, in contrast, were high, but could be covered by the profit margin of each deal. These occurred to varying degrees during each venture, and included: waiting time, entertaining customers and suppliers, drug consumption, transportation, accommodations, meals, and other such costs. One cocaine smuggler described some of his entertainment and related expenses:

Once I've got a load of coke in that I need to sell, I set myself up at the fanciest hotel in Swanky Hills. Then I call all my customers and tell them I'm in business. One by one, they fly into town from all over. Naturally, I pay for their plane fare, cab fare, and put them up in their own rooms. We'll stay up all night long snorting coke and drinking Dom Perignon champagne. I pick up the tab for everything. I always tip big—15 percent on top of the 15 percent written in. If we go out to dinner I pay for the meal. If they get in trouble, I trip for the attorney.

To recapitulate, the boom in air smuggling fostered the rise of a new breed of entrepreneur. Cars and campers were left to the amateurs, those who could not muster the finances or imagination to rise above the problems inherent in ground transportation and the constant harassment from the border patrol. Those who made the jump to the speed and range of airplanes were an elite group, capable of assembling highly sophisticated operations. As noted, air smuggling was a cooperative effort which required the carefully planned work of several persons. The size of each organization varied, ranging from the larger, more stable groups to the slapped-together, fly-by-night operations assembled for a single run. Within the marijuana trade, the minimum number of people filling specialized roles included a pilot, a driver, someone to receive the goods, and one or more smuggling partners to arrange for the personnel, equipment, and buying and selling connections. These four or five persons comprised a crew (occasionally referred to informally as a "family"), and contrasted with the simple one or two persons usually involved in ground-level smuggling.

WATER SMUGGLING

The third means of importing marijuana and cocaine into the country was by boat. Ocean transportation offered the advantage of extremely large capacity; up to 60 tons of marijuana could be loaded aboard the giant shrimp trawlers and freighters commonly used. Smugglers using these vessels thus supplied several major customers in a single run by arranging for multiple drop-offs as they proceeded northward up the coast. The disadvantage of water smuggling was the length of time involved: smugglers had to hold the drugs for several weeks before they could unload them in the States. If they desired a faster trip, they used smaller sailboats or motor-powered boats which held up to four tons. These made the trip in just a week or two.

Water smuggling operations commonly took two forms: those arranged by Americans, and those arranged by South or Central Americans (predominantly Colombians). During my research I had the opportunity to observe the initial dominance of one form and its subsequent replacement by the other. When I first began studying Southwest County smugglers, they organized and executed most of their own international water runs. Boat trips planned and conducted by Americans usually had a single destination. Commonly, a few individuals banded together for such maritime operations. They generally purchased about 3–4 tons of quality marijuana in Central or South America (Mexican marijuana was rarely imported by boat) and loaded it onto the ship. The smaller, faster crafts just described were usually preferred. Smugglers occasionally rented these, like planes, but because the marijuana remained in the hold for so long that its odor set in permanently, one of the partners usually bought a boat. A smuggling crew was then formed to navigate and man the boat. On arrival at the arranged location, the signals between ship and shore were exchanged to confirm the identities of the parties. Small crafts or motor-powered Zodiac rubber rafts which held up to one ton of marijuana per trip were used to bring the drugs to shore. Packaged in heavy plastic and further protected by 50-pound duffle bags to prevent water damage, the bales of marijuana were transported to land. Water smuggling was extremely troublesome, however, and loads of marijuana were, at times, washed ashore, their ownership unknown. One smuggler described how a run of his ended in disaster:

There were four of us who went in on a deal together to bring up four tons of Colombian grass in a boat. This one guy had the buying and selling connections and he owned a boat, but he was broke. Me and a friend put up the money to buy the pot and the fourth guy was to navigate the boat up to a certain beach. Well the three of us charted the boat up there and sat around for our friend to show up and unload the stuff. Turned out he got screwed up on PCP and was out of it for a week so he never showed. There we were sitting out there for a week, in the water with the boat and the stuff. And we didn't even know we were parked on some Naval testing site until the Coast Guard or the Navy started shelling the area. One shell hit part of the boat, caught fire, and the entire load burned.

When cocaine was transported by boat it usually was bootlegged onto a marijuana run. Its compact size did not warrant arranging an entire water operation just for it. But the vast holding space of boats often tempted American smugglers to add that extra bit of diversified cargo which yielded so much profit.

The successful herbicidal spraying campaign which eradicated most of the Mexican marijuana fields in the mid-1970s had a profound effect on Southwest County smugglers (as the introduction notes). After this time, instead of buying their marijuana (and to a lesser extent, cocaine) in Colombia and transporting it themselves, Southwest County smugglers began to be pushed out of large-scale international trafficking by Colombian-dominated smuggling enterprises. Their independent entrepreneurial resources (even when partnered or organized into crews) could not compete against the more extensive Colombian organizations.

The Colombians launched a series of marijuana water smuggling operations that were beyond the scope of anything Southwest County smugglers had ever attempted. Rather than using pleasure boats or yachts, Colombians loaded giant shrimp trawlers to transport hundreds of tons per trip. These "mother" freighters navigated up the coast, remaining outside of the twelve-mile U.S. territorial limit so that the Coast Guard could not bother them. American dealers who bought from them brought their small "feeder" crafts out to these big ships, picked up the merchandise, and made the trip back to the beach. These relatively short but extremely hazardous runs were usually conducted under the cover of night. Normally, the money was exchanged at the time of delivery, but in special cases, it was repaid in person at a later date. Colombian water smuggling operations serviced many customers per trip, attracting greater law enforcement detection and harassment than the smaller American ventures. However, because the cost of the drugs to them was so much cheaper, they could lose four out of five loads and still make a profit (National Narcotics Intelligence Consumers Committee 1981).

PRICING IMPORTED DRUGS

Several factors combined to influence smugglers' prices to their customers. Some of these were inherent in the smuggling operation or in the drugs themselves, while others resided in external market conditions. I will briefly discuss the major factors and their role.

Cost. Several investigations of illicit drug pricing (Carey 1968; Redlinger 1975; Waldorf et al. 1977) have suggested that the most important consideration influencing smugglers' prices to their customers lay in the structure of their own costs. Southwest County smugglers' purchase prices were affected by: how close to the source they obtained the drugs; their relationship with the supplier (although this was a fairly minor consideration); and the current availability of the drug (supply vs. demand) in both the local foreign market and the international market as a whole. Unlike dealing, though, where a more or less standardized profit (or, at least, one from among several possibilities) was tacked onto the drug's cost to determine its selling price, I found no established profit margin in smuggling, either per unit or per trip. Rather, profit was determined by the difference between the smugglers' overall costs and the prevailing domestic market prices. In contrast to what previous researchers have suggested, then, my observations revealed that the main effect of smugglers' purchase prices was to determine the amount of their eventual profit. Fluctuations in purchase costs did not significantly affect the domestic pricing of drugs unless they underwent a major shift (as they did following the paraquat sprayings).

A second dimension of smugglers' costs was determined by the kind of operation they ran. Fly-by-night smugglers who pieced together a single venture had considerably fewer operating expenses than did individuals who supervised large crews. Established smugglers had to support employee salaries, legal and bail bond protection services, legitimate business fronts, and equipment. But their operational costs also influenced their profit rather than their selling price. Thus, established smugglers kept less profit per run than their one-shot compatriots, but earned more over a long-term period because of the regularity of their business.

Prevailing Market Price. The most important factor in the smugglers' prices to their customers was the prevailing price range in the market where they sold the drugs. Prices were influenced by the location of the transaction and the availability of drugs at that particular time. Each domestic locale thus had an ongoing illicit drug market which resembled a competitive free market in any commodity (although they

were somewhat constrained by their illegal status). Before attempting
to buy or sell in any market, smugglers gauged the upper and lower
boundaries within which drugs had recently fluctuated. These limits,
varying by the drug's quantity and quality, constituted the prevailing
norms which informally governed the price smugglers could command for their product. Smugglers thus adjusted their prices to fit the
local market, cutting back on profit if they needed to keep their inven-
tory and cash flow moving, or inflating prices to the upper limit if
they thought the immediate demand for drugs outstripped the supply.
Smugglers also set their prices according to their particular style and
reputation, some specializing in carrying only the highest quality merchandise at high prices, while others offered the most "righteous"
(reasonable) prices, and still others charged high prices but offered credit
liberally. In general, smugglers assessed the local drug market and fixed
their selling price before they actually imported the drugs.

Location. A major component influencing the prevailing market price
for illicit drugs in any given community was its location. We have already seen that marijuana cost less in southern Mexico than in the
northern zones (giving smugglers who ventured farther south a lower
initial outlay). I observed a similar pattern within the United States.
Prices in coastal or border areas were considerably cheaper than those
in the northern or midwestern sections of the country. The difference
was partly based on the greater expense involved, through both transportation and labor, in moving drugs over longer distances. It was also
tied to the geographic patterns of drug flow around the country. Thus,
smugglers were attracted to major urban centers which served as distribution hubs around the country, where goods could easily be un-
loaded. These places had lower drug prices than smaller cities and ru-
ral areas located closer to the border or coast. Finally, drugs were less
plentiful away from the coastal and border areas, so the high demand
and smaller supply further north and inland enabled smugglers to charge
higher prices in these regions.

Risks. Moore (1977) has asserted that an increase in the threat of arrest
due to law enforcement pressure (risk) acts like a "tax," raising the price
dealers and smugglers charge for their drugs (see also Redlinger 1975).
Smuggling was by far the riskiest aspect of the drug business, carry-

ing the severest legal penalties and evoking the most vigilant enforcement efforts. The disproportionate amount of risk smugglers assumed, compared to dealers, was rewarded by greater financial
remuneration, but this was not caused by their individually setting or
raising their selling prices. Instead, the type and amount of risk they
assumed were built into structured variations in prevailing market prices.
Market prices reflected the differential risk associated with: the number of international borders smugglers had to cross with the drugs; the
length of time they had to hold the product; the distance they had to
transport the drugs domestically (especially if they had to transfer the
drugs from one mode of transportation and/or storage to another); and
whether they had to extend credit to their customer and risk his de-
fault on the payment.

Quality. Waldorf et al. (1977) have cited quality as a major consideration smugglers used in setting selling prices for cocaine. They noted
that prevailing price levels generally specify a range, within which most
sellers fix their prices, often according to the perceived purity of the
drug. The Southwest County cocaine smugglers I observed, however,
rarely worried about quality. The quality, in fact, was fairly consistent. They thus let the dealers to whom they sold worry about testing
and cutting the product.

Marijuana smugglers, in contrast, dealt with a much wider variation
in the quality of their product, handling everything from low-potency
commercial Mexican to high-potency Central American strains.
Smugglers who specialized in high-grade marijuana had to be concerned about quality. Domestic market prices were finely attuned to
both the marijuana's effects and its appearance. To command top value,
marijuana had to have well-shaped, intact buds, devoid of seeds, stems,
and shake, be exotically colored (gold, reddish, or pale green as opposed to brown or dark green) with distinct red "hairs" covering the
outer portions of the buds, and be pleasantly fragrant. The preferred
effects included energizing lightheadedness and smooth taste, in contrast to a harsh-tasting smoke which brought on excessive cravings for
food and sleep. If the marijuana lacked these features, upper-level dealers
would not pay up to $600 a pound to buy it (late seventies prices).
Quality was, therefore, a vital consideration.

The commercial marijuana market had completely different stan-

dards, however. While the ultimate consumers cared about the marijuana's looks or effects, smugglers and upper-level dealers did not. Here,
dealers relied exclusively on the smuggler's word as to its quality, buying
and selling it sight unseen. Quality, then, was mostly irrelevant to
smugglers' pricing structure; it was just another commodity to be bought
and sold.

Situational Conditions. Added to these logical dimensions was one last
set of criteria: serendipitous, situational conditions. For instance, a
desperate smuggler might be in need of money and lower his price to
unload his holdings quickly. This could be rooted in his real, anticipated, or imagined legal difficulties, or in some problem with his personal life. Occasionally, a smuggler's relationship with his customer
could even affect the price. While Waldorf et al. (1977) and Redlinger
(1975) have noted that friendship and trust between smugglers and their
customers resulted in a lower selling price, I rarely found this to be
the case. Smugglers gave noticeable price breaks to people they liked
better or had known longer on very few occasions. Perhaps this was
because major smugglers generally dealt with so few customers, stick-
ing almost exclusively to people they knew well. Their transactions
were generally business-dominated, with friendship considerations
developing, yet remaining on the side. In one instance, however, I observed a smuggler raise the price of his merchandise to a customer with
whom he was angry. Sometimes people who had been turned down
as customers because they were unreliable were willing to pay a higher
price in order to obtain drugs. In a few instances I saw smugglers raise
their prices and sell to such individuals when they had extra merchandise that their regular customers could not cover. Finally, another deal
(either previous, concurrent, or future) between the buying and selling parties could affect the price structure on the immediate one.

But because things were customarily done one way did not mean
they were done that way every time. Individuals went into the dealing
business partly because they wanted the freedom to wheel and deal:
to run their affairs by putting together business ventures as they spontaneously decided. They also lived in a world of drugs, and heavy usage
affected their perceptions, moods, and decisions at times, making them
prone to capricious whims inside and outside their business lives.

CHAPTER THREE

UPPER-LEVEL DEALING

Awaiting the outcome of each successful smuggling run was a community of dealers ready to begin the process of distributing the drugs on a wholesale level. There were many more people who specialized in dealing than in smuggling; a stateside funnel shape begins to form. Among the reasons for the vast disparity between the number of upper-level dealers and the number of smugglers were: (1) the cost—compared to the high overhead of most smuggling operations, dealing ventures were relatively inexpensive to establish and maintain; (2) the manpower requirements—while smuggling required a small army of people to handle and coordinate transportation, storage, legal and financial matters, dealing was often a solo enterprise; and (3) the legal penalties—the enforcement vigilance and the structure of criminal sanctions were more lax for dealing than for smuggling. Thus the highly elite enterprise of smuggling was succeeded by the somewhat less prestigious but more popular activity of upper-level dealing. In this chapter I examine the range of activities which comprise dealing, and consider the hierarchy of levels by which dealers are vertically stratified.

STRAIGHT DEALING

There were two basic forms of drug dealing: straight dealing and middling. Straight dealing involved purchasing drugs in one quantity and dividing them into smaller units to sell. Southwest County cocaine dealers thus bought in kilos and sold in pounds or bought in pounds and sold in ounces to dealers at lower levels. In the cocaine market this usually included cutting the product. Dealers decided to cut their cocaine according to two considerations: their dealing style and the drug's potency. Some dealers were adamantly opposed to "stepping on" (adulterating) their merchandise. One dealer explained his philosophy:

> I want to be known as a dealer of quality merchandise, so I never cut my product. I know Fred whacks [dilutes] everything he gets. He figures people will respect him for being a shrewd businessman. But my customers would never buy from him on a bet.

Other dealers argued that cutting cocaine was standard operating procedure and therefore acceptable, as one practitioner stated:

> Sure you have to cut the stuff. Otherwise how can you make any money? The way prices run for the different quantities you can buy and sell, the only way you can make a profit is to cut it in between.

For those who did dilute their product (at least two-thirds of the dealers I observed), the amount of cut they added depended on the quality of their merchandise. The purer the cocaine, the more filler they could mix in, thereby greatly increasing their profits. Commonly used cuts included mannitol (a laxative); sorbitol (a sugar substitute); inositol (a B-complex vitamin); procaine (an analgesic), and quinine. Dealers used various testing methods to determine their product's purity. Some dealers placed a small amount of cocaine on a piece of aluminum foil and lit a fire underneath, watching to see the amount and color of the residue which remained after the cocaine boiled away. Others immersed some cocaine in a solution of either Chlorox or methyl alcohol and waited to see how much dissolved. While cocaine was soluble, some of the cuts remained, either floating or sinking to the bottom. These tests were all rather haphazard and unscientific. The ultimate test was the snorting test (alone or in conjunction with one of the other methods). Most dealers were able to discern the quality of the merchandise and offer an educated guess about the nature of its adulterants. Finally, the greater the quantity involved in the deal, the more likely it was that dealers cut the product.

After a dealer received and cut the cocaine, he or she usually turned it over as quickly as possible. This was not only due to the risk of holding it for long periods, but also so that he or she could make a speedy repayment, if it was obtained on a front basis. This was especially true if there was a time stipulation built into the payback arrangement. One dealer's remarks illustrate this case:

We [the smuggler and himself] had agreed that it would cost me a "nickel" [$5] more a brick for each 24 hours after the first had passed. You can be sure that we always had the stuff sold and the money delivered before evening of the next day.

To raise the repayment fee, major and proven reliable customers were taken care of first, along with those who paid cash on delivery. Optimally, a dealer had several standing orders to fill, as one wholesale commercial marijuana dealer described:

I usually have two or three standing orders, mainly because I do such a steady business. One guy from up North takes 300 bricks and another guy always wants 150 bricks. I even have a customer who takes 75 bricks every time. To me he's a small fry but I deal with him because I like him and because he's consistent.

Most dealers, after making a drug purchase, immediately phoned their customers to tell them that they had drugs to sell. The more successful dealers usually had the entire amount sold and paid for within a day or two. They then turned around and "copped" (made a purchase) again immediately, repeating this cycle as often as three or four times a week. Less successful dealers often fronted their merchandise to others and had to wait until they were repaid before they could reinvest their money. Depending on the reliability of their associates, this process took from several hours to a week or more.

People who became known as unreliable fronting risks found it increasingly difficult to obtain merchandise on credit, especially from dealers who maintained high standards. One dealer described how he was eased out of some details:

Until my smuggling gets off the ground I've been trying to survive by whatever dealing I can. It worked out for awhile, but I lost a couple of pieces [quarter-ounces of cocaine] to some people I had fronted; they couldn't pay me back. People snorting too much stuff up their noses. Then I fronted a couple up to someone in Desert City and he couldn't get the money back in time. So I couldn't repay the guy who had fronted me. So it's getting a little harder to get it fronted to me because I couldn't get the money back fast enough. I don't know why they seemed to think it was my fault.

When dealers could not find reliable or cash customers to whom to sell, they eventually became desperate to sell their merchandise. In this situation they often fronted to individuals who had dubious reputations.

Among people who regularly dealt with each other, there was little distinction made between paying cash for drugs and taking them on credit. This corresponds to Waldorf et al.'s (1977:57) observation that fronting was a common selling arrangement at the highest levels of dealing. Doug told how he regularly vacillated between obtaining drugs for cash or for credit, depending on the financial condition of his concurrently run legitimate business:

When I *have* the cash I pay cash for drugs, but I don't always have it. It depends on my cash flow situation. I've been in a few businesses over the years and have had to make heavy capital investments from time to time, besides losing my shirt in that restaurant. So when I'm broke I just get it fronted. It's really no problem, I just have to work a little faster.

MIDDLING

The second type of transaction that upper-level dealers engaged in was middling. Here, individuals sold the drugs they purchased intact, without separating them into smaller units. Middling generally occurred under one of two circumstances. Occasionally, a dealer with a load to sell found a single customer who wanted to purchase the entire amount. The ease and convenience of this type of deal caused many dealers to ask around when they were offered drugs for sale, to see if they could set up a simple transfer by finding a buyer interested in purchasing this same amount. Then, they simply transported the merchandise from their supplier to their customer and extracted a profit for filling the function of middleman. Although the middleman, in effect, deprived the first supplier of the additional profit he or she could have earned by selling directly to the final customer, most dealers did not mind (or even preferred) working through middlemen because it provided them with an extra layer of insulation from strangers. This first type of middling was precipitated, then, by the supplier's offer of merchandise.

The second type of middling was customer-initiated. Dealers were often approached by people looking to buy a specific amount of drugs. In this case, potential customers let it be known that they had cash available for a purchase. Upon hearing such a request, most dealers shopped around to see if they could fill this order from someone else in town. If they matched a source of supply with a cash purchaser, they boosted the price and made money on the transfer. Because this was such a common practice, considered a service to both sides, middlers might even discuss their profit margin openly with one or both parties. They might elect to receive their payment in cash or in kind (or both). The one thing they could not do was to reveal the identity of the two parties to each other. This second type of middling was the most common form and occurred within all dealing levels and circles.

Once the right connections were made, several hundred dollars could be earned in a short period of time. Moreover, this was usually accomplished without middling dealers having to put up any of their own money. In most cases, the buyer advanced the purchase money or the seller fronted the merchandise long enough for the deal to be completed. While most dealers considered this compensation good for the effort and risk expended, the profits available from middling were limited compared to dealing. The real money in dealing came from dividing the product and selling it in smaller units. One financial result of middling, however, was to drive up the price of drugs for each buyer and seller down the line. Thus unlike smuggling, dealing prices were affected by the additional variable of how many individuals handled the product, as distributors added their share of the profit into the value of the drugs.

In contrast to straight dealing, dealers who middled rarely adulterated the drug. Rather, these people passed the drug directly from the supplier to the customer as they received it. This was particularly true when the drugs were obtained on a front basis, as Marsha explained:

I would just pick up a kilo of coke at a time, fly home with it sewn in my jacket, and sell it straight across. It always worked out fine. But I never stepped on it. If you don't own it you can't, 'cause God forbid you have to give it back.

A small quantity, however, was often removed for the middler's own personal consumption. In some cases this was replaced with filler, but more often the merchandise was just delivered "short" (under the designated weight).

Although dealers looked favorably on the act of middling, it occurred most regularly among peripheral members of the drug trade: those on their way either into or out of dealing, and those who struggled in the drug business, unable to successfully establish and maintain regular buying and selling connections. Moreover, most novices who middled did not adopt self-conceptions as drug dealers. Jean explained how she first got into dealing by doing this:

After my husband got busted I was left alone to support the kids. I had never wanted to deal but I knew a lot of people who did. When I started to get really hard up I decided to try to see if I could make some money off of knowing all these big dealers. It's not really dealing—it's just putting together two connections, but the trick is to keep them apart so they don't know who each other are and they need you to complete the link.

Individuals who were trying to quit dealing also favored middling because it could be accomplished without undue complication or involvement. For instance, several dealers and smugglers I observed who were trying to retire took up middling drugs on a temporary basis. They removed themselves from dealing, but used middling to keep themselves financially afloat until they got on their feet. The same was true for people who had quit dealing to enter a legitimate business, but who needed to make a quick, noncommital foray back into the drug world whenever their business did not earn enough money. Lastly, middling was popular among drug entrepreneurs who tried but could not consistently engage in straight dealing. Their failure was rooted in either their inability to secure and hold an adequate supply of reliable connections, or in their inability to store, divide, repackage, market, and transport the product to dealers at the next lower level (without consuming an excessive amount of the merchandise).

CULTIVATION

A third type of activity which developed and became increasingly popular among Southwest County residents after the mid-1970s was the commercial production of high-potency domestic marijuana (as noted in the introduction). In the Southwest County marijuana fields and greenhouses, I observed several sophisticated cultivation techniques designed to maximize marijuana's THC content and appearance, from genetic cross-breeding to fertilization, prevention of seed-formation, pruning, growing, hydroponics, harvesting, curing (drying), and manicuring.

Because of the common product these two industries shared, some individuals sidestepped into the cultivation business from dealing, while others attempted to move into dealing through cultivation. But marijuana growing was a time-consuming and dangerous business. Planting, irrigating, fertilizing, and pruning required that the grower exercise responsibility and remain close to the fledgling crop. Harvest seasons required the most vigilance, as the incidence of rip-offs was high. All growers, especially those with outdoor fields, had to guard their near-ready crops both day and night until the process of cutting, preparing, packaging, and distributing was completed. And unlike dealing, where violence was less common, a successful cultivation business required carrying and occasionally using shotguns, handguns, and rifles.

A very different range of activities was thus called for in this enterprise, overlapping occupationally only at the sale of the finished product. There was therefore only limited cross-involvement, as beyond their common drug world membership and the sympathetic nature of their industries, dealers generally stayed out of large-scale cultivation and growers usually lacked the orientation toward or interest in more full-time dealing.

VERTICAL STRATIFICATION

The range of business activities practiced by Southwest County drug traffickers—from smuggling to straight dealing, middling, and cultivation—was instrumental (although not exclusively determinant) in helping to stratify dealers along a vertical continuum, or hierarchy of levels. Although several dimensions existed for dealers potentially to stratify themselves in relation to each other (see Blum et al. 1972:47), the most important of these to Southwest County operators was volume of business. I will present the overall hierarchy of levels which existed in the commercial marijuana (early to mid-1970s) and cocaine (late 1970s) trades, examine the types of activities common at those ladder rungs which characterized Southwest County's upper levels of dealing, and discuss the variations in dealers' behavior which makes a scheme such as this inevitably ideal-typical.

Commercial Marijuana. My observations of commercial marijuana traffickers in and around Southwest County yielded a hierarchy with six levels (see table 3.1).

At the top of the ladder were *smugglers,* those individuals who purchased their drugs in a foreign country and transported them into the United States. Typically, they bought marijuana in lots of 1,000 bricks (weighing one kilo each) and smuggled it across the border in small jet

TABLE 3.1
Hierarchy of Commercial Marijuana Dealers (early to mid-1970s)

Type of Dealer	Buying Units	Selling Units
Smuggler	1 ton (1,000 kilo bricks)	1,000 kilo bricks 600 300
Wholesale dealer	600 kilo bricks 500 400 300	300 kilo bricks 200 100
Multikilo dealer	300 kilo bricks 200 100	100 kilo bricks 50 25
Middle-level dealer	100 kilo bricks 50 25	25 kilo bricks 10 5
Low-level dealer	25 kilo bricks 10 5	10 pounds 5 1
Ounce dealer	5 pounds 3 1	pound half pound quarter pound (lids) ounces

Source: Adapted from Waldorf et al. (1977:50).

planes. Once the marijuana arrived safely in the United States, smugglers followed one of two options for its disposal: they brokered it all to a single large customer or middleman, or sent it to a stash house and sold it in smaller lots to several wholesale dealers. Because of the organization and complexity required for their smuggling ventures, most smugglers preferred not to get too involved in dealing, especially if this entailed the additional overhead and risk of maintaining a stash house and employees. Delivering the entire load immediately to a single outlet yielded less overall profit, but it was a more popular alternative. Among those who could not find or who chose not to employ such a connection, the load was broken down and sold in lots of 300–600 bricks.

Wholesale dealers were the top level of dealers within Southwest County, buying directly from the smugglers. These individuals commonly bought from only one smuggler at a time, turning to another smuggler only when their regular source could not supply them. Relations between smugglers and wholesalers involved a good deal of trust and commitment, and were characterized by a strong sense of loyalty. Many out-of-town wholesale dealers traveled to Southwest County to buy their drugs directly from these smugglers so that they could obtain the cheapest possible prices. Depending on the condition of their and the smuggler's transportation and/or storage resources, the drugs were exchanged either in Southwest County or closer to the wholesale dealer's base of operation. This usually involved transporting marijuana domestically by van or truck, due to its bulk.

Local Southwest County wholesale dealers operated their own stash houses to store their marijuana. Some dealers employed "runners" to transport the marijuana bricks from their stash house to their customers' desired locations, while others operated a cash-and-carry business where customers shopped at the stash house and took their merchandise with them when they left. Since wholesale dealers usually sold in lots of 100 to 300 kilo bricks, a large automobile, van, or pickup truck was required for this transportation. These dealers did not employ sizable crews like smugglers, but they still made a considerable investment in their operations (i.e., a stash house, a stash house operator, and possibly runners or vehicles for transporting drugs). Wholesale marijuana dealers therefore tended to specialize in a single

commodity. If they wanted to obtain better-quality marijuana or cocaine for their own consumption they usually bought it by the pound
or ounce (respectively) from a dealer who carried these drugs. Such
specialization in a specific type of commodity was the norm the closer
one got to the top of the hierarchy.

Estimating the extent of their markup per unit was difficult because
it varied with the distance they transported the drug, whether it was
middled before they got it, and the prevailing local prices (which were
also affected by the seasonal availability of the product).

Multikilo dealers constituted the next rung of the hierarchy. These
middle- to upper-level dealers bought in lots of 100 to 300 bricks and
usually sold amounts from 25 to 100 bricks. While they had no contact with the smuggler, they generally had a few possible suppliers
with whom they did business (3 to 5) and several customers whom
they called when they had drugs to sell (4 to 7). These individuals
were strictly solo operators, buying, transporting, storing, and selling
the marijuana themselves. Like wholesale operators, multikilo dealers
often moved the drugs from one area to another to boost profits. Many
dealers who lived in Southwest County, for example, bought there but
sold their marijuana in other cities. Or, some multikilo dealers from
elsewhere traveled to Southwest County to buy their drugs, bringing
them back home to sell. Initially, commercial airlines were widely used
for transporting large suitcases stuffed with marijuana bricks from city
to city. The occasional use of pot-sniffing police dogs at airports, though,
eventually deterred some individuals from flying with their marijuana.

At this level, it was fairly common for multikilo dealers to handle
more drugs than just commercial marijuana. These were generalist
dealers, in business to sell drugs on a fairly large scale. They had no
special investments in employees, storage facilities, or transportation
equipment which would tie them to a single product. The only constraints on their branching out to other drugs were product knowledge, buying and selling connections, and personal preference. Some
multikilo dealers in Southwest County thus handled a range of other
soft drugs, including hashish, hash oil, Thai sticks, sinsemilla, amphetamines, and cocaine.[1]

Cocaine. For the cocaine business I isolated a hierarchy with five levels
(see table 3.2).

TABLE 3.2
Hierarchy of Cocaine Dealers (1979)

Type of Dealer	Buying Units	Selling Units
Smuggler	40 kilograms 30 ($10,000) 20 10	10 kilograms 5 ($65,000) 1
Pound dealer	10 kilograms 5 1	pounds ($30,000) pound half pound ($16,000–$17,000)
Ounce dealer	pounds half-pound	ounces ($2,000– $2,200)
"Cut-ounce" dealer	ounces	half ounce ($1,100–$1,200) quarter ounce ($550–$650) grams ($100–$120)
Gram dealer	half ounce quarter ounce	quarter ounce gram half gram ($55–$65)

Source: Adapted from Waldorf et al. (1977:50).

The *smugglers* I observed brought cocaine across the border by boat or plane in quantities ranging from 10 to 40 kilograms at a time. These were full-time operators who handled only cocaine and rarely got involved in dealing (i.e., purchasing domestically). Normally, smugglers who made regular cocaine runs did not cut their product. Rather, they turned it over, untouched, to the first level of dealers. On the other hand, individuals who engineered a single, or small, run were more likely to add cuts when they were weighing and packaging the product in smaller quantities for resale. These were usually upper-level dealers who occasionally smuggled and who were therefore used to adulterating their product.

Smugglers usually partnered together to plan and finance an importation run, dividing the cocaine among themselves after they packaged

it so that each member could sell his share separately to his own customers. For this reason, I rarely saw a single upper-level dealer or
middleman purchase an entire smuggled load, which I often saw in
the commercial marijuana industry. Major cocaine smugglers thus
specialized in the commodity they imported, restricting their trafficking to cocaine only. When they had brought and were ready to sell,
cocaine smugglers contacted their customers and met them to exchange the drugs for money. These meetings took place in either the
area where the customer worked, the area where the smuggler had his
base of operations, or neutral territory. Smugglers sold in quantities
ranging from 1 to 10 kilos at a time. The cocaine was then transferred
from the smuggler to the pound dealer in person, being sampled liberally by both parties. This personal handling was completely opposite from the trafficking norms in the commercial marijuana industry,
where the product was never present when the smuggler and wholesale dealer consummated their sale. Holding drugs on one's person was
the rule throughout the cocaine industry, though, from the top all the
way down to the bottom levels.

   Pound dealers were the highest level of cocaine dealers in the county.
They bought the cocaine in kilos from the smugglers and sold it in
pounds (or half-pounds) to their customers. They were most often the
first to cut the cocaine, beginning with a one-for-one cut (depending
on the quality), thereby doubling the amount. Like smugglers, pound
dealers handled their cocaine personally, transporting it themselves and
storing it on their premises in specially constructed secret caches. Pound
dealers often flew around the country via commercial airlines to market their product. Some bought in Southwest County and sold up north
or in the Midwest, while others bought elsewhere (Florida, New York)
and returned to Southwest County to sell. The profit they made on
changing from one market to another justified the travel and lodging
expenses associated with such methods of operation.

   Buying and selling relationships associated with pound dealing were
also very stable. As I will discuss in the next chapter in more detail,
pound dealers usually bought from a single smuggler, bought and/or
sold equal amounts among a circle of associates (4 to 6) on their level,
and sold to a small group of individuals (3 to 5) at the next lower level.
The turnover in personnel at these upper levels was much less than

further down the hierarchy, leading to relatively stable relationships. One further procedure differentiated pound dealers in cocaine from wholesale commercial marijuana dealers: the cocaine dealers occasionally smuggled. Unlike commercial marijuana, which was bulky and unwieldy, a couple of kilos of cocaine could be easily hidden and smuggled via commercial airlines through the regular customs checkpoints. Pound dealers with foreign connections thus occasionally deviated from their normal dealing routines to put together a smuggling venture.

Although cocaine was sometimes sold from dealer to dealer in only slightly diminishing quantities, the next operating niche I identified was the *ounce dealer*. Ounce dealers represented a shift away from the level of commitment characterizing smugglers and pound dealers, as they were neither as professionalized as traffickers at those levels nor as exclusively specialized in handling solely cocaine. They were likely to trade in a variety of drugs, depending on what was available locally, knowing people to buy from in both the marijuana and the cocaine worlds. Similarly, their customers were not likely to restrict themselves to dealing in a single drug.

Ounce dealers bought, transported, stored, and sold their product themselves, neither employing nor partnering with others. Like pound dealers, their basic *modus operandi* involved buying domestically, but some also tried to smuggle a pound through customs occasionally if they could make all the necessary arrangements. Most ounce dealers cut the cocaine in a one-to-one ratio after they bought it. As Waldorf et al. (1975:53) noted, however, to have coke was to use coke, and after several days of holding the drug many dealers snorted more than their anticipated "stash profits." They then usually resorted to adding more cut to the remaining cocaine in order to make up for their overindulgence (early customers thus got better deals). Ounce dealers generally sold their cocaine by the ounce and half-ounce.[2] They also sold grams, as samples, to their customers at discount prices, because their profit margin at this level could not absorb the heavy "tasting" (sampling) during transactions that smugglers and pound dealers offered. While the money and drugs they earned were adequate to sustain them comfortably without need for other employment (except, perhaps, as a legal front), ounce dealers did not make the kind of profits that smugglers and pound dealers made. Their buying and selling prices were more restricted by the narrow profit margins dictated by local market norms (unless they took the unusual step of traveling with their drugs). Finally, ounce dealers cultivated a larger clientele (5 to 15) than smugglers or pound dealers, since the people they sold to dropped out of the business and were frequently replaced by others.[3]

In evaluating these hierarchical schemes it is important to remember that they represent ideal types. I extrapolated these different levels of operation from the most common patterns of buying and selling. However, the rigidity and regularity that they suggest may be misleading. Drug entrepreneurs would rarely buy consistently in the same quantity and divide that amount into smaller segments to be sold in fixed units. Rather, they wheeled and dealed, as they flexibly varied quantity and style of operation depending on their mood. They thus often handled different amounts from one deal to the next, "stooping" on one deal and "reaching" on another, selling pounds one time, ounces the next, and buying grams in a third. They also bought and sold back and forth among dealers on their same level, acting as the supplier in one deal and the customer in the next.[4] Dealers, then, trafficked in circles of associates rather than in fixed quantities, their drug world relationships having greater importance than any customary level of operation. It is to these circles of associates that I now turn.

CHAPTER FOUR

SOCIAL ORGANIZATION

I have described Southwest County dealers and smugglers as composing a subculture or social world. Inherent in every social world is a system of social organization which patterns the relationships of its members. In this chapter, I examine the social organization of the Southwest County drug world, focusing primarily on the structure and type of relationships between the members. I present a model describing the concentric circles of diverse relationships in which dealers and smugglers were involved and then consider each type of association in detail, examining its intensity, propensity, and character.

THE SOCIAL ORGANIZATION OF DRUG WORLD RELATIONSHIPS

Southwest County dealers and smugglers lived in a world filled with multiple layers and types of relationships (see the figure). These expanded concentrically outward around each individual, surrounding him or her with associations that began as highly business oriented, but decreased in their business intensity as they took on an increasingly social nature. *Partnership* bonds were the most closely entwined business relations, being characterized by equality, sharing of profit, and self-interest. *Connectional* liaisons were critical to making transactions and often endured over long periods, involving customer-supplier relationships. Beyond these, Southwest County traffickers were associated with others by friendship *networks*, social affiliations with other drug world members that had business overtones. Each individual also belonged to a larger circle of *acquaintances* which was composed of dealers and smugglers the individual knew socially, yet with whom he or she had no business dealings. Finally, individuals were encircled by an *umwelt* of other dealers and smugglers known to them by reputation only, with whom they had no direct business or social

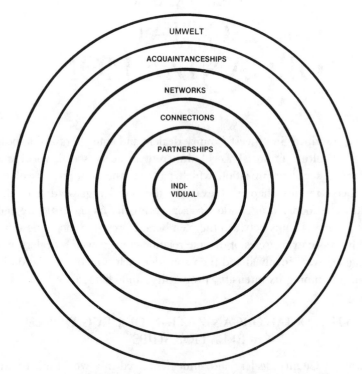

The Expanding Network of Drug World Relationships

bonds. This pattern of business and social relations surrounded each drug trafficker individually, framing and organizing his or her behavior. While the membership of each person's concentric circles varied, they partially overlapped.

PARTNERSHIPS

The closest of all relationships in the drug world were partnering ones, where people worked together toward successfully completing each transaction. Contact between partners, often occurring daily, was intense and frequent, requiring the greatest degree of mutual trust. Drug world partnerships were extremely varied in nature: they might endure for long or short periods; they might be augmented by business, social, or familial relations outside the dealing world; and they might be egalitarian or hierarchical in nature. Within Southwest County I found a range of partnering arrangements from working in crews, to groups, to working alone. These varied with the drug involved, the time period of the transaction, and the type of activity conducted.

The first partnering structure incorporated the closest, most enduring, and most intricate set of social relationships. Begun in the 1960s and made nearly obsolete by the mid-seventies, organized *crews* were primarily responsible for importing commercial marijuana. During this time large, stable, and highly specialized groups of individuals were needed to handle international air and local ground transportation, as well as a variety of other supportive roles. Ben's crew provided a slightly larger than average example, being composed of seven members, not including himself. Two of these were drivers and one a pilot. The dual role of driver and copilot was filled by a fourth man. Another pilot worked in the triple role as a smuggler with his own operation and as a side customer, flying loads for Ben when he was not busy. The sixth member was Ben's enforcer and stash house man, living in the place where the marijuana was stored, disbursing it to customers, and being available for acts of violence when Ben deemed it necessary. The legal and financial aspects of the business were handled by the seventh and final person. His job involved arranging for the lawyers and bail bondsmen when needed, laundering Ben's money, and providing him with a legitimate-looking business front. Most of these crew members also dealt on the side, having the choice of taking their payment in cash or in kind. Ben's role involved arranging the buying and selling connections, planning and financing the operation, providing the heavy equipment (planes, vans, radios, etc.), and recruiting, supervising, and replacing his crew members (which, between general attrition and Ben's security precautions, turned over about once every year).

Relationships within smuggling crews were very close, involving frequent and intimate contact. The smuggler presided over his crew, supporting them emotionally, picking up the tab for their extensive partying, and mediating disputes. They all associated together on a daily basis, intermingling their business and social contact completely. This could occasionally reach the point of exclusivity, where crew members became drawn into such a tight social circle that they cut off nearly all contact with others. They would then fluctuate in and out of this isolated stance, first expanding their circle to include other drug world members, and later bringing in nondrug friends. Periodically, however, they retreated once again to the security and total drug-using absorption of the crew base.

Relations between different crews sometimes took on a complex character, overlapping and becoming enmeshed. One pilot recounted how these associations occasionally extended beyond the social sphere into the realm of business:

The smuggler I worked for lived right next door to another smuggler who was as big or bigger than him. There was a lot of intermingling of their crews. Like his guys all dated my wife's circle of friends and sometimes we would blend into one big party at one house or the other. He was always trying to get us guys to work for him. I did a couple of gigs but I always checked first with my boss to see if it was all right or if he needed me.

Crew members were thus very committed to each other, sharing mutual interests and even showing relative longevity in their affiliation. Yet this form of partnership was based on a subordinate relationship. Smugglers and their crews had an employer-employee relationship, although the smuggler ruled in a paternalistic fashion and the atmosphere was fairly close and familial.

Beyond the crew structure, it was common for dealers and smugglers to work in *groups*. Group partnerships were the most makeshift, fluid, and diverse form of social organization in Southwest County's drug world. Generally ranging from two to four members, group partnerships varied in character along two major dimensions: by the relations that existed between the parties outside the dealing context, and by the stability of their relationship.

The most tightly bonded of all dealing and smuggling partnerships were those rooted in the nuclear family. Here, siblings or spouses worked in tandem, living together or in close proximity. There was usually a division of labor according to personality and social interaction: one person kept an eye on business profits, striving to drive a hard bargain, while the other provided the partnership with generosity, good will, and integrity. Relatives were the most trusted kind of partners because of the familial ties which bound them, augmenting the longevity of the association and ensuring that their interests were overlapping and mutually beneficial. Thus, through the lure of easy money and flexible hours, family members were sometimes recruited into the partnership from nondrug occupations.

Most often, partnerships were forged among friends met within the drug world. In lieu of loyalty and trustworthiness, friendship partnerships were rooted in pragmatic, business-oriented bonds, being centered around specialized divisions of labor. Commonly, one person bought the drugs, another arranged for their sale, and in multipartner situations, others might be responsible for raising the money or providing transportation. Some profit-sharing accommodation was then made. One dealer described an arrangement he had used:

I had a connection who was ready to supply me 700–800 bricks two or three times a week. He'd deliver them to a spot in Grass City and I had 24 hours to get rid of it and pay him. But there was no way I could turn all that stuff myself. So I got ahold of the heaviest cash dealer in town and sent the stuff to his house. I made him deal it all for me and I picked up the money the next day. We worked as partners and split the profits right down the middle. That's how I always like to work—an even share no matter who does what, how hard you have to hustle, or what the risks are.

Especially for smuggling, people with diverse expertise pooled their resources into partnerships, since it was nearly impossible for a single individual to be skilled, financed, and connected in all the highly diversified and changing dimensions of the business.

Some dealing and smuggling partnerships among friends were long-lasting, involving a firm commitment between people. This characterized the most stable, least common individuals in the subculture, those who followed a regular routine for the majority of their transactions. Generally, Southwest County's most seasoned veterans formed enduring partnerships because these individuals did not want to risk the dangers associated with constantly working with new people. In addition, the highly professionalized dealers and smugglers who took many security precautions (i.e., minimizing the number of people with whom they came in contact) to insulate themselves from robbery and arrest (as I will discuss further in chapter 6) formed these lasting relationships. One dealer explained the conditions of his partnership agreement:

My partner and I, we had an arrangement—we'd split whatever we could get either way. We wouldn't go around each other, even when we could buy more directly sometimes, to both help each other. We took care of each other, kind of a profit-sharing thing. It's a lot safer in the long run. But we always made it clear that if either of us ever got busted we would drop all contact with each other and never communicate again.

Such broad and enduring group partnerships were rare, though, since dealers and smugglers tended to traffic where the money and drugs were most readily available. Transitory partnerships of convenience were the most predominant, created for one or two transactions. While dealers partnered in this manner, these fleeting relationships were most characteristic of the smuggling profession during the post–commercial marijuana era. Once large-scale Colombian smuggling organizations displaced Southwest County smuggling crews from their dominant position in the regular, heavy-volume marijuana importation routes, flexibility, adaptability, and specialized expertise became more desirable than dependability. Group partnerships often were forged, then, according to the availability of personnel, their potential division of labor, and the type of smuggling run they were planning (i.e., boat vs. plane, marijuana vs. cocaine, Mexico vs. Colombia). Transitory partnering relations were especially prevalent among the "riff-raff" smugglers: the most careless, disorganized, and flighty operators (usually former members of another smuggler's crew who were trying to break out on their own), who never seemed able to establish and maintain a successful mode of doing business. These individuals needed to partner in both smuggling and dealing because they were incapable of putting together an entire transaction themselves, constantly fading in and out of sight as they alternately had money or went broke, or were forced to temporarily disappear because they were "hot" with the police or other dealers. For instance, Jack described how a partnership formed to smuggle marijuana resulted in a rip-off and violence:

I had tried smuggling gigs many times before but they never seemed to come together, so I went in on a run with Mack. Well, the only guy we could come up with to fly the plane was Bart. I knew he'd been involved in a rip-off some time earlier but he'd never ripped me off so I didn't worry about it. We talked, and it seemed like everything was cool. Bart left with 20 grand to go down and pick up the stuff, but he never came back. Never showed down there either. He's dead now. That Mack, he's kind of an excitable guy who doesn't take too kindly to these kinds of things.

The final alternative was to operate as an *individual*, partnering with no one. Conducting one's business alone occurred frequently among dealers, although as a social form, it was nonexistent for smuggling. "Lone Ranger" dealers set personal rules which dictated that they refrain from the type of close affiliation inherent in a partnership. This could be motivated by a combination of pride, greed, mistrust, and fear. One solo dealer elaborated on his feelings about unaffiliated dealing:

I've never trusted anybody completely in my career as a dealer and that's why I never worked with anybody as a partner, not even for one deal. There's an unsaid thing when you're doing a business deal that you're out to get as much as you can for yourself in an amenable arrangement. Having a partner would inhibit that. And also, I know cases of people who dealt with others for months and it turned out that they were narcs, that they ultimately put them in jail. That's why I always work alone.

The extent to which dealers operated as individuals was also tied to the pragmatics of their occupation: the connections and labor involved could be more easily handled by a single person than could the complexities of smuggling. Thus, especially when dealers were trafficking in cocaine or quality marijuana (the less bulky substances), and when they were working in the local area with well-established buying and selling associations, they saw partnering with others as unnecessary.

CONNECTIONS

Outside the relative intimacy found among smuggling and dealing business partnerships, the next closest form of relationship occurred between connections. While not as directly tied together by shared profit, connections were still tightly bonded by money and personal safety each time they came together on different sides of a business transaction. Relations between connections could be extremely friendly and enduring, with people compatibly working together over the course of years, or they might be furtive and short-lived, involving a single sale between people who never saw each other again. Relations between connections were also differentiated by the activities of straight dealing versus middling: the former involved a vertical transaction between people who were operating at least temporarily on different levels, while the latter was a horizontal transfer of goods among equals.

Suppliers (from whom goods were bought) were the most strongly coveted of all drug world connections because access to drugs was the first and most basic requisite for doing business. Individuals' relationships with their suppliers were also critical because these could affect the type of purchase arrangement involved, enabling them to get the goods fronted or forcing them to buy on a cash-only basis.

Supply connections varied between dealing and smuggling, and among the various levels of dealing. Smugglers usually operated with the fewest number of different suppliers, exclusively patronizing one or two foreign brokers. They cultivated their friendship and reputation with these connections carefully, as the smuggler in chapter 2 noted when he described a visit to his Mexican broker.

Upper-level dealers preferred to operate with a slightly larger selection of supply sources, although this varied with the standards for reliability and security that each individual operator maintained. The most professional dealers tended to buy from two or three connections only, calling upon one of these people when they needed drugs. They could thus be consistently counted on to have the desired substance themselves, and to offer it at a dependable quality. Their relations with their top suppliers, some of whom were smugglers, were binding and loyal, but not frequent or socially casual. Generally, smugglers did not party with their customers unless they were conducting a deal.

The less reputable upper-level dealers, who were inconsistent in their selling practices and/or reliability, usually worked with a larger number of suppliers (four to ten). These dealers often scrambled for connections, in part because the wholesalers or smugglers they bought from either offered an unsteady supply or refused to deal with them when they failed to make regular payment on previous deals. Their dealing activities involved a frequent process of supplanting old sources with fresh ones, while still seeking to maintain a steady flow of drugs for potential buyers. Tom, a multikilo marijuana dealer, described his perception of the dealing market as open:

Everybody is always shuffling around, getting new people to buy from, new people to sell to. Sources dry up, people retire. If you stay in the trade pretty actively it's not hard to make new connections. You're always running into somebody who has a good friend, somebody always has a deal; somebody always has a surplus because one of their buyers isn't around and is looking for somebody else they can trust. I'd say that's how you shuffle around quite a bit.

Relationships among these dealers were thus most likely to be capricious, affected by market demand and their current financial problems. The next mode of connections involved people who operated within a roughly equal range of quantity, often buying, selling, and middling back and forth among themselves. People in this type of relationship bonded with similar others into *circles*, one of the most common forms of dealing associations. Circles, numbering four to ten members, were characterized by both intra- and intergroup trading, although dealing within the circle was more predominant. Rob, a pound dealer in cocaine, discussed the nature of his dealing circle:

Sure, we'd buy and sell from the same people. It would go back and forth, depending on who had the product. There was no hierarchy. That circle of ten people was the hierarchy; we were on the same level with them for quite a bit of time, at least with five of them. . . . So there were five people with us and the other five right behind us. They were the intermediary, middle people. And the people right above us were the smugglers.

Dealing circles were generally very close, tightly knit groups who were mutually compatible personally, socially, and demographically. They attracted people of roughly the same age, race, and ethnic origin, who conducted their business along similar standards of security, reliability, involvement, and commitment. Kerry, another cocaine dealer, commented on the multifaceted intensity of the relationships within his circle:

It's good to keep friendships within the circle on both a business and social level because then you're friends on a daily basis; you see them all the time and so you're safe. If you socialize with the people you deal with there's more trust, you're sharing the same traumas. Hell, 75 percent of the people I'm involved with now I was involved with four years ago. Our circle has stayed really tight.

These groups, then, could be fairly steady in membership, often staying together over the full course of each person's involvement in the dealing world. They tended to jell early in dealers' careers and mature with them through the various changes that came with aging through the evolutionary course of the occupation. Members of younger circles, for example, took more risks and were more open to new practices and people than were those in established circles, whose goals narrowed their activities. Finally, only dealers organized themselves into circles, since smugglers had no reason to buy from or sell to other smugglers.

Customers, buyers to whom drugs were distributed, formed the third type of connection. Relations with customers were the most transient, being valued less highly than supplier or circle connections. Here a status differential was implied, as high-volume dealers carried more prestige within the community than the low-volume buyers to whom they sold. This relative prestige ranking was based partly (as Best and Luckenbill 1982:153–54 have noted) on the fact that demand nearly always outstripped supply, giving sellers a position of authority within the transaction. Customer connections were the least sought and most dangerous of all transactional relationships because of the illegality of the product. Dealers' and smugglers' reluctance to seek new customers was rooted in their awareness of the traditional "buy-bust" procedure, where police tried to make a purchase from someone and then arrest him once he sold them drugs (Manning 1980). Therefore, as one dealer explained, people were wary of selling to new faces since this represented the most dangerous form of exchange:

Trust is a risky business. Dealers get suspicious if a person is overzealous, if he's getting too much info out of you too fast. They'll often trust a broke person more than someone who comes running up to you saying, I've got 100 grand, get me something.

Dealers and smugglers varied in their practices concerning the number of customers they maintained and the stringency of the criteria they used for evaluating new potential customers. Smugglers had the strongest preference for selling to the fewest people; their energies were much more directed toward buying and importing drugs than toward maintaining a distribution network. At times, smugglers thus opted for a convenient and safe bulk sale, even if they might have achieved a larger profit through some other means. As noted, to accomplish this some smugglers dealt with a top-level middleman, turning all their goods over to him and thus avoiding involvement with dealing altogether. Burke, a wholesale marijuana dealer, described his role:

If a smuggler can't sell his whole load to one customer he'll turn it over to me. His specialization is importation, not sales. I know more dealers than any one smuggler knows so I am more or less in demand 'cause I know all the heavy people . . . mentally-wise, I know outlets seven times greater than any one smuggler in the county knows.

Like smugglers, two types of dealers also limited their number of customers: those who trafficked in the largest quantities, and those who had spent many years in the business. These people were more sensitive to the risks associated with dealing, usually having more to lose (i.e., possessions, family), and would rather moderate their speed of turnover than jeopardize their safety. They took on new customers only from the ranks of people whom they already knew.

Finally, some people were more open to having a wide, diversified, and changing group of sales connections. These were either the less reputable dealers who constantly maintained low standards of security, or those dealers trying to build their business by expanding their range of contacts ("up-and-comers"). Among these I found several types: the "vibes dealers" who disregarded the importance of references and reputation, considering themselves capable of judging an individual's reliability on the basis of his outward appearance and conversation; the "young bulls," upwardly mobile newcomers caught up in the dealing world's excitement, money, drugs, and power, who placed the dangers of dealing outside their zone of relevance; and the hustlers, often down-and-outers, who would do anything to make a quick buck. Mike, a multikilo marijuana dealer, described his basis for establishing trust and doing business with new people:

I basically operate under the vibes theory of dealing. If I meet someone new, say someone brings him over and introduces him to me, I'll sit down and rap with the guy. If I like what he's saying, like if I feel he's on the level, I'll sell to him.

People in these groups usually had several steady buyers with whom they kept in contact over the years, supplementing these regulars with a revolving pool of many others who passed into and out of their lives. Their rationales for selling were varied: they felt sorry for someone and wanted to give him or her a break; they were greedy for new markets and sold to anybody who seemed to have good prospects; or they suddenly became desperate to unload drugs when their supplier demanded immediate payment. These less reputable dealers therefore disregarded the general norms discouraging selling to strangers. Ironically, while they were the least successful exemplars of their trade, they were the individuals most likely to develop a wide reputation around Southwest County as drug traffickers.

Descending the chain of selling connections, I thus found a widening group of people involved in dealing. From the single outlet of the smuggler to the few, steady customers of the biggest dealers, to the many revolving clients of the less careful volume dealers, each level down the hierarchy was more heavily populated. As one dealer remarked:

Just as I have my circle, so do each of the people below me that I sell to. It keeps branching out like a family tree all the way down to the gram dealers.

NETWORKS

Partnering and connection relationships were primarily businesslike in nature, having a social dimension which grew out of mutual occupational concerns. The reverse was true, however, for the next ring of affiliations. Network relationships involved groups of dealers and smugglers who did not regularly deal with each other; rather, members were primarily linked by mutual interests, lifestyles, and friendship. Friendship networks thus cut across the different business niches, linking people who trafficked in different substances, levels, and circles.

Friendship networks did not overlap in the same exclusive way as dealing circles, where each member could list an identical roster of participants for his or her circle. Rather, they corresponded loosely, people sharing some friends in common, but maintaining other close friendships separately. Each individual had his or her own personal friendship network composed of people with whom they socialized, exchanged ideas and favors, and knew fairly intimately. However, because these relationships were within the drug world, business dimensions were never totally absent. Work-related development of network relations took a variety of forms.

For example, a person dealing in one drug could serve as a mentor to someone handling a different drug, offering advice on his or her *modus operandi*, security, and financial diversification. As one mari-juana dealer noted:

I'm very close friends with this guy who's involved in the cocaine market, even though we don't do any business together. I've always respected him because he's the top man, he has everything going for him. He's invested his money in apartments, boats, villas, and legal businesses. Whenever I'm unsure about something I always discuss it with him. He's a good friend and he gives me a lot of good advice.

Such counseling and leading by example were usually done within the context of partying, since upper-level dealers and smugglers rarely got together without consuming large quantities of drugs.

Another function of network relations was the exchange of information and aid. Money might be borrowed during financial crises, or loaned from one dealer to another as a short-term, high-interest investment for a particular caper. Ideas could be shared about the latest technological innovations affecting smuggling practices. Or, as one dealer explained, tips could be exchanged about police practices:

We know someone here who can call up the dispatcher at the local sheriff's department and find out who's been arrested and if you know them. If anyone in the network wants to know. Or the dispatcher will call him if there's been a drug bust.

Communications could thus be passed from circle to circle through friendship networks, helping people in other business spheres to stave off arrest. The network system also served as an informal credit rating service, where dealers and smugglers checked out potential connections for a past history of credibility or honesty. When people's network relations were extremely close they occasionally used them to forge business links, going in on deals together or picking up drugs for each other. Networks, then, served as avenues of occupational mobility, as they provided contacts for people to jump from one volume of business to another, or to move from trading in one substance to trading in another.

Drug world friendship networks (with their associated business overtones) were fluid, shrinking and expanding as people fluctuated in their desire to be involved with others. Dealers went through periodic cycles of unfolding and constricting their network alliances, as they were affected by energy, greed, security, family concerns, the police, and innumerable other factors. When they retrenched, they usually cut their contacts to dealing connections only, keeping a low profile and avoiding unknowns. But people who were looking to expand their business could find a world of dealers and smugglers by networking; by meeting friends of friends in a geometrically snowballing fashion, they could create an entire universe of contacts for themselves. Dave described how he used this technique to surround himself with a pervasive drug environment:

I had had some bad times and had to lay low for a while. But when I surfaced I was really ambitious to make something of myself. Through traveling around as a broker for one of the big smugglers I got to know all the heavy dopers around Southwest County and beyond. If one guy couldn't help me he might turn me on to somebody else: dealers, smugglers, crew people, and money people—private investors who charged high interest rates for short-term loans. I was circulating in a giant drug network that became my entire world.

ACQUAINTANCESHIPS

Beyond each dealer's and smuggler's close friendship network was a larger group of drug world members with whom they were acquainted. Circles of acquaintances comprised all those people who knew each other personally from seeing each other at various times and events, yet whose relationships had never taken on a more intimate tone. Drug world acquaintances knew each other's business in a general sense, had common friends, and socialized occasionally. Like friendship networks, not everyone's circle of acquaintances could be expected to overlap completely (there must be some interrelations between different circles of acquaintances), but there had to be a high degree of mutual selection. And like networks, acquaintance relationships were primarily social in nature but were continually infused with the overtones of possible business.

Social interaction among Southwest County dealing acquaintances was enhanced by the propinquity of their living and working arrangements: most people lived and operated their legal businesses within a fifteen-square-mile area. They ran into each other semiregularly at the bars, stores, restaurants, and recreational areas they frequented. More organized socializing occurred either in the context of small, intimate gatherings or at larger weddings, parties, and blowout bashes thrown by Southwest County dealers and smugglers. One marijuana smuggler described such a party:

I really dig throwing big parties where I try to get everyone loaded to the hilt. I invite all the dealers and smugglers I'm friendly with and they bring their friends. We really get it on with the coke and champagne flowing, a pretty lady on everyone's arm. People in the drug world jokingly refer to these as "dealers' conventions." They're not really for business but I get to catch up on the latest gossip and prices. Lots of times I meet new people there; I find a connection or try to get someone to work for me. I think this kind of pulls people into the business: they see the lifestyle and they're attracted to it.

Both camaraderie and business affiliation were thus fostered by the closeness, contact, and communication experienced by acquaintances within Southwest County's drug world.

UMWELT

Schutz's (1962) concept of *umwelt*, a world of relationships that are based not on concrete knowledge but on reputation, best describes the final circle of affiliations surrounding each member of Southwest County's dealing community. Someone might have known that Mike was a big dealer in town, that Greg was behind the recently busted cocaine operation, or that Dave and Phil were the smugglers who owned a local bar and hangout, without ever having seen or met any of these people, yet the feeling abounded that everybody at the upper level knew each other. Drug world acquaintanceships brought many people together, but the greatest bulk of mass relationships was based on reputational association. Dealers might circulate without ever having met, but feel that they were old friends when they finally chanced upon each other. One marijuana smuggler offered this example:

I was down at my real estate broker's office chewing the fat and talking about some property when Marty Morgan came in. I'd never seen him before but I knew that my broker handled some rental properties for him. You'd never have known that we didn't know each other though, because when the broker introduced us we just said, "Hi, Marty," "Hi, Bill," and smiled, like we saw each other every day. Hell, I know the guy's whole personal history—half the scams he's pulled, who he's dated, and where he's lived for the past three years.

Dealers and smugglers sometimes got an ego boost out of having their reputations precede their entrance. Their feeling of knowing about everybody's business also increased the social solidarity of the community. Yet there were times when the community's intermeshing was disturbing. An ounce dealer in cocaine recounted the following experience with a near stranger:

I was sitting at home in my living room when this guy came in looking for my roommate. I knew his name and that he'd recently started dealing with Cory, but I'd only met him once before. But before I knew it he sat down and started talking to me like we were old friends. He named off all of Cory's and my friends, who they do business with, how they do it, and who was bringing coke across the border. Jeez, it scared the pants off me. If this asshole knows all this stuff I've gotta figure the police know it too.

Thus, despite the obvious need for secrecy, a large amount of personal information permeated the drug world grapevine (see Adler and Adler 1980).

Such broad knowledge of others' activities fostered a feeling of Gemeinschaft within Southwest County's dealing and smuggling community. Even though they were in the minority, dealers and smugglers were powerful enough to impart a deviant flavor to this geographical area and to have a strong impact on the standards of the local culture. Most dealers and smugglers felt a sense of belonging to a group that was defined in its broadest sense only by a common enterprise, but was bound together by shared dangers, interests, values, outlooks, and lifestyles.

Drug world relationships, then, were neither exclusively social nor businesslike in nature, having a reciprocal spillover effect. Combined business and social bonding is characteristic of many deviant groups whose interests, lifestyles, and need for legal isolation do not permit easy social interaction with nondeviants. While these relationships were organized fundamentally around business, they led to the creation of a deviant social world that offered a refuge to its members, providing them with a community and a network of social relationships. It also served as a cocoon, buffering them, in part, from the outside world. Their social relationships, then, fulfilled the function of boundary maintenance, insulating dealers and smugglers from most others and delineating their outer social limits.

The social dimensions of the relationships dealers and smugglers formed also influenced their business activities. For drug traffickers, and deviants in general, transactional exchanges are by their nature problematic (Manning 1977). Unlike the legitimate business world where cash can be exchanged for goods without fear of theft or arrest, trust, at some level, had to be extended before a drug deal could occur. Drug traffickers had to rely on the associations they formed and on their community's informal credit rating to generate the sense of trust which was such an essential trading requisite.

SOCIAL ORGANIZATION AND MARKET STRUCTURE

As Reuter (1983) has suggested, a link exists between the social organization of illicit transactions and the structure of the illicit markets framing them. Few sociologists who describe illicit enterprise, though, have examined the market structure implied by the character and organization of their research subjects' criminal activities (the most notable exceptions are studies of the Mafia). I will therefore draw on the material I have presented thus far to describe and analyze the structure of Southwest County's drug market.

The structure of illicit markets has been alternately pictured as either *monopolistic* or *competitive*, as either a tightly closed system dominated by an entrenched organization or an open system where individual entrepreneurs trade freely in illegal goods or services. Much of the lay public has the impression that the former model best describes the upper levels of drug dealing and smuggling. Their view of the market is based on the organized crime image of illicit enterprise, featuring a centrally dominated organization with geographically diversified branches for whom the drug trade is only one of many criminal involvements. This portrayal emphasizes a formal, bureaucratic organization, intense familial commitment, ethnic homogeneity, rigid hierarchical structure, and a long-term pledge to group membership. This image has been fostered by the various Senate investigations into organized crime (President's Commission 1967; U.S. Congress, Senate 1951 [popularly known as the Kefauver Committee]; U.S. Congress, Senate 1965 [popularly known as the McClellan Committee]), the overall presentation of criminal activity featured in the news media, and popular novels, movies (the *Godfather* series), and television shows ("The Untouchables").

The contrasting view of illicit markets is that they have no such tangible, structural regulation but rather are relatively "disorganized" (Reuter 1983). Instead of being monopolistically controlled by a single, overarching organization, they are populated by a series of individual entrepreneurs who engage in the purchase and sale of their illicit wares. These individuals (and small organizations) operate under the mechanism of a free market economy that is characterized by pure competition, or some reasonable facsimile. Individual entrepreneurs in this kind of market structure have few long-term associations, little diversity of illicit activity, and answer to no superordinate criminal syndicate. Instead, in the classic model of "invisible hand" economics, the profit motive of each participant fuels and guides the operation of the market as a whole. Reuter has suggested that this view of illicit markets is unpopular with the public for two reasons. First, both academics and public officials have been slow to realize that the monopolistic, organized crime model was a market form that evolved in response to historical and political conditions of the 1940s and 1950s, which have since changed. Second, law enforcement agents, politicians, and the media cling to the Mafia image because it serves their political, sensationalistic, and budgetary interests. Thus, the view of illicit markets as competitive, disorganized, and entrepreneurial is only slowly gaining public and academic credibility.

Like the loansharks, numbers runners, and bookmakers Reuter described, the dealers and smugglers I studied operated within an illicit market that was largely competitive, or disorganized, rather than visibly structured. Participants entered the market, transacted their deals, shifted from one type of activity to another, and settled their disputes in a spontaneous and unrestricted manner. In fact, dealers and smugglers commonly referred to this market as "one of the last arenas of free enterprise in existence." While they cooperated with each other in setting up and executing deals, their behavior was guided by a competitive awareness of how others acted.

The Southwest County drug market also operated under a relatively open system, with low barriers to entry. Anyone who drifted into the dealers' and smugglers' social world through common interests or lifestyle could develop the connections necessary to put a deal together. This could even be done without a capital investment if the individual was liked and trusted by a supplier. The market was therefore populated by a large number of individuals. In contrast to organized crime markets, where participants display longevity and stability, Southwest County dealers and smugglers had a moderately high turnover rate. While they did not pass through drug trafficking as rapidly as middle- and lower-level operators (Anonymous 1969; Lieb and Olson 1976; Waldorf et al. 1977), their moderately frequent exits from and reentries into the occupation (see chapter 7) created an important and unstable atmosphere. The transitory character of their careers, then, affected the size of their operations: the "modal organization" (Soref 1981) for dealers was one or two persons, while smugglers' crews were generally composed of three to eight members. Reuter (1983) posited two factors which account for the relatively small size of illicit enterprises' modal organization. First, operations which do not endure for long periods rarely grow into large and complex entities. Building an organization manned by skilled crews, engaged in diversified activities, with layers of insulation, and a legitimate side business which laundered illegally earned money, required considerable time and commitment. Few drug traffickers were able to maintain their operations for long enough to establish these types of organizations. Unlike bureaucratic enterprises which function on the basis of abstract role relationships, Southwest County drug organizations relied on the charisma of their leader to provide them with cohesion. Thus, once he left, the crew rarely held together for long. Second, larger organizations, although potentially more profitable, were greater security risks. The more people a smuggler employed and the greater the volume of his business, the more likely it was that his entire operation would become known to the police.

This study thus joins with other studies of illicit enterprises (such as Langer 1977 and Redlinger 1975 on drug trafficking; Ginsburg 1967, Harris 1974, and Lloyd 1976 on homosexual prostitutes; Hindelang 1971, Lesieur 1977, and Reuter 1983 on bookmaking; Karp 1973 and Sundholm 1973 on pornography; and Hall 1952, Klockars 1974, and

Walsh 1977 on fencing) in suggesting that illicit markets are populated by individual entrepreneurs and small organizations rather than massive, centrally organized bureaucracies, and are therefore characterized by a competitive rather than monopolistic structure.

CHAPTER FIVE

THE DEALING LIFESTYLE

I have just described how the networks of social relationships which surrounded Southwest County dealers and smugglers provided an element of community and stability in their lives. Juxtaposed against this dimension of rational organization, drug traffickers' lifestyle of hedonism represented the irrational, compelling force.

Southwest County dealers and smugglers led lives that were seldom dull. Abandoning the dictates of propriety and the workaday world, they lived spontaneously and intensely. Drug traffickers rejected society's normative constraints which mandated a lifestyle of deferred gratification, careful planning, and sensible spending. Instead, they embraced the pursuit of self-indulgence. Whether it was the unlimited availability of their favorite drugs, the illusion of the seemingly bottomless supply of money, the sense of power and the freedom they attained, their easy access to sexual satisfaction, or merely the excitement associated with the continual dangers they faced, the dealing crowd was strongly driven by the pleasures they derived from their way of life. This lifestyle was one of the strongest forces that attracted and held people to the drug trafficking business. It was therefore largely responsible for the set of traits which comprised the dealers' personality; only those people who found the reward system enticing enough to merit assuming the risks were persuaded to strive for greater involvement in this world.

In this chapter I examine salient characteristics of the dealers' and smugglers' lifestyle and sketch a rough portrait of their common social psychological traits, in order to better understand the dual motivations of hedonism and materialism in the drug world's upper echelons.

THE FAST LIFE

The lifestyle associated with big-time dealers and smugglers was intemperate and uninhibited. Dubbed the fast life,[1] or "flash," it was characterized by a feeling of euphoria. So pleasurable was life that nobody worried about paying the bills, running out of drugs, or planning for the future. Dealers and smugglers plunged themselves fully into satisfying their immediate desires, whether these involved consuming lavish, expensive dinners, drugging themselves to saturation, traveling hundreds of miles to buy a particular item that caught their eye, or "crashing" (sleeping) for 15–20 hours at a time to make up for nights spent in unending drug use. Those who lived in the fast lane sought an intensity that disdained the boredom of security and the peace of calm quietude. They were always on the run, rushing back and forth between partying and doing business, often intermingling the two. Schedules and commitments were hard to maintain, since people were apt to pursue the unexpected at any time or get caught in a run of drug consumption that could last for hours or even days. One coke dealer commented on the frequency of his partying:

> When we're sitting around the house with friends that are into dealing it always turns into a party. We do a lot of drugs, drink a lot, and just speed rap all night. . . . It's a full time thing; we're basically decadent 24 hours a day.

Those who lived the fast life were the *beautiful people*, bedecked with expensive adornments such as flashy clothes, jewelry, and sports cars. When they entered a restaurant or bar they ordered extravagantly and tipped lavishly. They grew up to reattain a childlike innocence by escaping the unpleasant responsibilities of adult life, while seizing the opportunity to surround themselves with anything money could buy. In their own eyes, they were the ultimate "in crowd."

The dealers' and smugglers' fast life emulated the jet set with all of its travel, spending, and heavy partying.[2] Private planes were diverted to carry a smuggler's entourage off for a week in Las Vegas where they all drank, gambled, and saw the shows. At other times it was off to the Pacific Islands for sunbathing and tropical drinks, to the mountains for skiing, or to famous spas, where they luxuriously exercised and rejuvenated themselves. In contrast to those children of inherited wealth, though, dealers and smugglers had to work for their money.

Their lifestyle was characterized by a mixture of work and play, as they combined concentrated wheeling and dealing with unadulterated partying. Yet, like jet-setters, they ultimately became bored and sought ever-greater excitement, usually turning to drugs for their most intense highs.

Members of the "glitter crowd" were known for their *irresponsibility* and *daring*, their desire to live recklessly and wildly. They despised the conservatism of the straight world as lowly and mundane. For them, the excitement of life came from a series of challenges where they pitted themselves against the forces that stood in their way. Although they did not create arbitrary risks, dealers and smugglers were gamblers who enjoyed the element of risk in their work, being intoxicated with living on the edge of danger. They relished more than just the money; they reveled in the thrill-seeking associated with their close scrapes, their ever-present danger, and their drug-induced highs. Gone was the quiet, steady home life of soberly raising children and accumulating savings, as they set themselves on a continuous search for new highs. They exalted freedom, the ability to pick up and "blow" without having to answer to anybody. One dope chick who had spent the past several years moving from relationship to relationship with various big dealers discussed her sense of freedom:

Now I can do anything I want and not have to worry about someone telling me not to do it. One day I just woke up and said to my little girl, "Honey, pack your clothes. We're going to Hawaii."

Drug dealers lived for the present, surrounding themselves with the maximum pleasures they could grab. They did not, as the middle class ethos suggested, live in reduced comfort so that they could enjoy the fruits of their labor at a later date. In fact, the reverse was true. The beautiful people seized their happiness now and deferred their hardships for the future; they lived for the moment and let tomorrow worry about paying the tab. One dealer's old lady elaborated on this *mañana* effect:

It was always like, tomorrow, tomorrow. You write a check, you think you'll cover it tomorrow. It was like that. We went through a lot of stuff like that.

Money lay at the base of their exhilarating madness, more money than most could ever have imagined. The gigantic profits that could be accumulated after even a short period of smuggling or heavy deal-ing could run into hundreds of thousands of dollars a year,[3] which seemed like an endless supply to most participants. Sometimes they became so overcome by their material wealth that they just gloried in it. One novice dealer exclaimed:

We were like little children in a big fancy palace playhouse. We'd dump all our money on the living room floor and we'd roll in it.

Most initiates could not imagine how to spend this much at first, but they soon learned. After even a short period they found them-selves laughing when hundred dollar bills came out of laundered shirt pockets, crumpled and torn from the wash. By then money had be-come something to be spent without care on the fulfillment of any whim. One member of a smuggler's crew recalled:

Money meant nothing to me. Like, if some guy gave me a $100 bill I'd go out and burn it or cut it in half for all I cared.

This overabundance drove them to generate new needs, to search out new avenues of spending. As one dealer illustrated:

At the height of my dealing I was making at least 10 grand a month profit, even after all my partying. When you have too much money you always have to look for something to spend it on. I used to run into the stores every day to find $50, $60 shirts to buy because I didn't know what else to do with the money, there was so much.

Drugs were also a big part of the fast life. Smugglers and dealers took personal consumption for themselves and their entourage as a ba-sic cost of doing business, to be siphoned out before profits could ac-cumulate, so drugs flowed freely, without care for expense. High-po-tency marijuana and hashish were smoked in moderation by many, most noticeably among the marijuana traffickers. Alcohol, particularly wine and champagne, was consumed regularly, often along with other drugs. Cocaine, however, was used heavily, its presence pervading the entire dealing community. They typically "coked" themselves to sat-uration, and it was not uncommon for a dealer to snort more than an ounce a week (market value: $2,000–$2,200) during periods of heavy partying. One cocaine dealer estimated how much he and his old lady took out for their "own heads":

As much as we wanted, which was a lot. We used a couple of grams a day at least, that was nothing. We could go through a quarter [of an ounce], you wouldn't believe it. We used big ziplocs, the large size, for our personal stash. We'd stick a big spoon in it and just dump it out on the mirror. One time I dropped an ounce down the front of my shirt when I went to take a toot [snort] and the bag ripped. I just brushed it off, it was nothing.

One of the reasons dealers and smugglers went through large quantities of cocaine so quickly was that they built up a short-term tolerance to its effects. Early phases of contact with the drug usually brought on a subtle rush of warmth, and feelings of affection for surrounding people.[4] This might be accompanied by a brief seizure of diarrhea, a loss of appetite, and a feeling of acceleration. After a half hour or so the warmth faded and the speed effect intensified. The usual reaction was either to moderate this overintensity with alcohol or marijuana or to pass around another series of "lines" and snort some more. This pattern could continue for hours or days until the participants became so "wired" (tense) that they found themselves gritting their teeth and passing up further offers. Sleep usually came only with great difficulty, and then often did not last long, as individuals awakened, often exhausted, with a slightly bitter drip down the backs of their throats.

After people had been exposed to heavy cocaine use for a period of weeks, they usually noticed a slight change in its effects. They required larger quantities to generate and sustain that buzzing feeling of warmth ("the rush"). Their loss of appetite and sleeplessness diminished, so that people who used it to lose weight soon noticed a reduction in its effectiveness. These changes, although indicative of a shift in individuals' patterns and quantity of usage, were not associated with any physical withdrawal symptoms when the drug was unavailable, such as heroin and barbiturate users experience (Grinspoon and Bakalar 1976).

The great appeal of cocaine snorting rested on two main characteristics of its effects: internal and interpersonal. Psychologically, individuals achieved a sense of happiness and well-being. They felt as if their problems were temporarily solved and that everything was wonderful, that they could do no wrong. This was associated with great sensations of safety and power. However, coke was even more strongly a social drug, helping to facilitate intimate lines of communication between people. One pilot voiced a commonly held opinion concerning cocaine's aphrodisiac effects:

Coke and chicks! Yeah, man, whenever I have some I make sure all the ladies know, cause it really turns them on, they really dig it.

Beyond these casual relationships, serious coke users used the drug to enhance interaction with others. One ounce dealer described the effect it had within his group of friends:

Coke helps you get past the stupid front games. Our little sessions at night with coke show the closeness that comes from the coke raps. You have such tight friends in such a short amount of time—it's all right there.

Another dealer discussed how cocaine affected his relationship with his wife:

She and I have such a severe communication gap that it's probably 50 percent of the reason cocaine persists the way it does. When we get together in the evenings it smooths the way for us to relate, for us to have our special time together as lovers. We probably couldn't go on together for long without it.

Dealers and smugglers began consuming cocaine in even larger quantities in the late 1970s when "freebasing" became a popular fad. This involved altering the refined drug's condition into a smokable state. Chemical kits which contained the solvent that transformed coke into base became widely available in headshops. Jean described her fascination with this drug experience:

You start by mixing the coke with the solvent. You pour it out with an eye-dropper onto the dish and it fluffs up like little white trees—like snow, it's pretty. Half of the Jones [the high] is watching that stuff form, scraping it up, putting it into the waterbase pipe—you have to use a torch to keep the heat on it all the time—it forms oils and resins. And as it drops down through the pipe it starts to swirl—half the Jones is in that whole process of smoking it. The other half is in the product. It's like you got hit by a train, it hits you so heavy, but then it goes away so fast that you use so much.

Yet along with the intense highs came some equally intense lows. An experienced freebaser recalled some of his more unpleasant episodes:

Lows? It's like when you can't get up to go to the bathroom and your mind goes by itself. When you're up pacing the floor—your mind, but your body's not. When you're so wired and exhausted and you just want to sleep but you can't. You lie there staring at the ceiling for about 24 hours straight. You're so fucked up you're embarrassed to go out of the house. Falling asleep in public bars. I've been so fucked up I couldn't go in to work and my six-year-old kid had to call in sick for me.

Getting into the habit of consistently freebasing (called "being addicted" by some) broke several dealers and smugglers in Southwest County. Many individuals, once introduced to freebasing, found it increasingly difficult to moderate their drug use. It was an allure that compelled continuing use more than any other drug popular with this subculture. Because larger and more frequent doses of cocaine were used when smoking base, two people could easily consume a quarter to a half ounce of cocaine during a single night's "run" (sitting of continuous usage). Some heavy users freebased for as long as seven or eight days straight without sleep. One person I knew went through $20,000 worth of cocaine in a week this way, while another used $60,000 worth in a month. Only the richest and most successful dealers and smugglers could afford to sustain such an expensive drug diet. Freebasing, however, could become all-consuming, leaving little time for the business of earning money. Thus some people committed themselves to sanatoriums for rehabilitation when they realized that they had reached this level of involvement. Still others quit the business altogether (some with the help of Narcotics Anonymous), as one former pound dealer explained:

Once I got into base I realized I could never deal again, because you can't have the product or you might get into doing it again.

Another component of life for Southwest County's beautiful people was the *casual sex scene*. Although many members of the community were married and had children, they openly broke the bonds of marital fidelity to explore their sexual urges. Casual attractions, although not the only mode of sexual fulfillment, were a commonly accepted part of life. This open sexual promiscuity was legitimated by the predominance of the hedonistic ethos which infused the dealing and smuggling community. The ease with which they engaged in casual sexual relations indicated their openness toward sexual self-indulgence as a subculturally accepted norm, overriding the contrary sexual mores of the greater society.

Many male dealers and smugglers went out with their male friends to pick-up bars, looking for one-night stands. Some kept old ladies on the side and set them up in apartments. They also played musical old ladies, shifting from one to another as they got tired of each one. Extramarital flings were not limited to the men, though, as married women frequently went out for a night with the "girls" and did not come home until sunrise. Marital relationships often became taken for granted in the light of this emphasis on immediate attractions, and divorce was common.

Dealers' old ladies formed an interesting part of the drug scene, because although their role was occasionally active, it was more often passive. Some women ran their own drug businesses. Of these, most entered dealing through the connections they made while living with a male dealer. Typically, after a breakup, these women needed money and realized that they had the knowledge to attempt doing business on their own. Not all women who tried to establish themselves as drug traffickers were successful, however. This lack of success rested, in part, on certain qualities essential to the profession and in part on the reactions men had to working with them. Blum et al. (1972:47) offered a discussion of why there were fewer women dealers in their sample which is relevant to my sample as well:

Dealers suggest first that women do not always have the personality for it, that they are too paranoid. They also say that women are victims of the double standard; their being in the dealing business is generally disapproved. Some observed that women are less business-oriented in general and so are less likely to be entrepreneurs in peddling drugs. Some contend that women are in general less competent; others hold that women, as the girl friends or sexual partners of dealers and users, can get their drugs free and need not worry about drugs or money. Finally, some of our dealers point out that women cannot do as well in dealing because men, who comprise the majority of the business network, are not comfortable dealing with them or do not trust them.

Some Southwest County dealers echoed these sentiments, as one marijuana trafficker complained:

Among the guys I know, a lot of them are reluctant to deal with girls. Girls don't seem to bend as well as guys do. Like girls seem to be a lot more high-strung, or they get more emotional if something doesn't go down right. Like guys seem to have more patience involved in it. . . . And girls are a lot more greedier than guys, they want a bigger cut normally for some strange reason.

This was not a universal complaint. Others found nothing wrong with working with women and did not reject them as associates. One cocaine dealer gave his view on women dealers:

Out here there's lots of them, as equal with guys. The first person who gave me my first front was a lady and I'm still good friends with her. I really have no preference for dealing with either sex.

Most people agreed, though, that men chauvinistically bent the rules for the "ladies." For instance, women were given more time to pay back money they owed, and were less likely to have to adhere to standard operating procedures for dealing, such as weighing or performing tests for quality on drugs that they sold. This chauvinism could be favorably manipulated, as one female dealer admitted:

Chicks have a great advantage, especially when you use it in an unfair way, which you can when you're a chick.

Women, as I have discussed, were also used by male dealers and smugglers as employees. Smugglers felt that women were less vulnerable to the suspicions of police or border agents. Positions in which women were often employed included transporting money or drugs, locally, around the country, or across international lines, and operating stash houses.

The majority of women in Southwest County's drug world took a more passive role, however. A crowd of dope chicks formed part of the entourage which surrounded big dealers and smugglers. Universally beautiful and sexily clad, they served as prestigious escorts, so that dealers could show them off to other members of the community. The motivation for these women was to share in the fast life's drugs, money, glamor, and excitement, as one dealer's wife explained:

Some chicks use their looks as a way of getting a man or some coke or their money or whatever. Those girls are like prostitutes—they put themselves where they know they can accomplish what they're really looking for.

In return, they were expected not to intrude on any of their companions' social or business relations. One dope chick offered this explanation of the reciprocal relationship:

I guess he just wanted someone to look pretty and drive his Pantera, so that people would say, hey so-and-so's got a real foxy-looking chick.

Beyond appearance, dealers looked on these women as sex objects. A married smuggler explained the rules of the game:

Sex is important in that they can make love to that lady because they're stimulated by her. They're gonna live with her and ball her, but yet they can make love to another lady too.

When it came to personality, however, less dynamic stimulus was required. A major coke dealer was frank about his colleagues' attitudes on this point:

The guys want a chick who will hang on their arm and go places with them and they don't really have to relate to her, because they would actually prefer if the chick was dumb enough to where they could leave her with a couple of bottles of wine and say I'm going out to do some business, I'll see you in the morning. They want a chick who will accept where she's at and have enough brains to know when to shut up.

Children of the drug world experienced an upbringing that was very different from children of the larger culture. When their parents went out to a party they were often left home alone. Some were enrolled in boarding schools to offer their parents greater freedom. In divorced households they were often bounced back and forth from one parent to the other as the adults fluctuated in their financial and household stability. When parents dealt or partied in the home, only slight efforts were made to hide their actions from the children. However, as the party progressed or the children aged and became more aware, it was increasingly impossible to disguise what was happening. Other parents made no attempt to camouflage their promiscuous or drug-related activities. They took their children with them when they slept around or partied, allowing them to view what went on without censorship.

The result of this treatment was generally a premature precocity and independence on the children's part. Given the responsibility for viewing, understanding, and accepting this adult behavior, children adapted rapidly. They learned about the nature of drugs: what they were worth and what effects they generated. They also learned to amuse and take care of themselves in the absence of parental protectiveness.

In some cases, their experience with drugs came firsthand. From earliest infancy these children were "tinydopers" (see Adler and Adler

1978), becoming passively intoxicated through the inhalation of smoke in the air. As they got older, however, they were permitted to take an occasional toke on the communal marijuana cigarette. Parents varied in how regularly they gave their children drugs. Some made marijuana available to children whenever it was requested, either bringing them into the smoking circle or rolling "pinners" (tiny, thin joints) for the youngsters to smoke on their own. One dealer, when queried about the possible dangers of offering drugs to young children, replied:

What the hell! It grows in the ground, it's a weed. I can't see anything wrong with doing anything, inducing any part of it into your body any way that you possibly could eat it, smoke it, intraveneously, or whatever, that it would ever harm you because it grows in the ground. It's one of God's treats.

Other parents offered marijuana to their children only occasionally. These parents made the decision to let their children have access to marijuana for one of the following special reasons: (1) as a reward for a child's good behavior in the past, present, or anticipated future; (2) out of guilt, to compensate children for neglecting them in other ways; (3) as a source of adult entertainment, because children behaved amusingly when under the influence; or (4) as a medicinal aid, to help children fall asleep or to alleviate their cranky moods.

Children of the dealing crowd eventually outgrew their cuteness as tinydopers, however, and some graduated to become "tinydealers." Moving into junior high and high school, 13- and 14-year-old dealers were capable of making large sums of money by selling ounces of marijuana and grams or half-grams of cocaine to their peers. One smuggler commented on this second generation of dealers:

These are kids who've been raised with this lifestyle, easy money, drugs around all the time—their parents are still heavy dealers now. All these kids and all their friends have access to the drug and they're ripping off their parents. Or else they're dealing on their own through their parents' connections or through their parents' friends' kids. . . . What the hell are the parents going to do? They're not setting the example themselves so what can they do? They have no relating to the kids anyway.

Thus these children grew up in their parents' image. It is not unusual to see a community transmit its norms, values, and occupational preferences from one generation to the next. In fact, this commonly occurs with some regularity, even when that community constitutes a subculture that stands off from the norms of the greater culture. The unusual thing here was the fact that drug use and drug trafficking, acts which are usually reserved for more mature members of a community, were allowed for children, a sacred group in most societies. This violation of a cross-cultural taboo further stigmatized the drug dealing subculture as highly deviant.

THE DEALING PERSONALITY

Drug dealers and smugglers entered the business from many walks of life. However diverse their origins, though, they were all attracted to certain joys and pressures inherent in the dealing life. As a self-selecting group, they held key common traits which I have compiled into a portrait of their collective social psyche.

The most noticeable and significant characteristic was the *dealer's ego*. Dealers and smugglers had a highly elevated sense of self-esteem. This was, in part, based on their degree of success in completing challenging business transactions, where they had to constantly maneuver to overcome such obstacles as the law, untrustworthy dealers, human error, mechanical failure, climatic disaster, and a host of other unforseeable difficulties. Money also served to inflate their egos, not only because of the amounts they could earn but because of the consumable items on which they were forced to spend it (for security reasons). Another feature contributing to the dealers' egos was the *power* of their position. They controlled the flow of drugs to lower-level dealers, which affected others' ability to do business, to earn money, and to obtain a personal supply of drugs. They could thus make or break their associates through the extension or withholding of their favors.

Dealers and smugglers also derived ego-gratification from their social status in the community. Although many differences exist between the drug dealing culture and lower-class culture, Miller's (1958) discussion of the importance of "rep" among juvenile street gangs highlights the infamy dealers earned from their personal exploits: recognition among peers became an end in itself. They greatly enjoyed the *prestige* of others' knowledge about the deviant nature of their occupation, the volume they were capable of handling, and the amount of money they made. Many dealers thus relished the spread of their reputations, dangerous though this was, because it fed back to their egos and made them feel important.

Closely interwoven with power and prestige was the attribute of being *sexy*. It was part of a dealer's macho image of himself and others to be sexually attractive to women. One tactic they used to seduce women was to impress them with their status as dealers. Many females found this a "turn on" because of the glamor, money, thrills, and risk associated with evading the law and handling forbidden substances. Dealers were also known to have a ready supply of cocaine, which was perceived as an enticement and enhancement to sexual activity. During sexual hunting, then, a dealer might breach his safety precautions and reveal his identity and activities to an available woman.[5]

Interestingly, the dealer's ego stands in contrast to another egotistical personality syndrome: the "little man" complex. While the latter refers to a condescending attitude arising out of an inferior physical stature, dealers and smugglers as a group were overwhelmingly large in size. Before meeting a new drug trafficker I could expect that, at minimum, he would be six foot two and weigh 180 pounds. The reasons for this also lay in self-selection, for although violence was rare in Southwest County, it was fairly common in the drug world more generally. Regardless of whether an individual ever had to resort to violence it lay behind all business relationships as a lurking threat. As Moore (1977:43) has noted, "muscle" in the drug world refers to one's perceived capacity for violence more than its continued demonstration. Thus people who felt unsure of their ability to be aggressive or to physically defend themselves were less likely to venture into drug trafficking. This was also part of the reason why the dealing and smuggling ranks were more heavily populated by men than by women. The dealer's ego was the "big man's" ego.

Another characteristic of dealers and smugglers was the high level of *tension* which prevaded their existence. Inherent in their occupation were certain pressures of time, money, and the law, which made them highly vulnerable to emotional stress. Dave spoke about his underlying worries:

I realize I might lose everything again completely. I may get busted and go away for quite awhile. I guess I have a gambling sickness, like I'm gambling on my life. It's crazy. I try and push the worry about getting busted out of my mind but I think about it quite a bit. It's a heavy toll.

Tension also built up from the intensity of their lifestyle, as they both worked and partied to extreme degrees. Here, as the pressure to seek thrills mounted, dealers became more frazzled. This was exacerbated by their extended periods of heavy cocaine use which left them jittery, on edge, and prone to quick flare-ups of anger.

Set against this enduring mood of tension were more intense and short-lived spells of "paranoia."[6] All dealers and smugglers knew the feeling of paranoia. Although they generally rode the crest of enthusiasm and confidence, their constant flirtation with great risk caused them to occasionally experience flashes of vulnerability. These came when they claimed their drug-laden suitcases at airports, passed through metal detectors, crossed international borders while carrying drugs, or most often, as one smuggler described, for seemingly little reason:

You can be up for hours totally high on a utopia type of thing, but if things start going slow, like if a deal's going down and it seems to be taking too long, paranoia totally sets in, unbelievably sets in, like one minute after the load's supposed to arrive.

In order to deter such attacks of paranoia, dealers and smugglers developed a series of *rationalizations* which were multifunctional. One set functioned as "accounts" (Scott and Lyman 1968), helping drug traffickers to convince themselves that their activities were "cool," that for some reason they were safe from the law. One cut-ounce cocaine dealer attributed this to his "karma":

I really believe it's karma—cause and effect. What you're putting out gets back. The types of deals and business that I'm doing are so minor and nonoffensive that I don't think they want me.

Others based their sense of safety on their degree of caution, criticizing colleagues for their shady associates or loose behavior, while being blind to these very elements in their own mode of operating. These delusions were all part of their internal cover-up.

Dealers' and smugglers' rationalizations extended beyond their self-deceptions to their use of techniques of legitimation and neutralization (see Sykes and Matza 1957), designed to help them deal with society's reactions to their being deviant. They knew that they were breaking the law, but they saw nothing morally wrong with their activities. Providing a commodity that people eagerly bought did not give them criminal self-conceptions. One smuggler offered an analogy that combined both the "denial of injury" and "rejecting the rejector" neutralizing themes:

Even the straight people who've made a lot of money have done it illegally one way or another to get up there. Even look at the Kennedys—Kennedy was a bootlegger. I look at running grass and selling grass right now, is the same thing as the bootleggers did in the 1920s with booze. And nobody looks down on them. Like I don't feel like I'm pushing anything which is hurting anybody.

A final personality characteristic shared by dealers and smugglers was a sense of *invulnerability*, a feeling that they were surrounded by a protective shell so that nothing bad could happen to them. Despite the dangers and tensions with which they lived, drug traffickers did not always brood on disaster; in fact, they generally ignored that possibility. When not stricken by pangs of paranoia, they commonly felt inordinately safe, flaunting their illegal activities and gains within the group. Their moods thus vacillated erratically, seesawing up and down from one extreme to the other.

This trait was partly tied to their heavy drug use, as their extended cocaine consumption generated an aura of "magical omnipotence," a bubble which was artificially inflated only to be continually punctured and reinflated. Using cocaine also created a subtle detachment from reality so that they tended to forget about their ever-present danger. But dealers' and smugglers' feelings of invulnerability also indicated that they had developed a subconscious coping strategy where they removed constant worries about their personal safety from their immediate zones of relevance in order to normalize their occupation and lifestyle.

MOTIVATIONS FOR DEALING

Two dominant motivations fueled the drive to traffic in drugs: *hedonism* and *materialism*.[7] The latter was the more readily apparent of the two, and has been cited by most sociological accounts of other illegal occupations as the primary enticement (see Cameron 1964; Ianni 1972; Langer 1977; Letkemann 1973; Plate 1975; Sutherland 1937). Certainly, none of the dealers or smugglers I observed could have earned as much money in as short a time by legitimate means. Their drug profits enabled them to surround themselves with the kind of material possessions they coveted: fine food, clothes, cars, electronic equipment, and, above all, money itself, as a symbol of success and power. The lure of extravagant wealth thus served to both recruit and hold people to this enterprise.

A second source of motivation, more compelling than the first, however, was the hedonism inherent in the lifestyle. Southwest County drug traffickers pursued a style of life filled with the pleasures of unlimited drugs, sexual promiscuity, personal power, high status, freedom, risk, and excitement. Yet the acceptance of hedonism as a forceful motivation underlying criminal behavior remains controversial in the literature. Some studies, particularly those focusing on materialism, have decried this as a secondary, irrelevant, or nonexistent dimension of deviant occupations, considering illegal work as mundane as its legal counterpart (Inciardi 1975; Letkemann 1973; Sutherland 1937). Others, however, have pointed to the thrills, sexual opportunities, and deviant lifestyle as equal in their attraction and reward to materialistic compensations (see Jackson 1972; Maurer 1974; Roebuck and Frese 1976; Miller 1978). For Southwest County dealers and smugglers, the fast life became the central part of their existence. While they might have been initially drawn to trafficking out of materialism, they soon became addicted to it out of hedonism. Once people had become sufficiently exposed to the enchantment of the fast life, enamored with their feelings of importance, and used to wantonly consuming money and drugs, they were willing to continue drug trafficking to support themselves in this style. The myriad pleasures reinforced one another, overwhelming even the once soberly directed individuals. Thus, the dealing lifestyle, through its unmitigated hedonism, both attracted pleasure-seeking individuals into the drug business and transformed others, through its concentrated decadence, into pleasure seekers, combining its thrust with materialism in ensuring their continuance in this line of work.

CHAPTER SIX

SUCCESS AND FAILURE

Dealers and smugglers craved the material wealth and hedonistic life-style that their occupation offered, but entry into the world of drug trafficking did not automatically guarantee success. While some individuals found it an arena for easy money, others fell into a spiral of increasing debt. What separated the successes from the failures of the drug world? What facets of their nature, their behavior, or the social organization of their subculture were responsible for separating drug entrepreneurs along a continuum of varying degrees of success?

Ultimately, the difference between success and failure can be recognized as a structural dimension in the drug world, based on dealers' and smugglers' ranking on the *prestige hierarchy*.[1] Recognition, and especially respect, were very important in the drug world because, as Sutherland (1973:204) and Letkemann (1973:44) have noted, criminals must seek their social rewards within the criminal element. Dealers' and smugglers' self-images and feelings of power, then, were based largely on their social status within the community, the *umwelt* throughout which their reputations extended. Their rankings on the prestige hierarchy were based on their reputations for having certain styles of dealing and histories of past performance.[2] These criteria for stratification included: character, business acumen, and the ability to avoid legal entanglements.[3] In addition, dealers' and smugglers' reputations were based on their previous dealing-related behavior within the community. These factors could have a profound effect in determining individuals' success or failure, since they reflected on both their competence and their connections.

The prestige hierarchy was subsumed within the vertical hierarchy of trafficking described in chapter 3. Each vertical level of operators, from the smugglers down through the ranks, had its own hierarchy of prestige along which traffickers were secondarily ranked. This hierarchy encompassed individuals ranging from the more careful, security-conscious, professional operators, to the assortment of flim-flam hustlers and vibes dealers who recklessly wheeled and dealed. A chronic riff-raff dealer could conceivably have handled similar volumes to a more respected and successful dealer, yet he or she was looked upon as having less prestige.

Moreover, the two would be extremely unlikely to engage in a deal together because of the drug world's boundary maintenance, which served to repel outsiders and to differentiate along internal lines within the community. Thus, as Higgins and Butler (1982:215) have observed, what appears homogeneous from the outside may in reality be seen as heterogeneous by the insider.

In this chapter I examine some of the factors which determined the quality of dealers' or smugglers' styles of operation and hence affected the way they were stratified on the prestige hierarchy of success/failure.

CHARACTER

One of the first requirements for success, whether in drug trafficking, business enterprise broadly, or any life undertaking, is the establishment of a good personal reputation. To make it in the drug world, dealers and smugglers had to generate trust and likeability. The most important character trait in this regard was *integrity*. According to others, quality dealers were honest and fair in their business transactions, gave exact "counts" (full weight values), and made fairly accurate estimations of the quality of their product. Jean and Jim discussed how they developed an image of integrity:

> We worked on developing the best image we could get, something that would be known within the circle but not within the community. We dealt high quality, the lowest prices, and only to certain people, no one else. . . . Reputation is very important, because you're dealing with people who have so much money all the time that you need to keep their respect.

In contrast, deceitful people were considered mercenary profit-seekers who lied, cheated, and stole to fill their own needs. Fred, a marijuana dealer, represented one such example. By his own admission, he lacked integrity:

I said to others I had pot to sell. I guaranteed it would be good every time. I lied; I used my sales training to sell grass.

As more and more people received bad deals from Fred or were inadvertently ripped off by the failure of Fred's customers to honor their debts, he was cut off by one smuggler and dealer after another. Without his even realizing it, his reputation grew so bad that when his wife divorced him and started dealing on her own, she reverted to her maiden name to avoid any association with him. As she put it:

Fred's a typical person in the drug world: a total fuck-up. He's got the worst reputation. Everybody in town knows it. I'm embarrassed to even say I ever knew him. People who haven't ever met him know he's a total asshole. He owes one guy money, he's ripped another off. He beats people off, he lies, he cheats, and steals. He lies, and when he's caught, he still lies again.

Fred, however, did not represent the lowest rung of the prestige hierarchy because he began most deals with honorable intentions. He only slid into dishonesty when, because of his incompetence, things started to go awry. Beneath Fred were those individuals who intentionally ripped off other dealers, setting up deals for the express purpose of stealing money, drugs, and/or equipment. One marijuana smuggler explained how this happened to him:

This friend of mine had connections in the next county who were going in on a pot smuggling deal with us. They supposedly had the buying connections and the pilot, and we were going to sell it, but we had to come up with the plane. Well, every plane we found wasn't good enough. When we finally found a big enough one their pilot disappeared in it and so did they. I think the whole thing was a set-up from the beginning to steal the plane.

For obvious reasons, drug thieves were not a stable population in Southwest County; their reputations eventually caused them to be shunned by others as business associates. The lure of money and drugs, however, attracted a continuously regenerating population of such rip-off artists, the bottom rung of the drug world. Occasionally, too, dealers who usually displayed higher integrity became desperate enough to attempt a rip-off. These people disappeared with the goods and were never heard from again. Southwest County dealers and smugglers usually responded to such thefts angrily, and armed themselves with rationalizations designed to convince themselves that they were not to blame. Riff-raff operators brooded vengefully over their losses and threatened their associates with retaliation. With a few exceptions, though, these were just bravado displays, lacking in subsequent action. More reputable dealers and smugglers usually gave little serious consideration to a violent recourse. Rather, they bitterly accepted the loss, while besmirching the person's reputation around the local community.

Only on rare occasions did Southwest County dealers and smugglers react violently. In the following example, a cocaine dealer recounted an instance of theft which ended with a violent confrontation:

My friends from [state] were going to front me a pound of cocaine, so we agreed to meet at this heroin addict's place that was a friend of theirs, that was halfway in between here and there to exchange the stuff. Well, while we were there these three other guys came busting in with rifles and stole the stuff. You could tell the addict guy was in on it because they all got mad at him when they found out that it was a front deal, that there wasn't any money around. These guys were excited and we were all pretty scared. When one guy stepped over to look out the window I managed to grab his gun and shoot him in the arm. Then we all ran for it. That was enough for me, but my friends insisted on hiring some guy to track them down and shoot all four of them. I kept my mouth shut and went along because I was afraid they would think I was one more loose end.

For the most part, though, dealers and smugglers known for having high integrity were less violent in their approach, although they had to maintain the threat of violence.

A second character trait which promoted a good reputation was *generosity*. Dealers and smugglers liked doing business with righteous associates. By allowing people more time when they occasionally could not repay a front, or throwing in extra bits of drugs for their customer's personal use, or offering the loan of certain possessions (i.e., telephones, chemical kits, equipment, and legal connections), dealers built up good will with their colleagues in the community. "Chintzy" drug traffickers, on the other hand, often regretted their stinginess because it caused diminished esteem in the eyes of others.

One quality which fostered ill will was *greed*. While dealers and smugglers were largely attracted to the quick and easy money they could make in this business, the quickest way was not always the best way to become successful. One cocaine dealer described how a greedy associate developed a bad reputation:

A lot of people don't have much respect for Mike. If he has an ounce of cocaine he'll cut it in half before he sells it to the next guy. A few people who've bought from him have gone out and gotten the stuff tested. Then word gets around that because he's greedy for more profit he doesn't give good quality.

Thus, greed often separated the successes from the failures, dividing individuals who displayed patience and moderation from those who tried to extract the maximum profit out of every deal. From my observations, in fact, most instances of failure could ultimately be traced to individuals' greed, to the point where they displayed what Lyman (1978:233) called "a permanent restlessness, characterized on the one hand by the insatiable desire to acquire more and more, and on the other by the miserable but nagging apprehension that whatever one has or gets is not and never can be enough." One cocaine dealer concurred by offering this insight into what separated the successful operators from those who got busted or ripped off:

Greed, it's greed. People are so interested in making a deal that they're willing to ignore certain things, and it turns out it's a set-up.

Dealers and smugglers preferred to do business with connections who had proved their trustworthiness and *reliability* over the course of their dealing careers. This included making prompt payments for fronted merchandise, being accurate in estimations of the quality and availability of merchandise, and following through on commitments. Most drug traffickers who failed in this regard did not do so intentionally, but rather succumbed to self-delusion, or what Douglas (1977b:68–71) termed "self-seduction." They misled others because they fooled themselves, living in a world where "perhaps" and "maybe" were taken as signifying "absolutely." One associate complained about Mike and his chronic overoptimism:

That's the problem with trying to deal with Mike. He calls you up, says he's got a friend who wants X. I'll spend all day running around putting it together and then his friend doesn't want it. He's unreliable because of his overoptimism.

The problem of reliability was also linked to the battle between *self-control* and *self-destruction*. Hayano (1982) proposed this diametric polarity as a career tension that professional poker players face in their playing and betting aggressiveness, but it pertains to drug dealers as well, especially regarding the extent of their cocaine use. As Waldorf et al. (1977) have noted, the problem of overconsumption was pervasive among cocaine dealers. Consuming excessive amounts of cocaine caused many people to lose control over themselves, their dealing, and their lives, as Bruce, a riff-raff dealer, admitted:

Like that's what this trip is with coke when you're dealing. Once you start tooting with your friends you're so into it and having such a good time, you just keep bringing it out. If I was rich enough I could afford it, but we'll go through six grams in an evening of partying and you don't want to put a trip on anybody else about the bread [money]. Every morning I wake up and find we've gone through more than the profit I made on the day before and I just fall further into debt.

The final character dimension linked to developing a reputation for success was *courage*. Drug trafficking was an occupation which demanded risk-taking. Some risks were calculable in advance, while others arose spontaneously through unexpected turns of events. Dealers who wanted to persevere could not react in a cowardly manner but had to show others that they were willing to accept the necessary challenges. On occasion, this meant responding to rip-offs with either violence or social sanctions. One cocaine dealer commented on a group of riff-raff operators who damaged their reputations through their repeated lack of action:

All these guys are ripping each other off from one deal to the next. They all talk about how they're going to snuff each other out or hire someone to do their collections but none of them has the balls to do it. And because of that, no one else will deal with them. They have nowhere else to go.

I do not mean to suggest a universally direct relationship between courage, action, and success. In fact, this was not the case, because "balls," or guts, had to be tempered with the sense to know when to press on and when to pull back from potentially dangerous or unrewarding endeavors. However, without the nerve to assume certain challenges, no potential dealer or smuggler could thrive or advance in the business.

BUSINESS ACUMEN

Drug dealers' and smugglers' relative success or failure in their occupation rested not only on their character attributes (which built the type of reputation that attracted others as associates), but also on their entrepreneurial business skills. This included both natural aptitude and a range of specialized knowledge. The following characteristics thus represent an area of overlap between drug trafficking and legitimate business activities.

The first trait which enhances the functioning of any entrepreneur, whether legal or illegal, is a basic foundation of *business sense*. By this I do not mean intelligence, since intellectual ability does not necessarily correspond to business ability. Instead, business sense more closely resembles common sense, especially that instinct which fosters a good eye for profit and the capacity to wheel and deal. One cocaine dealer offered his associate as an example of the difference between integrity and business sense:

Steve is fanatically concerned with being known as a quality dealer. But he's the only guy I know who can lose $100 on an ounce of pure cocaine because it boosts his ego to sell uncut coke to little nobodys, and he's a soft touch for a sob story. As a friend I like him, but I can't afford to do business with him because he'd rather impress people with quality than with his ability to do business. That may keep his customers around but it sure won't keep him in suppliers.

Business sense in the dealers' world also contained an element of what Sutherland (1937:197) called "larceny sense": a set of wits, "front," and talking ability. Individuals who possessed this aptitude were more likely to become successful.

Would-be drug traffickers, however, had to supplement their innate abilities with *knowledge of how to operate* a dealing or smuggling enterprise. This type of specialized information exists in any field, from servicing, designing, or manufacturing in the straight world, to the "complex of techniques" Sutherland described for the criminal world. Many dealers viewed themselves as businessmen, putting the generic nature of their activities first and the illegality of their product second. As one dealer remarked: "A dealer is a middler, an agent. We have a commodity, we try to broker it the best we can."

The specific knowledge a drug trafficker possessed varied with the nature of his or her operation. Middling constituted a relatively straightforward transaction, but as individuals moved into dealing, or into the extremely intricate and difficult enterprise of smuggling, the knowledge required became more involved. Being successful in the drug business not only required the knowledge of how to import, evaluate, and distribute drugs, but required constantly up-to-date technical and strategy information to stay ahead of police techniques. Drug traffickers usually obtained information about the police only at the expense of colleagues who got arrested.

Operating a successful drug business also required *knowing people*, from connections to employers and employees. The more connections dealers or smugglers had, the easier it was for them to plan new ventures and staff their crews. But unlike legitimate business, knowing a lot of people in the drug world was a double-edged sword: the more people drug traffickers knew, the better they were known to both desirable and undesirable others. This made the type of people they knew very imporant, because developing a reputation with a crowd of low repute was distinctly dangerous.

The capacity to *collect debts* was also of paramount importance in running a profitable operation. No matter how professional a dealer's circle of associates were, there were always times when customers, either intentionally or inadvertently, reneged on debts. To accept nonpayment with equanimity was bad business and invited recurring loss. Yet dealers and smugglers lacked legal recourse: they could hardly sue. As noted, one option was to physically threaten their debtors. A few operators did this themselves; others hired nonprofessional enforcers to do the work for them.

A second option was to ostracize offenders and refuse to do any further business with them. This was a powerful sanction, especially in highly integrated dealing circles where a blackball from one member could cause all the other members to shun an associate.

A third option for collecting debts, as described by Roger, a marijuana dealer, was to go after replacement merchandise:

I knew if I didn't go after the $16,000 I had advanced to Ken to buy the dope, the two guys who fronted it to me were going to harm me pretty seriously. I can act when my life is on the line. So one day when he was out, I just pulled up to his house with a moving van and loaded everything he had into it. I took it straight to a used furniture dealer and got cash for it on the spot.

A fourth option, by far the most common, was to do nothing, accepting the "sting" with acrimony but inaction.

To avoid getting repeatedly stung, dealers and smugglers needed to be able to *evaluate people*. This evaluation had to be done before the deal was transacted, or it was of no use. One smuggler discussed the outcome of his poor judgment:

I had made a mistake and fronted nearly all of my load to this kid from [state] for the promise of a good price. I didn't realize until too late that this amount of merchandise was totally way over his head, and he lost the majority of it. Until I paid the Mexican broker back I had to do quite a few deals and make no money on them whatsoever.

Another attribute of successful drug entrepreneurs was *product knowledge*. As Langer (1977:381) noted, dealers ware expected to display expertise regarding the merchandise they carried. In Southwest County too, dealers had to competently display knowledge about their drugs, especially about additives used to cut cocaine. Dealers' reputations for honest product evaluation directly affected their sales. For example, customers routinely shopped around by phone to see what was available in the county before making a purchase, relying on suppliers' verbal descriptions of the merchandise to help them decide if they were interested. They would then be more likely to buy from dealers who were accurate in their assessments of their merchandise. As one dealer recounted, people who displayed inadequate product knowledge, who exercised poor judgment, or who were careless in checking either the quality of the drugs or the reliability of the supplier could easily get burned, ending with inferior or unsaleable merchandise:

I had around $7,000 of somebody else's money that I was going to invest in a dope deal before I handed it over to the guy. I had never bought in this kind of quantity before but I knew three or four guys who I could get it from. I was nervous so I got really stoned before I shopped around and I ended up being hardly able to tell about the quality. Turned out you just couldn't get high on the stuff. I ended up having to sell it below cost at some military base up north.

The final attribute which contributed to a dealer's business acumen was good *money management*.[4] Individuals who guarded their profits and reinvested them in their drug businesses were able to purchase larger quantities of drugs, to purchase and maintain more, newer, and better equipment, and to hire more employees. This allowed them further insulation from contact with the drugs. They could also channel some of this money into nondrug ventures, such as legitimate investments, businesses, or business fronts. Money directed into these areas increased the secrecy and insulation of their present operations and their savings for future retirement. Thus, individuals who wisely allocated their resources greatly enhanced their security and long-term business profitability. Yet, as I have stated, few dealers or smugglers acted with such rationality, especially when it meant curtailing the gratification of immediate desires. Southwest County drug traffickers regularly spent money impulsively, neglecting to distinguish between capital and profit, or business money and living money. When their earnings could support such a continuous drain, no significant problems arose. Most dealers considered personal consumption more important than savings. Problems of money management arose among dealers whose profit margin was not great enough to cover their overconsumption. This often led them to mingle their dealing funds with other sources of money. Bruce discussed how he comingled his drug money with the funds of the greenhouse business he managed:

A couple of times I've gotten into trouble by tooting up a lot of coke where there was anticipated profit, but then there was none. So I dipped into the greenhouse money to pay back my front, but like right now the greenhouse is on a borderline spot and so I had to pay for some ferns. I had some cash from some other coke that a guy had fronted me and I made a bank deposit to cover the checks I had written for the ferns. And as I would get new funds I would cover the old debt with the new cash, and as long as the new item kept coming in I could always keep the old one caught up. I ended up having to float $500 of "imaginary money" for over a week by writing checks back and forth between the greenhouse and myself until I was able to generate enough money to cover it all.

Bruce thus added embezzling, check-kiting, and other forms of secondary deviance to his original comingling in order to buy himself some time to get out of debt. This kind of money management represented bad business practice and was the mark of a disreputable and unsuccessful dealer.

AVOIDING THE LAW

While a range of talents and skills overlap between successful drug trafficking and success in legitimate business enterprises, the constant need to avoid the criminal justice system is one concern which dealers and smugglers share only with members of other criminal occupations.

Dealers' Perceptions of the Police. Considering their very real danger of arrest, Southwest County dealers and smugglers were surprisingly optimistic about their continuing ability to evade the law. This confidence rested partly on their belief that police and drug agents were basically stupid and/or inept. Dealers pictured law enforcement as an administrative jungle, a morass of loosely connected police agencies who were constantly involved in competitive in-fighting. According to their perceptions, the specific agents who worked on drug busts were usually low on the enforcement status hierarchy, such as local narcs, whom they thought made sloppy or illegal arrests frequently. Dealers and smugglers held some agencies in high esteem and feared them (the FBI and IRS), but according to subcultural lore, members of these agencies were not often assigned to drug work. They thus believed that the main task of catching them was left to the lower-echelon drug task forces and the unspecialized local patrols.

Dealers believed that the majority of arrests resulted from sheer happenstance. Varying circumstances led to accidental busts: after stopping a dealer for a traffic offense, one patrolman spotted drugs under the dashboard; once, a truck full of marijuana pulled into a gas station to refuel and a nearby policeman smelled the odor; as a dealer walked down a hotel hallway, his briefcase opened and marijuana bricks fell out, and while looking for one type of offender the police accidentally stumbled onto another. These are actual instances which befell people whom I studied, and illustrate why dealers believed that the law of averages functioned to maintain a myth of police effectiveness in the eyes of the public.

According to dealers, planned arrests usually followed the traditional buy-bust method. With the help of an undercover agent (rare) or informant (more common), police purchased illicit drugs and then arrested the seller in the act. Whenever possible, they added conspiracy charges to increase the damage. Once jailed, the suspect was pressured to turn informant and "arm lock" friends by setting them up for future busts. Marty, a marijuana and cocaine dealer, discussed how he was nearly trapped by this procedure:

I'm out of business now, that's for sure. Turns out I was dealing with somebody who was a paid informant. That guy was ratting because he had been busted on one beef and was on probation. They told him they would send him back to prison unless he helped them get the goods on certain people. They gave him a list of five known heavy dealers they would like to bust and my name was one of them. Someone else told me about it at the time, but I was so screwed up on coke, drugs, and amphetamines that I didn't take it seriously. I finally realized it when a heavy bust came down in the area and all my friends got picked up. That's why I had to split the country. I may be hot now, I don't know.

Although none of my respondents would admit to having turned informant (and I believed them), they had all encountered such people or heard about this happening to their friends. One ex-boyfriend of a female dealer I interviewed was reputedly receiving money from the police for each person he set up, and had admitted it to her. People who turned informant in Southwest County soon outlived their usefulness to the police, however, and fled the area to avoid possible retaliation from their victims.

Acting with an awareness of these methods, dealers and smugglers planned their activities to avoid being caught. One marijuana dealer explained the commonly prevailing sentiment:

Usually you make a set of rules that you're gonna follow, and then abide by them. If you break them, then it's your fault and you get busted.

Thus, aside from accident and the collusion of informants, dealers and smugglers attributed most arrests to their own negligence, to their failure to observe routine security precautions.[5] Being arrested, then, not only brought stigma from conventional society, but within the subculture it reflected on the competence of people's dealing styles and contributed to their overall placement in the hierarchy of success/failure. Drug traffickers' rules for staying out of legal trouble took the form of three reactive strategies—secrecy, insulation, and manipulation—based on their perceptions of how police operated.

Secrecy: Avoiding Arrest. Dealers' and smugglers' first lines of defense were measures designed to prevent police from discovering their operations. "Laying low" and guarding against obvious excess was one means of avoiding detection. Heavy partying and spending money in local restaurants and nightclubs was a tip-off that they had cash. Many dealers and smugglers believed that these establishments were frequented by narcs and thus were places to avoid.

Another common policy, along similar lines, was to avoid dealing in their own backyard. Buying and selling drugs in the area where they lived increased the likelihood that they would come in contact with local agents. Doing business elsewhere was comparatively quick and safe: they were never there long enough to establish predictable patterns of action (see also Carey 1968).

Acquiring a legal business front was essential for hiding illegal activities and income. Without this, straight neighbors, friends, relatives, and ultimately the police, were apt to become suspicious about their means of support. The IRS was also perceived as a threat, since it was known to work in conjunction with drug enforcement agents. One smuggler described the role of the IRS in his recent court case:

It turns out that once they had the goods on me, that they knew they were going to bust me, they sicked the IRS on my case. They had an agent tail me around for four months and write down every penny I spent. Then when they busted me they threw on the tax evasion charge too. They couldn't make the bust stick, but they got me on the tax evasion. Then they multiplied the money they saw me spend by five—that's the magic number—and they accepted that in court as my illegal income. So now I'm into them for $200,000 in back taxes.

Because of a healthy respect for the IRS, careful dealers and smugglers tried to manage the money they spent as well as the money they earned. Too many expensive purchases of traceable tangibles were dangerous, so illegal earnings were usually spent on consumables that left little evidence. Creative ways of accounting for earnings were also necessary; businesses with a large cash flow where the books could be juggled (i.e., restaurants, retail stores, self-employed professions and enterprises, specialized services, etc.) became havens for dealers to aid their passing (Goffman 1963) as legitimate businessmen. Dealers and smugglers used a variety of "disidentifiers," such as falsified records and bills of sale, erroneously reported gambling earnings, and money laundered through private trading in gems or real estate as props to help support their performances. Some dealers held jobs and dealt on the side (or tried to, for a while). This gave them the advantage of both a cover and a supplemental source of income, but often proved an excessive hindrance by cutting into the time and spontaneity they needed to deal.

The most secretive tactic drug traffickers pursued was to avoid meeting new people altogether. One smuggler, in the business for a dozen years, refused to go anywhere he might encounter a dealer he did not know. He preferred to sit outside in the car while his associate did a deal inside rather than risk having his name become known in dealing circles. He based this behavior on the philosophy that what the dealers knew, the police also knew, a common observation among criminal subcultures (see Letkemann 1973:43).

Insulation: Avoiding Ties to Evidence. While some dealers, especially novices and unsophisticated operators, believed that the police were ignorant of their identities, the more experienced and professional drug traffickers, like other criminals (see Klockars 1974, Letkemann 1973), assumed that they were known. One marijuana dealer described her attitude:

You always have to think they're [the police] on to you, have to figure your phone is tapped. You have to act under the assumption that they're watching you in everything you do.

Taking police knowledge of their identities as given, experienced dealers focused their energy on preventing police from proving that they were involved with drug trafficking by insulating themselves from contact with illegal substances or activities.

Routine means of insulation included using elaborate telephone codes to avoid mentioning drugs directly, discussing business only from pay telephones, changing their residences frequently (see also Carey 1968), and maintaining distance from the substance. This last was more common among marijuana than cocaine dealers.

Dealers and smugglers with a sophisticated type of organization could use buffers in the sampling, paying, or collecting ends of the transaction rather than being personally involved. This technique was used principally by smugglers, who had crew members they employed for such tasks. One smuggler I observed used his brothers and sister as buffers, but most others placed a hired employee in this position. Mark, a buffer unrelated by family ties, described his job:

I was taking orders directly from the smuggler, but I was the only one he contacted. Then I'd talk to the drivers and pilots, and I'd travel up and down the coast selling the pot to his customers. They knew I wasn't the actual smuggler, but they didn't know who was. They did all their dealings with him through me.

This type of insulation put an additional wedge between a smuggler and his crew members and connections, keeping him one step further removed from the illegal activities, while at the same time safeguarding his identity.

Another area where dealers and smugglers insulated themselves from danger involved extending or withholding trust from potential connections. Southwest County drug traffickers followed widely variant criteria for evaluating new customers. The most broadly followed precaution was a prohibition against dealing with strangers; only the least reputable dealers risked engaging in a business transaction with a completely unknown person. More careful dealers regarded such dealers as security risks themselves, as one cocaine dealer related:

When I first met Mitch I thought he'd be a good steady customer because he knew a lot of consumers and was always wanting to buy ounces or quarters [of cocaine] off me. But after awhile I found out how he was operating and since then I've kind of backed off. Shit, the guy's a walking drugstore—he hangs out on the streets loaded with stuff, looking for customers.

Normally, the minimum security precaution followed was to sell only to those individuals who were guaranteed by friends. Here, the guarantor had to be someone they knew well and trusted. More cautious individuals sold only to their friends directly, refusing to do business with anyone else, as one marijuana dealer stated:

When a friend brings his friend along who wants to buy dope from me I tell him my business is with the guy I know only. If he wants to sell it to the next guy for no profit that's his business, but I'm not getting involved.

These drug traffickers tried to work with relatively few buyers. They did not entirely rule out new connections, but tried to keep the number of their business relationships to a minimum.

Finally, some drug traffickers only worked with people they had encountered in the past. These highly cautious individuals avoided forming new distribution routes altogether (once their steady circle was established), preferring to restrict their dealing to those who had already been proven reliable. Jean and Jim discussed their security rules and the sanctions they invoked on people who violated them:

We would deal only to certain people, no one else. If you ever brought anybody we didn't know to the house you didn't get sold anything and you were never allowed to come to the house again. No one else around us would have anything to do with them. And we stuck to that. We did it to quite a few people who made that mistake of having a friend come up with them if they were middling something. They would try things, like park behind the garage or something, but we always knew.

Another bolster to security involved shunning "hot" associates, such as colleagues who had recently been busted or jailed. Within the dealing and smuggling community the myth of the "code of honor" circulated, suggesting that dealers adhered to a high standard of intragroup ethics and mutual self-protection. Like the "honor among thieves" Sutherland (1937) found within the subculture he studied, Southwest County dealers paid lip service to their loyalty to each other and to the group. Mutual loyalty and honor were further enhanced by the pragmatic importance of their reputations, within the drug world grapevine, for future business endeavors. Yet the success of police tactics in turning informants belied this image. Just as the countercultural antimaterialist, turn-the-world-on ideology was replaced by the driving self-interest of profit-motivated capitalism, so too did the "save your own skin" rationale become prevalent in the dealing subculture. This is not to suggest that dealers were universally devoid of scruples, informing on each other at the slightest provocation, but that the prevailing notion of universal self-sacrifice and mutual commitment did not accurately reflect how people reacted when subjected to the threat of personal harm. Enough stories circulated of people who succumbed to police pressure to make dealers and smugglers wary of those who had just emerged from an encounter with the law, especially if they appeared to have gotten off lightly. Dave described the effects of his prison experience:

When I first got out of the joint [jail] none of my old friends would have anything to do with me. Finally, one guy who had been my partner told me it was because everyone was suspicious of my getting out early and thought I had made a deal.

Thus, while arrest and/or incarceration are fairly common experiences among those who violate the law, the significance of these rites of passage was somewhat different for upper-level dealers and smugglers than for other criminals. Although many studies of criminal groups (see Klockars 1974 on fences; Sutherland 1937 and Letkemann 1973 on thieves; Cameron 1964 on shoplifters, and even Langer 1977 on middle-level drug dealers) have stated that being arrested was considered a positive social benchmark which enlightened participants as to police procedure and elevated their status within the group, Southwest County dealers and smugglers looked on arrest as a step toward failure. Like the dealers Goode (1970) studied, arrest was seen as a "status transformation," a ceremonial rite that downgraded individuals in the eyes of significant others. Being arrested made them recipients of undesired police scrutiny, for themselves and for their associates. It also suggested an often arduous legal process that was financially draining, beginning with the confiscation of merchandise and ending when they no longer had the money to sustain a legal defense. Even worse, being arrested suggested that they might be informing to the narcs. Temporarily, at least, they ceased to be desirable business connections. Thus, in the drug business, locked up often meant locked out from all those who had come to constitute their circle of friends.

Manipulation: Avoiding Incarceration. Once their strategies of avoiding arrest failed, dealers and smugglers tried to exploit the criminal justice system. A coterie of dope lawyers who specialized almost exclusively in drug issues were employed to protect their clients' constitutional and legal rights. These lawyers found loopholes in the arrest proce-

dures or negotiated advantageous plea bargains. Some smugglers kept
a lawyer employed on a retainer basis so that they could have the advantage of continuous legal counsel. These professionals made smugglers aware of legal technicalities or changes in the law which affected
police practices. In addition, some dealers and smugglers had ties with
bail bondsmen who paid for a person's release once the court had set
bail. By quickly liberating associates from jail, dealers and smugglers
hoped to reduce the chances of their informing. Thus, while drug
traffickers were wary of doing business with colleagues who had been
arrested, they did not abandon them altogether. As one cocaine dealer
said, "one of the biggest rules is that you take care of the people you
sell to."

When dealers or smugglers were known by reputation among
bondsmen, they could get bail posted for their associates on their word
alone. Without this recognition, the money had to be collateralized with
concrete assets. One smuggler owned a piece of property he kept
available on a rotating basis, renting it out to friends, for a fee, as bond
collateral. In such a case, the jailed dealer had to pay the property
loan fee in addition to the bail bondsman's fee and the lawyer's fee.

When legal maneuvers failed, dealers and smugglers turned to the
most direct route to freedom: bribery. It was rare in Southwest County
because the drug traffickers were only loosely connected individual
entrepreneurs, lacking the tight organization necessary to come up with
large amounts of regular bribe money. Police in the vicinity also had
a reputation as generally honest and incorrupt. However, individual
officers were reputed to have warned a smuggler or dealer before a
planned raid or set-up, to have prevented suspicion from falling on an
individual or crew, or to have destroyed police evidence once an arrest
had occurred.

Style Variations and Temporality. I have presented three reactive strategies, secrecy, insulation, and manipulation, which Southwest County
drug traffickers used to avoid the law. For the most part, I portrayed
these strategies ideal typically, depicting only the most meticulous
modes of operation. These highly cautious modes, though, were not
employed by all. Vast differences existed in styles of operation. While
those at the higher end of the reputational spectrum lived well and

surrounded themselves with the finest-quality possessions, food, and drugs, they also lived discreetly. They partied privately, within a small network of drug world associates, mostly inside each others' houses. Their wilder spending sprees in public occurred when they were out of town on vacation or conducting deals in private hotel suites. Less well-respected dealers and smugglers, on the other hand, followed considerably fewer security tactics (although all of them had some minimum rules they followed). Those on the lower end of the spectrum displayed big bankrolls in local bars, readily admitted their dealing status when trying to pick up women, pursued no legitimate work, filed no tax returns, and dealt with a wide range of other drug traffickers (who, not surprisingly, were also at the lower end of the prestige spectrum). Idiosyncratic dealing styles between these two polar extremes also existed, and were practiced by people who adopted some of the rules but were not careful (or paranoid) enough to follow others. Their place on the continuum of prestige corresponded closely to their degree of success or failure; people who were more adept at avoiding legal entanglements lost less money and drugs to law enforcement agents, suffered fewer interruptions in the flow of buying and selling, and hence were rated as more desirable business associates by other reputable operators.

In reality, all dealers and smugglers were inconsistent in their adherence to these practices, however (see also Carey 1968; Moore 1977). Their behavior varied from one year to the next or, for some, from one day to the next. Some fluctuations were due to their freedom, since, as self-employed entrepreneurs, they were able to break their rules whenever they wanted. They saw this, in fact, as a benefit of their nonroutine occupations. In addition, many dealers began with an ideal view of the appropriate strategies but gradually slipped into looser behavior as their use of drugs and quest for hedonism took over. The most radical inconsistencies, though, were due to the fundamentally unstable nature of their careers. Events in their lives (ranging from business considerations such as the seasonal availability of drugs to social factors such as their romantic interests) created a cyclical syndrome where they vacillated between relatively stable periods of behavior to unpredictable ones. Some individuals were able to settle into a dealing niche, maintaining one style of operation for years, but more commonly, niches disintegrated and were replaced by a series of evolving, shifting patterns.

Jean is a case in point. In eight years, she went from being a casual and careless middle-level marijuana middler, to being a well-respected major cocaine pound dealer with stringent and rational rules for three or four years, to quitting the business when she got divorced. After failing in a legitimate business venture, she got back into trafficking by doing small deals and muling drugs across the border (the most risky of all operations). Deep in debt and strung out on drugs, she became unreliable in her business dealings. Her shifts in operating style, although major, were fairly commonplace for Southwest County drug traffickers. Moreover, she illustrates a common sequence of prestige mobility. Once established in the cocaine trade, she worked hard, reinvested all her profits, and built a carefully run empire, complete with a legitimate business as a cover. After quitting and reentering the business, though, she was desperate, reckless, and foolhardy. Her life spiraled downward, her social and business relationships dwindled, and she lost the reputation for insulation and success which she had worked so hard to achieve.

Once dealers or smugglers established a reputation within the community for adhering to a certain dealing style, their future prestige mobility was more likely to be downward than upward. Their early rationalism, goal-orientation, and self-control usually gave way to the heavy partying, impulsive behavior, and present-orientation so prevalent within the subculture of hedonism. Pleasure-seeking, decadence, and irrationality formed an environment ripe for breaking rules and failure. Drug traffickers thus often neglected their standards for security to an increasing degree, the longer they remained within the drug world. Once their reputations had declined, they found these harder to rebuild than to initially establish.

THE PRESTIGE HIERARCHY AS THE "INVISIBLE HAND"

In chapter 4 I contrasted the monopolistic and competitive models of illicit market structure. I concluded that the organization of Southwest County's dealers and smugglers was closer to the latter model. A further dimension differentiating monopolistic and competitive markets, however, is their regulatory mechanisms. Some of the data in this chapter have shed light on the drug market's formal and informal regulatory mechanisms, further reinforcing the view of this illicit market as competitive.

Monopolistic markets are associated with "visible hand" forms of regulation, such as coercion and force. Most common to illicit markets of this kind are police corruption (Cressey 1969; Ianni 1972; Reuter 1983), arbitration (Reuter 1983), and violence (Ianni 1972; Moore 1977; Reuter 1983). First, large syndicates such as the Mafia which seek to dominate a market monopolistically generally develop connections with law enforcement agents. Syndicates use police to protect their members and operations, while driving their competitors out of business. However, because Southwest County drug traffickers were entrepreneurial and disorganized, their ability to corrupt drug agents was insignificant at best. I heard rumors about dealer-police contacts, but none of them were ever substantiated. Second, monopolistic markets have structured, illicit venues where participants can present disputes for arbitration. For example, Reuter described how in New York City the Mafia had exclusive control over settling arguments for illicit operators who had irresoluble disagreements. No group filled such a function in Southwest County. Drug traffickers had either to accept the actions of others or to settle their differences personally. Third, monopolistic markets are especially known for participants' proclivity toward violence to make others follow their wishes. This "competitive violence" (Reuter 1983) involves the use of force to control an individual's or group's share of the market, to keep new people from entering the field, to protect territory, or to make others pay a "tax" to the dominant group. I saw very little, if any, of this kind of violence in Southwest County. The rare incidences of violence I observed were "noncompetitive" (Reuter 1983), primarily oriented toward collecting debts and only secondarily aimed at getting revenge. Violent behavior was least prevalent in the upper echelons of the prestige hierarchy. Individuals at these levels generally excluded others from their business dealings if they committed offensive acts. Ostracism was considered sufficient retaliation for burns, rip-offs, security violations, and other disreputable behavior. At the lower end of the prestige hierarchy, where rip-offs and burns were more common, drug traffickers chased, threatened, and occasionally hit each other. In the end, though, the guilty parties usually either capitulated to the threats or fled the area and hid. Ultimately, little violence occurred even among this group.

Competitive markets are characterized by "invisible hand" forms of regulation rather than by force. In these markets, people are not coerced or cornered, but voluntarily choose their actions to further their own self-interests. While they may act only for their own benefit, the un-intended consequence of their pursuit of personal gain is the good of the market and the group as a whole (Smith 1937). This self-guided and informal regulation of market behavior was apparent in dealers' and smugglers' competitive alignment of their actions to correspond with others', and in their adherence to market norms and conventions.

The Southwest County drug market's informal regulatory mecha-nism lay in its prestige hierarchy, which served to influence drug traf-fickers' degree of success and failure. First, dealers and smugglers ad-justed their prices, services, and credit policies to fit within the range of prevailing local customs. This enhanced their reputations as sup-pliers, attracting customers to them and increasing their ability to sell their drugs easily and replenish their capital. At the same time, their competitive behavior ensured that an orderly market in drugs would be maintained, where buyers and sellers could know what to expect. Second, most dealers and smugglers followed the conventions of the local market. This enhanced their reputations as desirable customers, since suppliers preferred to sell to individuals who operated discreetly and repaid their debts promptly. Those dealers who followed the norms shielded themselves from outsiders. This affected their success or fail-ure because many of the norms served to protect them from being dis-covered, arrested, or imprisoned. For example, drug traffickers who took care of their customers when they got arrested did so because it was in their interest. By bailing busted customers out of jail, lending them money, or fronting them drugs, suppliers sought to discourage their customers from informing. The bail custom also had two unin-tended consequences: (1) it benefited the customers by helping them regain financial solvency, and (2) it benefited the community as a whole by strengthening the group's cohesion.

The social and economic order of this illicit market was maintained, therefore, not by the monopolistic "visible hand" of corruption, arbitration, and violence, but by the competitive "invisible hand" of self-interest serving to indirectly ensure the good of all. In a competitive market, the informal mechanisms ensuring order are those which determine individuals' success or failure—in this case, the prestige hierarchy.

THE STRUCTURE OF SUCCESS AND FAILURE

In chapter 4, I showed how the drug world's social solidarity supported an information network capable of spreading gossip throughout the community. This information diffusion was the mechanism by which people were stratified along the prestige hierarchy. The need for self-regulation often ensured that behavioral norms were enforced by stricter standards than they were within conventional society. Dealers could not afford to rip off or burn people in the drug community too often or they found themselves out of business or, at best, only dealing with other losers.

Success and failure in the drug world thus continually regenerated themselves. When Hayano (1982) noted that for professional card players, "being on the tilt can become a way of life," he referred to this syndrome. In his theory of momentum, Adler (1981) analyzed the way failure, or "negative momentum," took a downward spiral, and showed how negative consequences fed back to successively lessen the quality of individuals' behavior until they became trapped in a situation characterized by lost confidence and diminished positive effort. For dealers and smugglers, each lost load or unpaid debt worsened their overall reputation in the community. Desperate to make up for the last failure, they acted rashly, broke rules, or dealt with dangerous associates. This intensified the cycle, as Bruce, with his increasing debt, so vividly exemplified. Being labeled a failure, by first a few individuals and increasingly a growing segment of the community, became a self-fulfilling prophecy; dealers and smugglers were then forced to deal with people of questionable repute, and the unreliability or malfeasance of others compounded their own. Conversely, success bred success. Drug traffickers who established and sustained high standards of secrecy generated the positive rewards which led to a set of associates where bankruptcy, notoriety, arrest, conviction, and imprisonment were much less likely to occur. The prestige hierarchy was thus the ultimate determinant of success or failure as all the environmental, psychological, business, social, and legal contingencies combined to form a continuum which regenerated and reified itself.

CHAPTER SEVEN

DEALING CAREERS

Southwest County upper-level dealers and smugglers pursued drug trafficking as their primary, full-time occupation. While many dabbled in side businesses, the bulk of their time, money, energy, and self-image was lodged in their drug careers. In this chapter I outline dealers' and smugglers' sequential career patterns throughout their involvement with drug trafficking. I begin by examining the process of becoming a drug trafficker, then consider the various routes to upward mobility. Next, I describe how the experience of aging in the career changed them from the "beautiful people" described earlier to fearful and cautious individuals looking to return to conventional society. I outline the multiple, conflicting forces which repeatedly lured them out of and back into drug trafficking, and their resulting pattern of career oscillations. I suggest a variety of paths dealers and smugglers pursued out of drug trafficking, and discuss the problems inherent in leaving this deviant occupation.

BECOMING A DRUG TRAFFICKER

Becoming a drug trafficker was a gradual process, where individuals progressively shifted perspective as they became increasingly involved in the social networks of dealers and smugglers (Lieb and Olson 1976). As Ray (1961) has noted for the careers of heroin addicts, joining these social networks required a commitment to the drug world's norms, values, and lifestyle, and limited the degree of involvement individuals subsequently had with nondeviant groups.

Recruitment. I observed three entry routes to this deviant career. These routes were different for dealing and smuggling, and varied according to the level of trafficking where individuals entered the field.

DEALING. Individuals began dealing drugs through their own initiative, entering the occupation via *self-propulsion.* They fell into two groups, marked by different levels of entry and characterized by significantly varied experiences.

People who began dealing with a low-level entry followed the classic path portrayed in the literature (see Anonymous 1969; Blum et al. 1972; Carey 1968; Goode 1970; Johnson 1973). These initiates came from among the ranks of regular drug users, since, in practice, using drugs heavily and dealing for "stash" (one's personal supply) were nearly inseparable. Out of this multitude of low-level dealers, however, most abandoned the practice after they encountered their first legal or financial bust, lasting in the business for a fairly short period (see Anonymous 1969; Carey 1968; Lieb and Olson 1976; Mandel 1967). Those who sought bigger profits gradually drifted into a full-time career in drug trafficking. Their careers as dealers were therefore entwined with their careers as drug users, which usually began by late adolescence (between the ages of 15 and 22). Because of this early recruitment into dealing, low-level entrants generally developed few, if any, occupational skills other than dealing. Although it was difficult to attain the upper level of the drug trade from these humble beginnings, a small but significant percentage of the dealers I observed in Southwest County got their start in this fashion.

A larger percentage of Southwest County dealers made a middle-level entry. Future big dealers usually jumped into transacting in substantial quantities from the outset, buying 50 kilos of commercial marijuana or one to two ounces of cocaine. One dealer explained this phenomenon:

Someone who thinks of himself as an executive or an entrepreneur is not going to get into the dope business on a small level. The average executive just jumps right into the middle. Or else he's not going to jump.

This was the route taken by Southwest County residents who had little or no previous involvement in drug trafficking. For them, entry into dealing was precipitated by their social relations with local dealers and smugglers (naturally, this implies a self-selecting sample of outsiders who became accepted and trusted by these upper-level traffickers, based on mutual interests, orientation, and values). Through their friendships with dealers, these individuals were introduced to other members of the dealing scene and to their fast life. Individuals who found this lifestyle attractive became increasingly drawn to the sub-culture, building networks of social associations within it. Eventually, some of these people decided to participate more actively. This step was usually motivated by their attraction to the money and the life-style. Dave recounted how he fell in with the drug world set:

I used to be in real estate making good money. Through my property man-agement and investment services I started meeting some rich people. I was the only person at my firm renting to longhairs and dealing with their money. They all paid me in cash from a giant wad of bills. They never asked for a receipt and always had cash, 24 hours a day. I slowly started getting friendly with them, although I didn't realize how heavy they were. I knew ways of buying real estate and putting it under fictitious names, laundering money so that it went in as hot cash and came out as spendable income. I invested their money in gems, metals, cars. But the whole time I never asked any questions. I just took my commission and was happy. Then one guy asked me to clear some checks for him through my bank account—said he was hiding the money from his ex-wife and the Treasury people. This was the beginning. I slowly got more and more involved with him until I was neglecting my real estate business and just partying with him all the time. My spending went up, but my income went down, and suddenly I had to look around for another way to make money fast. I took the money I was cashing for him, bought some bricks from another dealer friend of his and sold them out of state before I gave him back the cash. Eventually I started to deal with him too, on a front basis. Within six months I was turning 100 bricks at a time.

Once individuals decided to try dealing, they rarely abandoned it after one transaction. Earning money was intoxicatingly alluring, stimulating their greed for more, while losing money usually necessi-tated becoming involved in another deal to recoup what they lost.

People who entered drug dealing at these middle levels were usually between the ages of 25 and 35, and had worked in some other occu-pation before dealing seriously. Many drifted into the lifestyle from jobs already concentrated in the night hours, such as bartending, waiting tables, and nightclub door bouncing. Still others came from fields where the working hours were irregular and adaptable to their special sched-ules, such as acting, real estate, inventing, graduate school, construc-tion, and creative "entrepreneurship" (more aptly called hand-to-mouth survival, for many). The smallest group was tempted into the drug world from structured occupations and the professions.

SMUGGLING. Smuggling, in contrast, was rarely entered in this self-directed manner. Only a small minority of upper-level dealers were able to make the leap into importation on their own. The rest became involved in smuggling through a form of *solicitation*. The complex task of importing illegal drugs required more knowledge, experience, equipment, and connections than most people possessed. Those who got into drug smuggling usually did so at the invitation of an established smuggler. About half of the people smugglers recruited had not dealt before, but came directly into importation from the drug world's social scene. This implies, like middle-level entry into dealing, that recruits were attracted to the drug crowd and its lifestyle, and that they had prior acquaintance with dealers and smugglers. The other half of the recruits were solicited from among the ranks of middle-level Southwest County dealers.

Recruits who were solicited were likely to have some skill or asset which the experienced smuggler needed to put his operation together. This included piloting or navigating ability, equipment, money, or simply the willingness to handle drugs while they were being transported. One smuggler described the criteria he used to screen potential recruits for his smuggling crew:

Pilots are really at a premium. They burn out so fast that I have to replace them every six months to a year. But I'm also looking for people who are cool: people who will carry out their jobs according to the plan, who won't panic if the load arrives late or something goes wrong, 'cause this happens a lot . . . and I try not to get people who've been to prison before, because if they haven't they'll be more likely to take foolish risks, the kind that I don't want to have to.

Learning the Trade. Once people experienced some initial success in dealing, their attitude shifted from hesitancy to enthusiasm. Despite the amount of time and effort they invested, most people felt as if they had earned a lot of money for very little work. This was because dealing time and work differed structurally from legitimate work: the latter usually took place within a well-defined physical and temporal framework (the 9-to-5 hours at the office), while dealing was accomplished during discretionary, or recreational, hours and settings.

As business began to go well, the danger translated into excitement, making it seem like fun. Novice drug traffickers felt as if they were earning "gravy" money while simultaneously enjoying themselves. This definition of the situation helped them overcome any remaining reluctance and plunge themselves more deeply into the occupation. They then became eager to learn more about concrete strategies of conducting business safely and successfully.

Learning the trade involved acquiring specific knowledge of potential business connections, ways of organizing transactions profitably, ways of avoiding legal detection and arrest, ways of transporting illegal goods, ways of coordinating participants, types of equipment, and myriad other details. This knowledge was acquired through either *on-the-job training* (Miller and Ritzer 1977:89) or *sponsorship*.

Dealers underwent on-the-job training, refining their knowledge and skills by getting experience and learning from their mistakes. Their early experiences often included getting burned with inferior merchandise (as one novice dealer described in chapter 6), getting "short counted" with low volume, and getting ripped off through carelessness in selecting their dealing associates. While some people abandoned dealing because of these early errors, many returned, better educated, to try again.

Socialization into the technical aspects of smuggling was not as isolated as it was for dealing. Most future smugglers were recruited and trained by a sponsor with whom they had an apprentice-mentor relationship.[1] Those who had been dealers previously knew the rudiments of drug transactions. What they learned from the smuggler was how to fill a particular role in his crew. From there they became familiar with many other roles, learned the scope of the whole operation, and began to meet suppliers and customers. This mentor relationship often led apprentices to form an enduring loyalty to their sponsor, as I discussed in chapter 4.[2]

Identity Shift. Developing a dealing or smuggling self-conception involved more than simply committing illegal acts. A transition in the locus of self was required. Some people assumed the dealing identity immediately and eagerly, having made a conscious decision to pursue dealing as an occupation. Others displayed a more subtle identity shift, as they gradually drifted into membership in the drug world (Matza

1964). Many individuals, then, became drug dealers by their actions well before they consciously admitted this to themselves. One dealer described his transformation:

I had a job, school, and I was doing volunteer work, but I was also deviant and the deviant part was the part I secretly got off on. I was like a Dr. Jekyll with a Mr. Hyde side. When I got into my dealing bag people would pay homage to me; I'd get respect and recognition. . . . Eventually the two worlds intermingled and the façade [dealing side] became the reality.

Becker and Carper (1956) have asserted that individuals' identities are based on their degree of commitment to an occupation. Thus, those people who maintained their ties to other occupations took longer to form a dealing identity. They did not become fully committed to dealing until some external event (i.e., an arrest, or the conflicting demands of their legitimate and illegitimate businesses) forced them to make a conscious choice. One dealer related how he faced this decision:

I had been putting off thinking about it for all those months but the time squeeze finally became such a thing that I couldn't ignore it any more. I was working at the office all day and staying up dealing and doing drugs all night. My wife was complaining because I'd fall asleep at odd hours and I never had any time for the kids. I knew I had to choose between my two lives—the straight and the dealing. I hated to give up my job because it had always been my security, and besides, it was a good business cover, but I finally decided I was more attracted to dealing. I was making better money there in fewer hours and this way I'd have more time to be with my kids during the day.

UPWARD MOBILITY

Once they had gotten in and learned the trade, most dealers and smugglers strove for upward mobility. This advancement took different forms, varying between dealing and smuggling.

Dealers experienced two types of upward mobility: *rising through the ranks* and *stage-jumping*. The gradual rise exemplifies the way upward mobility has historically been portrayed in the sociological literature on dealing (Anonymous 1969; Carey 1968; Redlinger 1975). Individuals from the lowest levels expanded their range of contacts, realized that they could earn greater profits by buying in greater quantities, and began to move up the hierarchy of dealing levels. Rick described his early stage of involvement with dealing:

I had dealt a limited amount of lids and psychedelics in my early college days without hardly taking it seriously. But after awhile something changed in me and I decided to try to work my way up. I probably was a classic case—started out buying a kilo for $150 and selling two pounds for $100 each. I did that twice, then I took the money and bought two bricks, then three, then five, then seven.

This type of upward mobility, while characteristic of low-level dealers, was fairly atypical of the upper-level drug crowd. Two factors combined to make it less likely for low-level entrants to rise through the ranks to the top. The first was psychological. People who started small thought small; most had neither the motivation nor the vision to deal large quantities of drugs. The second and more critical factor was social. People who started at the bottom and tried to work their way up the ladder often had a hard time finding connections at the upper levels.[3] The few people who did rise through the ranks generally began dealing in another part of the country, moving to Southwest County only after they had already progressed to the middle levels. These people were lured to the region by its reputation within drug circles as an importation and wholesale trafficking market.

More commonly, dealers and smugglers stage-jumped to the higher levels of drug trafficking. Beginning at a middle level, and progressing so rapidly that they could hardly acclimate to their increasing involvement and volume, these people moved quickly to the top. Jean described her mode of escalation:

When I started to deal I was mostly looking for a quick buck here or there, something to pay some pressing bill. I was middling 50 or 100 bricks at a time. But then I met a guy who said he would front me half a pound of coke, and if I turned it fast I could have more, and on a regular basis. Pretty soon I was turning 6, 7, 8, 9, 10 pounds a week—they were passing through real fast. I was clearing at least 10 grand a month. It was too much money too fast. I didn't know what to do with it. It got ridiculous, I wasn't relating to anyone anymore. I was never home, always gone. . . . The biggest ego trip came when all of a sudden I turned around and was selling to the people I had been buying from. I skipped their level of doing business entirely and stage-jumped straight past them.

Southwest County's social milieu, with its concentration of upper-level dealers and smugglers, thus facilitated forming connections and doing business at the upper levels of the drug world.

Within smuggling, upward mobility took the form of individuals *branching out on their own* (Redlinger 1975). By working for a smuggler, some crew members developed the expertise and connections to run their own operation. There were several requirements for such a move. They could fairly easily acquire the technical knowledge of equipment, air routes, stopovers, and how to coordinate personnel after working in a smuggling crew for six months to a year. It was difficult to put together their own crew, though, because skilled employees, especially pilots, were hard to find. Most new smugglers borrowed people from other crews until they were established enough to recruit and train their own personnel. Finally, they needed connections for buying and selling drugs. Customers were plentiful, but it often required special breaks or networks to serve a foreign supplier.

Another way for employees to head their own smuggling operations was to take over when their boss retired. This had the advantage of keeping the crew and style of operation intact. Various financial arrangements were worked out for such a transfer of authority, from straight cash purchases to deals involving residual payments. One marijuana smuggler described how he acquired his operation:

I had been Jake's main pilot for about a year and next after him I knew the most about how his operation was run. We were really tight, and he had taken me all up and down the coast with him, meeting his customers. Naturally I knew the Mexican end of the operation and his supplier, Cesar, since I used to make the runs, flying down the money and picking up the dope. So when he told me he wanted to get out of the business, we made a deal. I took over the set-up and gave him a residual for every run I made. I kept all the drivers, all the dealers, all the connections—everything the guy had—but I found myself a new pilot.

In sum, most dealers and smugglers reached the upper levels of doing business not so much as a result of their individual entrepreneurial initiative but through the social networks they formed in the drug subculture. Their ability to remain in these strata was largely tied to the way they treated these drug world relationships.

AGING IN THE CAREER

Up to this point I have discussed dealers and smugglers separately because they displayed distinctive career patterns. However, once individuals rose to the highest levels, they faced a common set of problems and experiences. I will therefore discuss them together below.

Once they entered the drug world and established themselves at its upper levels, dealers and smugglers were capable of wheeling and dealing on a major scale. Yet this period brought with it a growth of malaise. As they aged in the career, the dark side of their occupation began to surface.

The first part of their disillusionment lay in the fading of glamor and excitement. While participation in the drug world brought thrills and status to novices, the occupation's allure faded over time. Their initial feelings of exhilaration began to dull as they became increasingly jaded by their exorbitant drug consumption. Already inclined toward regular use, upper-level dealers and smugglers set no limits on their drug intake once they began trafficking and could afford all the cocaine they desired. One smuggler described how he eventually came to feel:

It was fun, those three or four years. I never worried about money or anything. But after a while it got real boring, there was no feeling or emotion or anything about it. I wasn't even hardly relating to my old lady anymore. Everything was just one big rush.

After a year or more of serious drug trafficking, dealers and smugglers became increasingly sensitized to the extreme risks they faced. Cases of friends and associates who were arrested, imprisoned, or killed (because of natural hazards) began to mount. The probability that they were known to the police increased. They gradually realized that the potential legal consequences they faced were less remote than they had earlier imagined. Many individuals became convinced that continued drug trafficking would inevitably lead to arrest ("It's only a matter of time before you get caught").

Dealers and smugglers generally repressed their awareness of danger, treating it as a taken-for-granted part of their daily existence. Periodic crises shattered their casual attitudes, however, evoking strong underlying feelings of fears. One dealer talked about his feelings of paranoia:

You're always on the line. You don't lead a normal life. You're always looking over your shoulder, wondering who's at the door, having to hide everything. You learn to look behind you so well you could probably bend over and look up your ass. That's paranoia. It's a really scary, hard feeling. That's what makes you get out.

These feelings caused dealers and smugglers to assume greater security precautions. After especially close brushes with danger, they intensified their precautions temporarily, retreating into near-isolation until they felt that the heat was off. They also gradually incorporated more precautions into their everyday routines, abandoning their earlier casualness for greater inflexibility and adherence to their rational rules of operating (see Lieb and Olson 1976). This went against their natural preference, and they found it unspontaneous and cumbersome.

Drug world members also grew progressively weary of their exclusion from the legitimate world and the series of deceptions they had to manage to sustain that separation. Initially, the separation had been surrounded by an alluring mystique. As they aged in the career, however, the mystique was replaced by the hassle of everyday boundary maintenance and their feelings of being expatriated from conventional society. One smuggler described the effects of this separation:

I'm so sick of looking over my shoulder, having to sit in my house and worry about one of my non–drug world friends stopping in when I'm doing business. Do you know how awful that is? It's like leading a double life. That's what makes it not worth it.

Thus, while the drug world was somewhat restricted, it was not an encapsulated community. As Reuter (1983:174) has noted, criminals maintain an involvement with the legitimate world:

Criminals do not inhabit a social and physical world that is different from the rest of society. They walk the same streets, dine in the same restaurants, and send their children to the same schools.

This constant contact with the straight world reminded them of the comforts and social ease they had left behind, and tempted them to go straight.

For upper-level dealers and smugglers, then, the process of aging in the career was one of progressive *burnout*. With the novelty worn off, most dealers and smugglers felt that the occupation no longer resembled their earlier impressions of it. Once they had reached the upper levels, their experience began to change and they changed with it. No

longer were they the carefree people who lived from day to day without a thought for the future. No longer were they so intoxicated with
their glamor that their only care in the world was the search for new
heights of pleasure. Elements of this lifestyle remained, but they were
tempered with the harsher side of the reality. In between episodes of
intensive partying, veteran dealers and smugglers were struck by anxiety. They began to structure their work to encompass greater planning, caution, secrecy, and insulation. They isolated themselves from
the straight world for days or weeks at a time, imprisoned and haunted
by their own suspicions. They never renounced their hedonism or
materialism, but the price they paid increased. Eventually, the rewards of trafficking no longer seemed to justify the strain. It was at
this point that the straight world's formerly dull ambience became
transformed (at least in theory) into a potential haven.

SHIFTS AND OSCILLATIONS

Despite the gratifications dealers and smugglers derived from the easy
money, material comfort, freedom, prestige, and power associated with
their careers, most of them decided, at some point, to quit the business. This stemmed, in part, from their initial perceptions of the career as temporary ("Hell, nobody wants to be a drug dealer all their
life"). Supplementing these early intentions was the process of rapid
aging in the career, where dealers and smugglers became increasingly
aware of the sacrifices their occupations required and got tired of living the fugitive life. As the dealing life began to look more troubling
than rewarding, drug traffickers focused their energies on returning to
the straight life. They thought about, talked about, and in many cases,
took steps toward getting out of the drug business. But like entering
the field, disengaging from drug trafficking was rarely an abrupt act
(Lieb and Olson 1976:364). Instead, it more often resembled a series
of transitions, or oscillations[4] out of and back into the business. For
once out of the drug world, dealers and smugglers were rarely successful at making it in the legitimate world because they failed to cut
down on their extravagant lifestyle or drug consumption. Many thus
abandoned their efforts to reform and returned to deviance, sometimes picking up where they left off and other times shifting to a new

mode of operating. For example, some shifted from trafficking in cocaine to trafficking in marijuana, some dropped to a lower level of
dealing, and others shifted their role within the same group of traffickers. This series of phase-outs and reentries, combined with career
shifts, endured for years, dominating the pattern of their remaining
involvement with the business. It also represented the method by which
many eventually broke away from drug trafficking, for each phase-out
had the potential to be an individual's final departure.

Phasing Out. Making the decision to quit a deviant occupation is difficult.[5] Several factors served to hold dealers and smugglers to the drug
world. First, the hedonistic and materialistic satisfactions were primary. Once individuals became accustomed to earning large amounts
of easy money, they found it exceedingly difficult to go back to the
income scale of the straight world. They were also reluctant to abandon the pleasures of the fast life and its accompanying drugs, sex, and
power. Second, dealers and smugglers formed an identification with
and commitment to the occupation of drug trafficking. Their self-images were tied to that role and could not be easily disengaged. Their
years invested learning the trade, forming connections, building reputations served as "side-bets" (Becker 1960), strengthening their involvement with both the deviant occupation and the drug community.
And since their relationships were social as well as business-oriented,
members' friendship ties bound them to dealing. As one dealer, in the
midst of struggling to phase out, explained:

The biggest threat to me is to get caught up sitting around the house with
friends that are into dealing. I'm trying to stay away from them, change my
habits.

Third, dealers and smugglers hesitated to voluntarily quit the field
because they knew it would be difficult to find another way of earning
a living. They feared that they would be unable to account to pro-
spective employers for their years spent in illicit activity. This narrowed their occupational choices considerably, leaving self-employ-
ment as one of the few remaining avenues open.

Once dealers and smugglers made the decision to phase out, they
generally pursued one of several routes out of dealing.[6] The most fre-

quent pattern involved resolving to quit after they executed one last big deal. While the intention was sincerely uttered, individuals who chose this route rarely succeeded; the big deal too often remained elusive. One marijuana smuggler offered a variation on this theme:

My plan is to make a quarter of a million dollars in four months during the prime smuggling season and get the hell out of the business.

A second pattern involved individuals who planned to get out immediately, but never did. They announced that they were quitting, yet their outward actions never varied. Bruce, with his problems of overconsumption and debt escalation, described his involvement with this syndrome:

When I wake up I'll say, "Hey, I'm going to quit this cycle and just run my other business." But when you're dealing you constantly have people dropping by ounces and asking, "Can you move this?" What's your first response? Always, "Sure, for a toot."

In the third pattern of phasing-out, individuals actually suspended their dealing or smuggling activities, but did not replace them with an alternative source of income. Such withdrawals were usually spontaneous and prompted by exhaustion, the influence of a person from outside the drug world, or problems with the police or other associates. As one dealer's case illustrated, these phase-outs usually lasted only until their money ran out:

I got into heavy legal trouble with the FBI a while back and I was forced to quit dealing. Everybody just cut me off completely, and I saw the danger in continuing myself. But my high class tastes never dwindled. I borrowed money here and there. Before I knew it I was in hock over $30,000. Even though I was hot, I was forced to get back into dealing to relieve some of my debts.

In the fourth pattern of phasing-out, traffickers attempted a move into another line of work. Alternative occupations they tried included: occupations they had pursued before dealing or smuggling; front businesses maintained on the side while they were trafficking in drugs; and new occupations altogether. While some people successfully accomplished this transition, there were problems in all three alternatives.

Most people who tried to resume their former occupations found that these had changed too much while they were away from the field.

In addition, they themselves had changed: they enjoyed the self-directed freedom and spontaneity associated with dealing and smuggling, and were unwilling to relinquish it.

Those who turned to their legitimate front business often found that these businesses were unable to support them. Designed to launder rather than earn money, most of these ventures had become accustomed to operating under a continuous subsidy from illegal funds. Once their drug funding was cut off, they could not survive for long.

Many dealers and smugglers utilized the business skills and connections they had developed in drug trafficking to create a new occupation. For some, the decision to prepare a legitimate career for retirement followed an unsuccessful attempt to phase out into a front business. One husband-and-wife dealing team explained how these legitimate side businesses differed from front businesses:

We always had a little legitimate scam going, like mail-order shirts, wallets, jewelry, and the kids were always involved in that. We made a little bit of money on them. Their main purpose was for a cover and a legitimate business both. But [this business] was different; right from the start this was going to be a legal thing to push us out of the drug business.

Dealers and smugglers often formed these legitimate side occupations by exchanging their illegal commodity for a legal one, going into import/export, manufacturing, wholesaling, or retailing other merchandise. One former dealer described his current business and how he got into it:

A friend of mine knew one of the major wholesalers in Tijuana for buying Mexican blankets, ponchos, and sweatshirts. After I helped him out with a favor when he was down, he turned me on to his connections. Now I've cornered the market on wholesaling them to surf shops and swap meet sellers by undercutting everybody else.

The most future-oriented dealers and smugglers thus began gradually tapering off their drug world involvement, transferring their time and money into a selected legitimate endeavor. They did not try to quit drug trafficking altogether until they felt confident that their legitimate business could support them. But like spontaneous phase-outs, many of these planned withdrawals into legitimate businesses failed to generate enough money to keep individuals from being lured back into the drug world.

In addition to the voluntary phase-outs dealers and smugglers attempted after they became sufficiently burned out, many of them experienced an involuntary "bustout" at some point in their careers. Forced withdrawals from dealing or smuggling were usually sudden and necessitated by external factors, either financial, legal, or reputational. Financial bustouts generally occurred when dealers or smugglers were either burned or ripped off by others, leaving them in too much debt to rebuild their operation. Legal bustouts occurred when individuals got so hot from arrest or incarceration that few of their former associates would deal with them. Reputational bustouts occurred when individuals burned or ripped off others (regardless of whether they intended to do so) and were banned from business by their former associates. One smuggler gave his opinion on the pervasive nature of forced phase-outs:

Some people are smart enough to get out of it because they realize, physically, they have to. Others realize, monetarily, that they want to get out of this world before this world gets them. Those are the lucky ones. Then there are the ones who have to get out because they're hot or someone else so close to them is hot that they'd better get out. But in the end when you get out of it, nobody gets out of it out of free choice; you do it because you have to.

Death, of course, was the ultimate bustout. Some pilots met this fate because of the dangerous routes they navigated (hugging mountains, treetops, other aircraft) and because of the sometimes ill-maintained and overloaded planes they flew. However, despite much talk of violence, few Southwest County drug traffickers died at the hands of fellow dealers.

Reentry. Phasing out of the drug world was usually only temporary. For many, it represented merely another stage in their dealing careers (although this may not have been their original intention), to be followed by a period of reinvolvement.[7] Depending on the situation, reentry into the drug world represented either a *comeback* (from a forced withdrawal) or a *relapse* (from a voluntary withdrawal).

Most people forced out of drug trafficking were anxious to return. They had never decided to withdraw, and their desire to get back was based on many of the same reasons which drew them into the field originally. While it was possible to come back from financial, legal, and reputational bustouts, it was difficult and not always successfully accomplished. Dealers and smugglers had to reestablish their contacts, rebuild their organization and fronting arrangements, and raise any necessary operating capital. More important, they had to overcome the circumstances surrounding their departure; once they resumed operating they often found their former colleagues suspicious of them. They were therefore informally subjected to a trial period in which they had to re-prove their reliability before they could once again move easily through the drug world.

Dealers and smugglers usually found that reentering the drug world after they had voluntarily withdrawn from it involved a more difficult decision-making process, but was easier to implement. As I noted earlier, experienced dealers and smugglers often grappled with conflicting reasons for wanting to quit and wanting to stay with the occupation. When the forces propelling them out of the drug world were strongest, they left. But once out, these forces weakened. Their images of and hopes for the straight world often failed to materialize. Many could not make the shift to the norms, values, and lifestyle of the straight society and could not earn a living within it. Yet the factors enticing individuals to resume drug trafficking were not the same as those which motivated their original entry. They were no longer awestruck by the glamorous lifestyle or the thrill of danger. Instead, they got back in to make money both to pay off the debts they had accumulated while "retired" and to build up and save so that their next phase-out would be more successful. Dealers and smugglers made the decision to reenter the drug world, then, for some very basic reasons: the material perquisites; the drugs; the social ties; and the fact that they had nowhere else to go.

Once this decision was made, the actual process of reentry was relatively simple. One dealer described how the door back into dealing remained open for those who left voluntarily:

I still see my dealer friends, I can still buy grams from them when I want to. It's the respect they have for me because I stepped out of it without being busted or burning someone. I'm coming out with a good reputation, and even though the scene is a whirlwind—people moving up, moving down, in, out— if I didn't see anybody for a year I could call them up and get right back in that day.

People who relapsed thus had few problems obtaining fronts, reestablishing their reputations, or readjusting to the scene. Yet once back in, they generally were again unsuccessful in accumulating enough of a nest egg to ensure the success of their subsequent phase-outs. Each time they relapsed into drug trafficking they became caught up once again in the drug world's lifestyle of hedonism and consumption. They thus spent the money they were earning almost as fast as they earned it (or in some cases, faster).[8] The fast life, with its irrationality and present orientation, held a grip on them partly because of the drugs they were consuming, but most especially because of the pervasive dominance of the drug subculture. They thus started the treadmill spinning again so that they never got enough ahead; they never amassed the stockpile that they had reentered the drug world to achieve.

Career Shifts. Dealers and smugglers who reentered the drug world, whether from a voluntary or forced phase-out, did not always return to the same activity, level, or commodity which characterized their previous style of operation. Upon returning after a hiatus, many individuals underwent a "career shift" (Luckenbill and Best 1981) and became involved in some new segment of the drug world. The shifts were sometimes lateral, as when a member of a smuggling crew took on a new specialization, switching from piloting to operating a stash house, for example. One dealer described how he used friendship networks upon his reentry to shift from cocaine to marijuana trafficking:

Before, when I was dealing cocaine, I was too caught up in using the drug, and people around me were starting to go under from getting into base. That's why I got out. But now I think I've got myself together and even though I'm dealing again I'm staying away from coke. I've switched over to dealing grass. It's a whole different circle of people. I got into it through a close friend I used to know before, but I never did business with him because he did grass and I did coke.

Vertical shifts moved operators to different levels. For example, one former smuggler returned and took up dealing; another wholesale marijuana dealer came back to find that the smugglers he knew had disappeared and he was forced to buy from other dealers.

A third type of shift relocated drug traffickers in different styles of operation. One dealer described how, after being arrested, he tightened his security measures:

I just had to cut back after I went through those changes. Hell, I'm not getting any younger and the idea of going to prison bothers me a lot more than

it did ten years ago. The risks are no longer worth it when I can have a comfortable income with less risk. So I only sell to four people now. I don't care
if they buy a pound or a gram.

A former smuggler who sold his operation and lost all his money during his phase-out returned as a consultant to the industry, selling his
expertise to individuals with new money and fresh manpower:

What I've been doing lately is setting up deals for people. I've got foolproof
plans for smuggling cocaine up here from Colombia. I tell them how to mod-
ify their airplanes to add on extra fuel tanks and to fit in more weed, coke, or
whatever they bring up. Then I set them up with refueling points all up and
down Central America, telling them how to bring it up here, what points to
come in at, and what kind of receiving unit to use. Then they do it all, and I
get 10 percent of what they make.

Reentry did not always imply a shift to a new niche, however. Some
returned to the same circle of associates, trafficking activity, and commodity they worked with before their departure. Thus, drug traffickers' careers often peaked early and then displayed a variety of shifts
from lateral mobility, to decline, to holding fairly steady.

A final alternative involved neither completely leaving nor remaining in this deviant occupation. Many individuals straddled the deviant
and respectable worlds forever by continuing to dabble in drug trafficking. As a result of their experiences in the drug world they had
developed a deviant self-identity and a deviant *modus operandi*. They
did not want to bear the social and legal burden of full-time deviant
work, but neither were they willing to assume the drudgery of the
straight world. They therefore moved into the entrepreneurial realm,
where their daily activities involved some sort of hustling in an assortment of legitimate, quasilegitimate, and deviant ventures, and where
they were their own boss. In this way they were able to retain certain
elements of the deviant lifestyle and to socialize on the fringes of the
drug community. For these individuals, drug dealing shifted from a
primary occupation to a sideline, but they never abandoned it altogether.

LEAVING DRUG TRAFFICKING

This pattern of oscillation into and out of active drug trafficking makes
it somewhat problematic to speak of leaving deviance in the sense of a

final retirement. Clearly, some people succeeded in voluntarily retiring. Of these, a few managed to prepare a postdeviant career for themselves by transferring their drug money into a legitimate enterprise. A larger group was forced out of dealing and either did not or could not return; their bustouts were sufficiently damaging that either they never attempted reentry or they abandoned their efforts after a series of unsuccessful comeback attempts. But there was no way of determining in advance whether an exit from the business would be temporary or permanent. Here, dealers' and smugglers' vacillating intentions were compounded by the complexity of operating successfully in the drug world. For many, then, no phase-out could ever be definitively assessed as permanent. As long as individuals had the skills, knowledge, and connections to deal, they could potentially reenter the occupation at any time. Leaving drug trafficking was thus a relative phenomenon, characterized by a trailing-off process where spurts of involvement occurred with decreasing frequency and intensity. This disengagement was characterized by a progressive reorientation to the legitimate world, where former drug traffickers once again shifted their social networks and changed their self-conceptions (Lieb and Olson 1976).

SUMMARY

Dealing and smuggling careers were temporary, fraught with multiple attempts at retirement. Veteran drug traffickers quit their occupation because of the ambivalent feelings they developed toward their deviant life. As they aged in the career their experience changed, shifting from a work life that was exhilarating and free to one that became increasingly dangerous and confining. Just as their deviant careers were temporary, so too were their retirements. Potential recruits, therefore, were lured into the business by materialism, hedonism, glamor, and excitement. Established dealers were lured away from the deviant life and back into the mainstream by the attractions of security and social ease. But once out, retired dealers and smugglers were lured back in by their expertise, by their ability to make money quickly and easily. People who were exposed to the upper levels of drug trafficking found it extremely difficult to quit permanently. This stemmed, in part, from their difficulty in moving from the illegitimate to the legitimate business sector. Even more significant was the affinity they formed for their deviant values and lifestyle. Thus few of the people I observed were successful in leaving deviance entirely. What dealers and smugglers intended, at the time, to be a permanent withdrawal from drug trafficking can be seen in retrospect as a pervasive occupational pattern of shifts and oscillations.

CHAPTER EIGHT

TOWARD AN EXISTENTIAL PERSPECTIVE ON DRUG TRAFFICKING

Throughout this work I have discussed specific dimensions and details of drug dealers' and smugglers' activities. My aim in this chapter is to draw generic conclusions about ideas which have been implicitly presented in various parts of this book, thereby unifying the previous chapters into an integrated portrait of upper-level drug traffickers. I begin by drawing together three perspectives on drug trafficking—the organizational, the occupational, and the hedonistic—and evaluate their role in affecting dealers' and smugglers' commitment to this deviant behavior and subculture. I then discuss the relationship between people's existential brute beings and their decision to quit conventional society and enter the dealers' subculture of hedonism.

IMAGES OF DRUG TRAFFICKING

Many perspectives can be used to enhance our understanding of drug trafficking as an illicit enterprise. In the following discussion, I take three sociological images of illicit enterprise and apply them to drug trafficking. Throughout my discussion of these images I consider their role in fostering dealers' and smugglers' commitment to this deviant activity.

Criminal Commitment. The relatively recent shift in focus away from criminal etiology to the study of illicit careers (Rains 1982) suggests that sociologists have become increasingly concerned with why people remain in deviance once they enter it. I look at commitment as a dependent rather than independent variable and try to identify those features of drug dealing and smuggling which foster commitment. The concept of commitment is multifaceted and can be studied most effectively by analyzing several of its dimensions. Nieves (1978) has proposed a total commitment index, consisting of three components: normative, economic, and social. *Normative* commitment involves individuals' acceptance and internalization (Kelman 1958) of a group's, organization's, or profession's values and mores. *Economic* commitment is rooted in individuals' rational cost-benefit analysis of the advantages inherent in pursuing a given line of activity (Blau 1964; Homans 1950) and the associated involvements, or side-bets (Becker 1960), which are further tied to their remaining associated with this behavior. *Social* commitment refers to the interactional dynamics of the people involved in the enterprise (Sheldon 1970) and to individuals' self-images (Huntington 1957), role relationships (Della Cava 1975), integration into the group (Gouldner 1960), and identification with the group (Kelman 1958). To these I add a fourth component, *egoistic* commitment, which incorporates the degree of personal enjoyment, satisfaction, and fulfillment individuals derive from being involved with a given enterprise.

Drug Trafficking as Organized Crime. There can be no question that drug trafficking requires considerable planning and systematic execution. Unlike crimes of passion, which are spontaneous and often unintended, drug dealing and smuggling constitute a form of organized criminal activity. However, what remains unanswered is the degree and type of organization required to engage in this illicit enterprise.[1]

The most organized depictions of illicit enterprise are those which describe the structure and functioning of organized crime, specifically the Mafia. The official view of the social organization of organized crime syndicates was best summed up by the President's Commission (1967:1):

Organized crime is a society that seeks to operate outside the control of the American people and their governments. It involves thousands of criminals working with structures as complex as those of any large corporations, subject to laws more rigidly enforced than those of legitimate governments. The actions are not impulsive but rather the result of intricate conspiracies carried on over many years and aimed at gaining control over whole fields of activity to amass huge profits.

This image of illicit enterprise has been reinforced and legitimated in the academic community by sociological reports and analyses of racketeering activities (Bell 1953: Cressey 1969; Ianni 1972; McIntosh 1973; Wilson 1975).

The next level of organization of illicit enterprise is found among groups of "professional" criminals (Best and Luckenbill 1982:55–65). These mobs or crews are highly cohesive, use a specialized division of labor, and are composed of individuals who make a life commitment to criminal activity. When in trouble they band together, pool their resources, and have been known in the past to fix cases with the courts or police (Cameron 1964; Letkemann 1973; Maurer 1964; Plate 1975; Prus and Sharper 1977; Sutherland 1937). A major factor differentiating crews of professional criminals from organized crime families lies in the former's flexibility and independence. They can function when, where, and how they want, adjusting their membership according to the feelings of the group.

Generally, the organization of Southwest County dealers and smugglers was neither as highly bureaucratic and centralized as the organized crime image of trafficking, nor as binding, extensive, or professionalized as illicit mobs. Although smuggling crews bore some resemblance to mobs in their division of labor, mutual aid when arrested, close friendship, and team organization, they were neither as professionalized in their attitude nor as committed to a lifelong criminal career. The majority of dealers, like members of many other deviant occupations (Miller 1978), displayed, instead, peer relations (Best and Luckenbill 1982:45–54).

Peer relations are characterized by a subculture which provides functions for its members that increase their social solidarity. The peer subculture is instrumental in the recruitment and socialization of new members, transmitting the jargon, norms, and values surrounding both business and social relations. It also provides individuals with the necessary skills and ideology. This includes the technical knowledge required for trade in addition to the rationalizations and neutralizations which explain and justify members' problems, thereby helping to insulate them from the denigrations of conventional morality (Higgins and Butler 1982:192; Miller 1978:228). Peer relations commonly emerge within illicit marketplaces, where illicit goods or services are sold. Deviants organize as peers in these meetings to foster the spread of information they need about the marketplace and to enhance their enjoyment of the deviant activity by socializing with others.

Members of the Southwest County drug subculture provided support for each other in various, although occasionally limited, ways. Moral support was always available; material support could be obtained for the right price; and legal support was offered when an unincarcerated person helped a jailed partner or customer. Their peer social organization was enhanced by the drug world grapevine, which enabled them to make judgments about potential customers, partners, or suppliers by checking out reputational ranking. Like other groups characterized by deviant peer associations, drug dealers and smugglers shared their participation in the illegal act. Drug trafficking was by its nature social, requiring individuals' cooperation and contact with at least two other parties: a supplier and a customer. The combined efforts of connections and close associates such as partners enhanced individuals' opportunities, supplementing their weak areas with diversified knowledge, capital, and specialized skills. Such shared participation also ensured a certain amount of companionship, creating an overlap between members' business and social activities. Increasing this interface between work and leisure diminished drug traffickers' alienation from their work, a common complaint of nondeviant workers. It thereby enhanced their commitment to this illicit enterprise by giving participants mutual social satisfaction (Miller 1978:228).

While the social organization found among Southwest County dealers and smugglers was neither as extensive nor as binding as that which characterizes organized crime, elements associated with the organization of deviant relationships had to be present for smoothly efficient and successful deals to occur: trust had to be extended; alliances formed; a specialized division of labor created; and secrecy and security ensured. Both the normative and the social dimensions of commitment are represented here. From the former, dealers and smugglers displayed a subscription to the overall norms and values of both their immediate business and social groups and the greater drug community (umwelt). They hated police, felt a kinship with other drug traffickers, operated according to spoken and tacit understandings which were generally honored, and in smuggling crews, some exhibited intense loyalty. Like organized and professional criminals they looked on dealing as a career, involving their identity and self-image (at least temporarily) in this occupation. The organizational aspects of their pursuit also enhanced the social commitment dealers felt. Through their work they became integrated into a formal (smuggling) or informal (dealing) network of associates where they formed business and social relationships that strengthened their solidarity and identification with the group. This membership functioned as a social involvement, or side-bet, further binding them to continuing illicit enterprise.

Drug Trafficking as Work. The organizational perspective on deviant behavior and on the type of criminal commitment associated with it does not fully describe the dealing subculture. This is partly a deviance as work situation, since the affiliations forged for each transaction often failed to endure beyond that temporary time frame. The resources which most members had at their disposal to assist their fellow traffickers were relatively limited and the turnover rate within the occupation was moderately high, especially among novices. Moreover, many people betrayed their colleagues rather than risking death or imprisonment. Their concerns focused primarily on their own well-being and comfort. Income was thus a far more powerful motivation than group membership or loyalty.

Drug dealing, as an occupation, thus bears great similarity to the world of work. The occupational perspective on deviant enterprise has long existed within sociology.[2] Although the parallels between deviant and respectable work are limited, deviant occupations can be characterized by many of the same work problems, motivations, rewards, and experiences found in the legitimate world. The occupational perspective has also come to dominate the current sociological imagery of drug dealing, replacing the hippie ethos and communal ideology portrayal which was recognized as defunct by the mid-1970s (see Langer 1976, 1977; Lieb and Olson 1976; Waldorf et al. 1977). Drug dealers organized, planned, and executed their ventures in similar ways to other businessmen. They relied on an occupational body of knowledge which new recruits had to learn. A modicum of business acumen was required for success. It was also important to have contacts and networks of associates. Finally, dealers' occupational involvement took the form of a career, with the same entry, socialization, and retirement stages found among all workers, albeit manifested rather differently.

Certain features of deviant occupations, however, differentiate them from legitimate careers. Drug dealers and smugglers valued their occupation for its distinct working conditions. In contrast to the bureaucratization and rationalization of most conventional forms of work, drug dealing and smuggling were flexible, creative, exciting, and personal enterprises. Drug traffickers were self-employed, and could therefore usually schedule their working hours and locations around their leisure pursuits. They made all their own decisions, often on the spur of the moment, uninhibited by the constraints of bureaucratic rules. In addition, the structure of their careers was fluid rather than rigid. They frequently made shifts within the occupation that moved them either vertically or laterally. They quit trafficking and returned to it at the whim of their vacillating intents. These oscillations into and out of the business were partly due to dealers' and smugglers' initial perceptions of their trafficking as a steppingstone to a more secure, legitimate occupation. This ideal scenario hardly ever occurred, though, because they became engulfed by the drug world and seduced into continuing deviant involvement.

Dealers' and smugglers' work roles and relationships were imbued with individuality, feeling, and meaning. People dealt with other traffickers as individuals rather than with impersonal offices. This made character attributes a very important part of doing business. They relied on either the reputational grapevine or intuitive feelings before selling to others. They were creative in their work, forging new connections, evading the police, and putting together last-minute makeshift arrangements when someone failed to show up, the weather changed, or technical equipment broke down. Drug traffickers were thus personally involved with all aspects of their work, from its planning through its execution, and had a low degree of alienation from their labor.

Dealers and smugglers found their work thrilling, but it could also become dangerous. These individuals were thrill-seekers and risk-takers, but they were not gamblers. They did not create artifical risks to pit themselves against for the sport of it, but rather pursued an occupation that offered high profits precisely because of its inherently high risks. Thus, despite the freewheeling character of their illicit work, they still approached it with a businesslike orientation. They derived status from their drug trafficking and the fact that they were top-level professionals. Their actions were fueled by a driving profit orientation. They therefore organized their business behavior in a rational manner. Individuals who allowed their hedonism and impulsive self-expressionism to lead them too far astray from the security precautions they all consciously knew eventually found themselves either bankrupted, incarcerated, or dead.

These occupational aspects of dealing and smuggling show the economic dimension of their commitment. Members were attached to the large sums of money they could make in relatively short periods of time. They quickly acclimated themselves to a high standard of living which they could not maintain by most forms of nondeviant work. This emphasis on personal materialism heightened individuals' self-interest and diminished their commitment to the group (Miller 1978:227). Like other deviant workers, dealers and smugglers were attracted into and stayed with drug trafficking partly because of their autonomy regarding work activities and relationships. A number of economic side-bets were involved here as well: if individuals abandoned this line of work they lost the value of their acquired knowledge and skills, their business networks, the drug world reputation they had established, and the years of their lives they had already invested in this career.

Drug Trafficking as Fun. Like the organizational perspective, the occupational perspective also fails to provide a complete explanation of drug dealers' and smugglers' motivations. While the crime-as-work approach highlights the business, or rational, aspects of these organized criminals, it generates an image of crime as being like any other business, an activity which individuals enter for the same reasons people might enter any legitimate business. It suggests that occupational criminals are primarily motivated by their pride in being rationally organized and professional. Southwest County dealers and smugglers, though, were fundamentally just the opposite. They were rationally organized and professionalized because that was the way it had to be done, in spite of the fact that they themselves were not rationally organized people. Rather, they were driven by a search for fun and pleasure.

Deviant behavior has only occasionally been conceptualized by sociologists as pleasure motivated. Juvenile delinquency was considered
to be a rejection of society's norms and values, a mode of escape, and
a striving for kicks (Cohen 1955; Miller 1958; Tannenbaum 1938;
Thrasher 1963). Countercultural deviance has been similarly viewed
as a rebellion against the establishment and an attempt to obtain alternative forms of pleasure, especially through drug use (Carey 1968; Cavan 1970; Geller and Boas 1969; Goode 1972; Mouledoux 1972; National Commission on Marijuana 1972; Suchman 1968). Finally, some
deviance has been seen as "simply fun and really nothing more" (Riemer 1979; Sykes 1972).

Drug dealers and smugglers were above all motivated by hedonistic
materialism. They were committed to living the fast life. Primary to
the fast life was abundant drug consumption, generating intense pleasures. They wanted these pleasures now and for all time, not ten years
from now when their investments or pension plans matured. Drug
traffickers were Dionysian, disdaining the sober responsibilities of the
workaday world. They wanted the freedom to live intensely and
spontaneously, following any whim. They wanted to experience lust-
ful and passionate sex, unbridled by the normative bonds of marital
fidelity. They wanted to feel the excitement associated with gambling
on the unexpected. But euphoria was the excitement they craved, not
paranoia. Only the intense hedonism of living high and fast could
overcome the paranoia they experienced intermittently from the very
real dangers of capture, imprisonment, and death. Profit was for pleasure, permitting them to surround themselves with fancy clothes, jewels,
and sports cars. But the huge profits also became an intense pleasure
in themselves: greed fulfilled instantaneously. Thus, in between the
lows of "crashing" and paranoia, the dealers' life was one of peak experiences, following their emotions, indulging their impulses, and
thereby allowing the existential core of the brute being (see Douglas
and Johnson 1977) to direct their lives.

Only these intense feelings could motivate them to rationally organize and to run the risk of the terrible constraint and painful nongrat-
ification of prison. While organized crime of an earlier day may have
been the more mundane activity of Apollonian men, the rational organization of drug dealing and smuggling in Southwest County is only

understandable when it is seen in the service of irrationality. Thus in order to fully understand individuals' commitment to this deviant life, it is necessary to see the irrational that lies behind and makes sense of the rational organization. Ironically, it was their very quest for unmitigated decadence which caused them to impose rational constraints on their existence.

Accompanying the existential perspective on deviance as fun are its associated forms of commitment: social and egoistic. Socially, dealers and smugglers remained tied to their occupation as a result of the pleasurable relations shared with colleagues, friends, and lovers. The bonds people formed when they pooled their resources, risked their lives, and took drugs together were very strong. Even more important, dealers built commitment through the ego gratification they derived from drug trafficking. Their self-images were lodged in the power they wielded over others by withholding or supplying them with drugs (for both business use and personal consumption). Dealers reveled in their social status, occasionally breaking their rules of secrecy to reveal their occupation to outsiders. This extended the range of their prestige beyond the limited confines of the drug community. Their access to drugs further made them sought-after sexual partners, an aspect of the occupation many individuals found particularly satisfying. Finally, these illicit entrepreneurs enjoyed a style of life which they were loath to relinquish. Their indulgence in the fullest pleasures of hedonistic decadence served as both a motivation for entering the career and a reward structure enhancing commitment and deterring departure.

HEDONISM AND THE EXISTENTIAL SELF

While the associational ties and work dimensions constituted key components of Southwest County dealers' and smugglers' deviant experience, these were not the most vital elements attracting them to drug trafficking. Dealers and smugglers, above all else, pursued deviance to live freely and wildly, to make their hedonistic way of life possible. This was the domain where their existential selves were lodged. Their entry into the drug world represented their rejection of conventional society so they could find satisfaction for their brute inner drives in the subculture of hedonism.

The Repression of Brute Being. It was Weber who first called attention to the growing trend toward rationalism in society. As early as the turn of the century, he foresaw the coming routinization and bureaucratization and theorized that it would lead people to become disenchanted with the world. Existential sociologists have called our modern society absolutist, one that has achieved the bureaucratization that Weber warned us about (Douglas 1971). Our everyday lives have been affected by such trends as homogenization and massification, so that we function within an environment that is progressively losing much of its individuality and flavor. In addition, as Weber also foresaw, the criterion of sterile efficiency has largely come to dominate more personal evaluations based on loyalty, leadership, charisma, and character. Roles within bureaucratic organizations have become increasingly impersonal and inflexible, based on fixed rules governing role content. Relations within conventional work contexts have focused around abstract roles and offices, and we have lost the ability to creatively play with, in, and around these roles. People's ability to generate meaning and identify themselves through these roles has thereby diminished, so that we can no longer infuse these roles with many feelings and emotions (Burfoot 1984). In fact, as Weber pointed out, feelings have no place in a modern bureaucracy, which relies on rational, calculating systems of thought (Gerth and Mills 1946). This stifling of the creative character of work roles and the displacement of the "irrational" elements of behavior have, in fact, created a growing disenchantment with our bureaucratized society.

The giant bureaucracies of conventional society have also robbed us of meaningful emotions in other ways. They have forced us to repress the core feelings that are part of our fundamental brute beings, such as the desire to avoid pain, the desire to achieve pleasure, and the desire to increase our pleasure. Such expressions of overt hedonism run contrary to the norms of conventional social behavior and are not tolerated. Therefore, from earliest childhood, people are forced to adapt to a rationalized society and repress these feelings. This repression (what Freud would have called the suppression of the id) has been accomplished by harnessing other, more powerful feelings, such as fear, shame, and guilt to inhibit hedonistic self-expression. Because we fear the shame and ridicule associated with violating our reference group's moral rules, we have internalized the repressive norms and values of the conventional society. Our thoughts also fuse with these powerful feelings of fear, leading us to rationalize the importance, propriety, and moral righteousness of behaving in an instrumental, controlled manner (Douglas 1977a; Douglas and Johnson 1977).

But such culturally induced repression has not altered the nature of brute being. Congruent with Freud's theory of the persistence of the id, our brute feelings do not change, regardless of how much we are culturally trained or socialized. At the core of our existential selves, our brute beings teem with the feelings that are trapped inside, unable to find vent or satisfaction. Although our existence within conventional society requires that we strive for achievement and defer gratification for the future, our existential selves want to feel that gratification now. Humans are feeling beings who search for and crave feelings. We want to dare to risk, to feel the fear, to exalt our successes, to indulge our desires, to sense our pride. Yet such extreme degrees of living and feeling are not consonant with the standards of socially acceptable behavior. Living within conventional society thus creates great inner conflicts between our desire to live freely, with personal integrity, and our fear of becoming shamed for violating the norms of our reference group, regardless of whether we work within a bureaucratic organization or merely in a bureaucratized society. We become frustrated, socially pressured to restrain ourselves from seeking the ultimate goal of our brute beings: the satisfaction of our primal feelings. These structural conditions create a climate which encourages individuals to drift away or, in this case, seek alternatives to living and working within conventional society.

The Revolt of Brute Being. The upper-level drug dealers and smugglers I studied represent one group of individuals whose brute beings have revolted against the rationalist shackles of conventional society. These individuals have chosen to follow their emotions in a search for personal satisfaction. For some, the dissatisfaction with conventional society preceded their awareness of this deviant subculture. Others only began to feel overly confined by the traditional norms and values once they were exposed to the existence of an alternative lifestyle. Yet at some point in the process, they all shared the same feelings of alienation from their conventional reference groups and chose to change the moral rules surrounding them by changing reference groups. But rather than seeking out antimaterialist, sixties-style communes, these people retained (even intensified) the value of materialism which pervades our society. What they revolted against was the normative edict that materialism is tied to rationalism.

Most outsiders who had the opportunity to experience a taste of the fast life found its passion for indulgence inherently attractive. They freely welcomed the feelings of excitement, spontaneity, glamor, and self-importance they derived from drug trafficking and the dealing lifestyle. Their move to active hedonism involved more than just letting go of old restraints, however. Through interacting with others, new members learned the norms, values, and beliefs of the group, supplanting their old attitudes with this reformulated ethos. They also learned the cognitive rationalizations and neutralizations designed to block and/or alleviate the guilt they developed from committing illegal acts and abandoning the antihedonistic ethos of the conventional society. Douglas and Waksler (1982:147) have noted, however, that "values and beliefs become effective determinants of action only when (1) they have been fused with feelings through experience and (2) they give direction to the expression of those feelings."

In shifting their reference group, Southwest County dealers and smugglers effected a shift in the locus of their self-identity from what Turner (1976) has called an "institutional" to an "impulse" form of self-lodging. When they separated from the mainstream culture and ideology, they abandoned their predominantly instrumental, goal-seeking, controlled, and future-oriented behavior. They ceased to think of their selves as something to be "attained, created, achieved," and focused instead on discovering and satisfying their deep, unsocialized, inner impulses. They therefore sought self-expression in those acts which resulted from lowering their inhibitions, freeing themselves from rational planning, and indulging in "mad desires and errant fancies." Satisfying their immediate pleasures thus came to take precedence over planned behavior.

CONCLUSION

In Langer's (1976) analysis of a middle-level dealing subculture, he discussed the dissolution of the "hang-loose" ethos and its replacement by a profit motivation and business orientation. He attributed this transformation to the growth of rationalism in society, implying that rationalism similarly came to pervade the dealing subculture. He therefore posited a relationship between the dealing subculture and conventional society. I have also discussed the process of rationalism in society and its effect on the dealing subculture, but my conclusions differ from Langer's. It is precisely the rationalism of conventional society that has driven upper-level dealers and smugglers away from it, toward the hedonism and irrationality of their deviant subculture. They are profit-minded and business-oriented, but at this level of trafficking, individuals have always been. The dealing subculture is thus not a mirror of society, but a radically different alternative which serves as an escape from routinization and repression.

In conclusion, my data show that drug dealers and smugglers did not quit conventional society and enter a life of deviance because of blocked legitimate opportunity structures (Cloward and Ohlin 1960; Merton 1938), or because they were failures within their conventional reference groups (Kaplan 1980). Rather, their entry into deviance combined several other elements. First, their brute beings craved pleasure and the gratification of many other drives and urges. Second, conventional society repressed their pleasure-seeking and routinized their existence through its bureaucratization and impersonality, thereby fostering their disenchantment, alienation, and inner conflict. Yet not all people in this situation turned to drug trafficking. This path was only chosen by individuals who became aware of the upper-level dealing and smuggling subculture (which signifies that they were drug consumers), who were attracted to its freewheeling lifestyle of hedonism and illicit enterprise, and who developed the associations and knowledge necessary to traffic in drugs.

CHAPTER NINE

DEVIANT CAREERS
AND REINTEGRATION

"Cactus Inn," the gruff voice of the motel operator answered as he picked up the phone on the fifth ring. It was early in the morning and he had not yet finished his first cup of coffee.

"Yes," I responded politely, "may I please have room 154?" He transferred me without acknowledgment. What did I expect from an operator at a low-life motel? A few seconds later I could hear the ringing begin again. After several rings a groggy male voice picked up the receiver and I could tell I had awakened him. He sounded young, I thought. This must be Scott, the 26-year-old who was the latest in Dave's series of sidekicks. He had come from Australia and fallen in with Dave and his boys in Florida when Dave was running a surf shop. He worked for Dave in the store, and when the operation folded, as they all did, he moved back west with them. Dave was probably 43 by now, but he had always liked to hang out with people he considered less "together" than himself. It made him feel good about himself. Personally, I thought it was one of the reasons his business ventures never turned out better than they did. I had heard about Scott and Dave's latest residence at the Cactus Inn from a mutual friend, someone with a lifestyle more stable than Dave's whom I could usually reach when I wanted to get in touch with Dave. She knew where to reach him, even though their relationship had been on and off over the years and seemed to be more toward the off side now. So I called her up and asked if she knew where he was. She gave me his number and also promised to deliver the message that I was trying to get in touch. The next day I got a message from Dave that I should try him at the motel around 7:30 the following morning. I thought it was an early time to suggest, but I dutifully complied.

"Is Dave there?" I asked the person on the other end of the phone. There was a pause. No response. "Hello?" I once again queried.

"Yes, I'm here."

"Is Dave there?" I repeated my question.

"No," came the answer. "He's not here."

"Oh," I puzzled. "Did I call too late? Has he left for the day already?" Was such a thing possible, I pondered, knowing the habits of my long-time friend, which did not include rising early. "Or did he not come in last night?" Despite the fact that he had asked me to call, I considered this the more likely option.

"That's right," he responded. "He didn't come in last night."

"Oh," I said disappointedly, but not surprised. Dave was not really the reliable sort. "It's just that he left a message that I should call now." I felt guilty for waking this poor fellow up so early for nothing, so I offered my account. "Would you tell him that it's his friend Patti Adler trying to reach him?"

"Oh, Patti Adler?" was the now somewhat more interested-sounding response. "Just a minute. He's right here."

Between 1974 and 1980 I had the fortunate opportunity to be allowed entry into a community of upper-level drug dealers and smugglers in the southwestern region of the United States. For six years my husband and I lived among these drug traffickers as friends, neighbors, and confidantes, gathering ethnographic data on their hopes and fears, motivations, lifestyle, business operations, and careers.

More than ten years have now passed since we moved out of Southwest County and left behind both the scene and my drug trafficker friends. Over those years I have maintained contact with a couple of our closest respondents and through them have managed to stay somewhat current with a few more. Change has come rapidly to the drug scene since that time, with many transformations occurring, especially in the popularity of various drugs, the strategies of law enforcement, and the structure and organization of the drug business. Ten years out seemed a good time to return to the field, to see what had become of my former friends and subjects, to consider the effects of their experiences in drug trafficking, and to reflect on some changes in drug trafficking.

I therefore made a trip to Southwest County in the spring of 1991 to see who I could find in person or by telephone. Things looked different; several of the stores and restaurants I had frequented were out of business. My informants had not worked in many legitimate concerns, so I could not begin my search for them in public establishments. Going from contact to contact, I picked up the trail as best I could, trying to track them down in their dispersed and/or hidden locations. Either directly or indirectly I was able to get in touch with thirteen of my former subjects, in Southwest County and around the country. Once returned home, I continued to search for my subjects on the phone throughout 1991 and into 1992. By snowballing from this group, I was more successful in locating people this way than I had been in person. While my original group of subjects had never been a random or necessarily representative sample of all upper-level drug traffickers, the sheer number of people I observed ensured that they covered a range of motivations, behavior, and social organization. This group had consisted of several different types of people: dealers and smugglers, pilots and drivers, money launderers, storage personnel, dope chicks and wives, hangers-on, and members of the general social circle. In addition, they were divided by their relation to Peter and me; there was a core group with whom we were the most intimate (those we had once seen on at least a weekly basis), and there were others who fell more under the category of acquaintances. Of the original sixty-five people in our sample, roughly two dozen fell into the former group.

Despite its smaller size, the follow-up sample serves as a good representation of the original group for several reasons. First, the follow-up sample was drawn exclusively from among members of the core group. This core group had served as the center of the study, with others extending out from them. Their social and work styles were thus repeated, to a certain extent, within the more peripheral group. By not including these peripheral members, I merely lost those who tended to replicate the core group's behavior. Second, the members of the core group I was able to recontact encompassed the full range of dealing styles, from the successes to the failures, the lone operators to the organizers, the aggressive to the casual, the longer-term to the more briefly involved, thus fairly well representing the entire spectrum of dealing activities that I had seen. Third, the new group was characterized by an appropriate gender diversity. Ten of the people I recontacted were men and three were women (plus the wife of one of the men who had not herself been a dealer). This corresponded fairly accurately to the gender breakdown of the original sample. These factors thus gave me confidence that the group I found might be typical of former Southwest County upper-level dealers and smugglers.

DEVIANT CAREERS

Scholars have noted that individuals' involvement in deviant or criminal activities displays many of the characteristics of legitimate careers, often comprising a beginning, ascension, peak, decline, and exit. The stages of these careers most often discussed in the literature are the entry and exit periods, as they mark the boundaries of people's involvement in deviant worlds (Luckenbill and Best 1981). Yet for many individuals these careers encompass only a brief phase in their lifespan, as they age and move out of deviance (Shover 1985). What, then, happens to them? How do they make the transition into conventional society and its legitimate economy?

The issue of reintegrating deviants has received scant sociological attention. Braithwaite (1989) has discussed the role of others in shaming individuals out of brief forays into deviance, Brown (1991) has studied how people capitalize on their former deviant status and experiences to forge counseling careers, and Ebaugh (1988) has analyzed the effects of ex-roles on people's subsequent lives. Only a few studies (cf. Chambliss 1984; Shover 1987; Snodgrass 1982) have traced the lives of former deviants with the intent of discovering the paths they have taken and the effects of their former activities on their subsequent lives.

In this new addendum to the second edition, I offer a follow-up glimpse into the lives of thirteen of the former upper-level drug dealers and smugglers I studied in the 1970s. In earlier parts of this book I have described their active criminal careers and the attempts they made, often temporary and unsuccessful, to exit the drug world after years of trafficking and find another way of making a living. Those members of my original sample that I was able to locate in 1991 and 1992 were all involved in other pursuits. While they were, to varying degrees, reintegrated into more mainstream society, their lives had been indelibly affected by their years spent trafficking. This, then, formed the post-dealing phase of their deviant careers.

In this chapter I describe the life paths of these former occupational criminals. I then analyze the factors affecting their degree of success in reintegration, the segments of society into which they move, and the influence on their current lives of their years spent out of the mainstream in a criminal occupation and subculture.

SOUTHWEST COUNTY REVISITED

Dave was the first person I looked for when I went back to Southwest County in 1991. Through him I was able to find some others and hear about a couple more I could not find. Given the covert, unsteady nature of the business, where people commonly leave no forwarding address, I was not surprised to encounter such a small group out of my original sample.

I knew what Dave had been up to since I left Southwest County, although I did not always know where to reach him, since he was such a transient. Dave was the kind of key informant who became my friend, to whom I got so tied through the research bond and its tightening effects on our friendship that I became connected to him for life. We were too important to each other for too many years for time or distance to weaken our friendship, me bailing him out of financial scrapes, or him cheerfully stopping at my house for a few days on his way across the country to some business venture. Dave was an on-the-road kind of guy, always hopping into some beat-up old van that he had just got a "deal" on from some guy who owed him money. These vans often ended up on the accident heap, and then there was Dave in action again, in the insurance claim business. Not that he hadn't honestly hurt himself. It's just that he liked to milk it. Just part of the general "getting over" mentality.

Dave had bottomed out of the drug market after losing so much money and reneging on so many fronts that no one would do business with him any more. He had tried to get back into real estate, where he had been working as an agent before he met the Southwest County dealers and smugglers who brought him into business with them, but his license had been revoked when he was sent to prison. Over the years he made numerous attempts to petition the real estate board for reinstatement, but had been repeatedly turned down. He then transferred his entrepreneurial buying and selling skills first to the flea market and county fair business, where he sold a variety of faddish but inexpensive items, and then to the import business, buying legitimate goods (mostly clothing) from Mexicans he had met while dealing. He eventually opened up a series of his own surfing stores under a variety of assumed names (for the credit rating), but these went bankrupt one after another. He never achieved the financial success he had during the early drug years because he never found a product that consistently enjoyed the same high level of consumer demand, and his business practices failed to improve.

But Dave was getting older. After years of consuming drugs in large quantities and failing to take care of his body, he was feeling tired and less resilient. His two boys, who he had dragged around the country from shop to shop, were growing up and didn't want to keep moving around. Now in their early twenties, they were living on their own and trying to go to college part-time, while also partying and chasing girls. They were torn between their parents' example—following one scam after another and thinking that this was what life was all about—and trying to find something more stable. As I was finishing these updated chapters to the book I got a call from Dave that his younger son, Kai, 20 years old, had been killed in a motorcycle accident on his way home from a bar one night. After he failed to return home that night Dave and Jean searched the road for two days before they found his body in some bushes. He lived a turbulent life and died a turbulent death.

In his mid-forties, Dave was no longer a party animal. "I can't handle doing coke anymore," he confided to me, sounding somewhat wistful. Another of those nasty reminders of aging that seem to pop up all the time, I thought. "It affects me in bad ways. I can't do it at all."

"What do you mean?" I asked, recognizing that this sounded like more than the ordinary aging process.

"I mean it kind of turns me into an epileptic. I can't think straight, can't communicate."

Boy, this sounds bad, I thought. "Like how?" I responded sympathetically.

"I get spastic. I can't form words."

"Wow," I exclaimed quietly. "Do you think this has something to do with after effects?" He had been known to lay a line out on the table and snort it up with the best of them.

"It's gotta be," he said, that familiarly sheepish tone creeping into his voice. "Doing so much of it. Not all people get the same effect, though, you know. I just don't get the euphoria anymore. If I ever get some and I do it, then I become sorry right away that I did it. So because of that I have to really keep away from the people that do it." Now Dave was definitely out of the drug business, even as a sideline.

"Oh," I said aloud, thinking to myself what a change of lifestyle this had to signify. All those hours he used to spend in the card rooms until the late hours of the night, stepping out into the parking lot for a little refresher. Nearly all of the people he associated with had been cokeheads to one degree or another.

Dave was not only tired, he was bored. "I miss being on the road," he confided. "I haven't been out of town for nine months, and I'm stuck here staring at the walls of this motel room. I have nowhere to go. I have all this merchandise in storage, but when I try to open up a store I can't break even. Even last Christmas season. The economy is just terrible."

Dave was sad. He felt like a failure. He was starting to use that term in talking with his kids, they told me. Even his ex-wife Jean was worrying about him.

"He can come back," she said. "He was a good real estate salesman, he can really sell. He just has to learn that one scam after another is not the way to go. Maybe this will help him."

Seven other people that I managed to track down were also out of the drug business, for one reason or other. Marty quit after being busted and then stayed away from his former dealing friends. He was a big dealer and had gotten "hot" while I knew him. He was one of those people whose name showed up on a drug agent's list, so he knew they were watching him. He vowed to "be careful." But he was not careful enough. He had a new wife when he got busted and her feelings along with the weight of all these factors made him decide to retire for good. He described his attitude following his arrest:

It was like my life was smashed. It was all I could do to just hang in there. I was smoking three packs of cigarettes a day. So I just said to myself, "Marty, you just have to be Mr. Joe 'Good Citizen,' you just have to get your life together." When you stand up there in front of that judge, you really feel the full weight of the law.

Marty had been a school teacher before he began dealing, and he eventually settled down with his wife and was able to reacquire a teaching job.

Another former pilot who had gotten hot was Jeff. Originally from upstate New York, Jeff's family was in the trucking business. But he moved out west to go to college and started flying on the side. Eventually he got his pilot's license and started flying regularly. He was recruited into piloting by a coalition of Southwest County guys who wanted to put a smuggling run together. One had the connection, one had the sales outlets, one had the capital to buy and outfit the plane, but none of them could put it together alone. He flew runs, either for them or himself, for about five years, with some successes and some failures. Eventually the government began inquiring into his activities and following him around. This made him nervous. At around the same time he had a major break-up with his live-in girlfriend and she threatened to turn him in to the authorities. Abandoning a plane that he believed was under surveillance on a runway, he quit the drug business and went to work flying for a commercial airline. When I contacted him he was still with this firm, and had risen through the ranks into a high management level.

Lou came from a mill town in the Midwest. Although his family was middle-class, none of his siblings had gone to college. Most of his brothers and sisters worked as machinists and auto mechanics. Although the youngest, he was the emotional leader in the family. He therefore brought all of his family members and high school friends into the drug business when he started dealing. He was known in Southwest County as someone who could move large quantities of marijuana. He spent a lot of time traveling back and forth between his home town, where his distribution network was located, and Southwest County, where he obtained the drugs. Eventually his brothers and one of his sisters moved out west. He would occasionally also work for one of the smugglers as a driver or unloader, and organize others to do the same. But Lou eventually got arrested with a large quantity of marijuana and was convicted for conspiracy to sell. His case dragged through the court system for almost five years before he finally went to jail. He ended up spending 40 months in jail and returned to his home town after his release. He currently lives back home with his parents, surrounded by his large group of high school friends and associates, and works as an auto mechanic.

One of the more flamboyant characters from the Southwest County scene was Rolf. Originally from the Midwest, he was large, good looking, and drank a lot. He had a hot temper and was easily inclined to get into bar brawls. Out of high school he had gotten a football scholarship that paid for his college education, and he went into the Air Force immediately following graduation. In the Air Force he flew B-52 bombers for the Strategic Air Command, but he was discharged because of his emotional volatility. After his discharge he went to visit a friend in Southwest County and was recruited by a smuggler there to fly runs for him. He worked with varying degrees of success, flying some runs, crashing some runs, until he settled down and decided that he would be better off organizing the runs and generally finding someone else to do the flying. He then became a major dealmaker and operated a fairly successful smuggling operation for several years. One time when he and a copilot were flying a run for himself, however, he stopped into a Southwest County airport for fuel on his way to flying a load-up to some customers in the Northwest. The airport personnel became suspicious of his plane and cargo, and managed to detain him on the ground while they called the police. He was arrested with 1,100 pounds of marijuana. His case dragged through the courts for several years while he was free on bail. During this time he flew several more highly risky runs to amass a stockpile of money. He eventually decided that things looked bleak and that with his temper he could not handle spending time in prison, so he jumped bail. While his copilot was sentenced and served 15 months in jail and 12 months of work-release time, Rolf fled to Europe. He spent most of his time traveling around Europe or the Caribbean on a huge yacht, occasionally putting new deals together, and returning to the United States for visits under a forged passport and set of identity papers. While Rolf got out of the business with a considerable sum of money, this dissipated quickly. He had spent much of it on legal expenses and his plane was confiscated at the time of his arrest. His living style was also expensive, as he had no firm home base. On one of his trips back to the States he explained why most of the people who quit the business with money never seem able to hold on to it:

It just kind of slips through your fingers, you know, and I'm not the only one. It's not just because of the way I live. But the other ones, when you are used to having so much money you just sort of treat it differently. You get out, you try to find something to do with it, and you may make a lot of bad investments. And when people know that you have money, they come to you for loans, and you have a hard time saying no, so there goes more of it. And then the rest just goes into your lifestyle. You know, you don't really think about how much the average person saves through a regular habit of living a frugal life. They keep the thermostat turned down, they buy their plane tickets ahead of time so they can get the supersaver rates, they make their phone calls after eleven o'clock, and they buy their clothes on sale. All of this comes second nature. But when you get into the big money and the fast life you sort of get out of the habit of watching money like that. So even if you don't blow it all on drugs, it slips away through your fingers and it doesn't last long.

Two others, Ted, a former pilot-dealer and Ben, a major smuggler, ended up "hustling for a living." They had escaped without ever having been arrested, which put them among the fortunate ones. Now they were in business for themselves pursuing whatever deals they could, while never finding a permanent stake in any line of legitimate work. Ted worked on books and screenplays for a while, which he attempted to peddle in Hollywood, and then made some money traveling around the country taking slides of railroad cars, which he sold to collectors. Ben opened a restaurant with some partners that closed after six months, then tried to broker Zodiac rafts to specialty groups with little better fortune. At the end of his years in the business he had a long decline. His best times were during the era of commercial marijuana importation. He never did as well in cocaine. When the cocaine trade rose to prominence he began to indulge in overuse and he became less careful about his business dealings. Ben stayed in the business for longer than anyone I knew. During his latter years people did business with him as a favor, based on who he was and what he had meant to them. Over time, these people, too, quit the business and there was no one left who knew Ben from the old days. He had become recluse, a habit he had picked up during his smuggling days, and he was reluctant to reenter the legitimate world, though he was finally forced to when his money ran out. By this time his wife had left him.

The seventh, Barney, was in the airplane business. A "trust-funder" from an upper-middle class background in the Midwest, his father had been a scientist and an inventor. Barney had always liked flying and got his license while he was enrolled at the state university. After college, he and his wife, Betty, moved to Southwest County and they used the freedom afforded them by his family income to avoid the shackles of nine-to-five employment. Barney gave flying lessons and flew for a small commuter airline. He used his free time to transport family and friends around the country for vacations. After a short while they were drawn into the fast life by former college and newly made friends. Within two years of his entry into the drug crowd he was recruited by a smuggler to fly runs for him. He worked transporting marijuana and partying for several years, but got caught in a near-bust in South America. Reacting quickly, he was able to escape, one step ahead of the drug agents. Terrified by this close call, he returned home and fled Southwest County with Betty and, by this time, their two children. They moved to a new state, established themselves, and Betty got a job. Barney could not bring himself to quit hanging around airports, however. He had some money saved from his drug profits which he used to establish an entrepreneurial business for himself, buying, fixing up, and selling used airplanes. He supplemented this unsteady income with money from his trust investments, by working on planes, and by giving flying lessons. He had never been one of the heavier drug users, and now slipped into a lifestyle of quiet sobriety.

I tracked down Jean through Dave's two boys. Her situation had had its ups and downs. Along with her sister, Marsha, she had become a major cocaine dealer in her own right after she divorced Dave. She then remarried and subsequently divorced Jim, her second husband and successful dealing partner, blaming the erosion of their relationship on drugs:

Too much cocaine. We were always doing it. Seemed like we needed to do it to have a good time. But then we were doing it separately from each other. He would go into his study, where he kept his secret stash and toot it up. I would go into the bathroom, where I kept mine, and toot. Eventually we got so wired up that we weren't connecting with each other at all.

After the divorce they each tried to stay in the dealing business separately, but neither was successful. Together they had complemented
each other, she providing the hard-driving business acumen and security-conscious rules, he serving as the nice guy to round out her hard
edges and frame their operation with class and generosity. When they
tried to operate alone Jean drove people away by being too demanding
and Jim lost money by being too lackadaisical. He eventually moved
out of town, vowing to stay in touch with her two children, whom he
had fathered for five years. He did maintain some contact with them,
and eventually invited the boys to visit him and his new wife at their
house in Hollywood. Starting from scratch, he had managed to establish a successful venture catering parties and dinners for "the stars."
Catering had been his and Jean's former legal front during their heaviest dealing years, and they had always groomed it to serve as their line
of work after retirement.

In the catering business they were partners with another couple,
Bobby and Sandy, who owned the local fish store. Jean and Jim
became friendly with Bobby and Sandy while buying fish and then
discovered that they were heavy cocaine dealers themselves. Jean was
struggling to establish herself as a dealer after breaking up with Dave,
and had been selling mostly to her girlfriends and to Jim's old high
school friends back east. Jean and Jim at first bought cocaine from
Bobby and Sandy, but their rise to trafficking in larger quantities was
so rapid that they were soon dealing on the same level, fluidly selling
back and forth as availability and connections dictated. They also did
business with Jean's sister Marsha, who sold to her younger circle of
friends. With Jean and Sandy's shared interest in food, they launched
the catering business together. Jim joined them soon afterward when
his drug use intensified to the point where he could no longer hold a
steady photography job. The catering business was fun and successful
for several years. (I partly supported myself through graduate school,
in fact, prepping food and working parties.) At this time money was
rolling in from the drug business so strongly that they did not need
the extra income, and so the work was sporadic and seasonal. The
catering business came undone through drugs. By 1980, both couples
began freebasing rather heavily. Bobby used up all of his and Sandy's
money on a two-month run and then checked himself into a rehabili-

tation clinic. Sandy moved out and returned to live with her parents. They divorced. Jim and Jean also got to the point where they considered their drug use out of control. They were sneaking behind each other's backs to snort cocaine at all hours. They went on freebasing runs that made them forget their obligations. They could not keep up with the catering business.

Upon my return to Southwest County, I learned through Jean that Bobby had since moved to Hawaii and opened a fish store. Sandy was living in San Francisco, married to a chef, and was cooking in his restaurant. Jean and Marsha had had a terrible fight over Marsha's boyfriend, Vince, and they had not spoken for several years. On a lead, I was able to locate Marsha in another state, now married to her former boyfriend. He was still working as an artisan, selling blown glass to stores, in fairs, and in mall shows. She worked in an office, but helped out with his business during the months preceding Christmas, when they did most of their yearly business.

After Jean split up with Jim she hit the bar scene for a while, picking up men and drinking a lot. She moved into a remote area and got a job in a bar where she had once worked right after her divorce from Dave. Over the years she drifted from bar to bar, waitressing, bartending, and serving as a bar, restaurant, or country club manager. She got fired from most of these jobs, once for having her hand in the till, other times for irregular attendance, and was arrested several times for drunk driving. When I spoke to her she was working at a country club as a bartender, serving at the club's catered events on the side. By her own admission, age had not dampened her ability to "party"; she could still get loose and have a good time far better than most of her contemporaries. After several years she had settled into an on-again-off-again relationship with Cliff, a man seven or eight years older than she, and they lived on three acres of land in the hills with three dogs, five chickens, and a large bird. Cliff was a former motorcycle racer and hang glider who now worked driving bulldozers and other heavy equipment. He had a substance abuse problem that was more serious than Jean's and he was occasionally physically abusive in their relationship. She fled on several occasions, but she always returned because she had nowhere else to go. During their good times she spoke of getting married; during their bad times she hid out from everyone.

Reflecting back on her dealing years in reference to her current life Jean had mixed feelings:

I wouldn't change a thing from the past, even if I could. Those years were great. Having as much money as we wanted, never having to worry about spending it. I really had a good time and I learned a lot from it. Not many people get to do all the things we did, and we did a lot of crazy things back then. But I'm not looking for the end of the rainbow anymore, all the scams and loose money. It was a wonderful thing to always have money, but we paid a price. I wouldn't want to live like that anymore. Now I like the comfort of my life. I like having a steady job. I like not having to worry about going to jail, having a driver's license that's legal.

Barney's reflections were similarly mixed:

Looking back on those years I have the full gamut of mixed emotions. It was a wonderful time in history when things were wide open. The government was running guns and drugs, and they weren't busting people very much. I lived every boy's dreams of cops and robbers, guns and knives, hide and chase. It had all the hardware and software, the glamour, the exotic settings like out of a James Bond movie. It was really cool. But there were bad times too. I have the worst tragedy stories and the best elation stories. When I think of those times I feel happy and sad, I remember the excitement, the fun, the thrills, but also the horror stories and the paranoia. I don't know if things would have turned out any differently in my life if I hadn't gone through those years. Who knows? I might still be here tinkering around with airplanes just like I did before.

My revisitation thus yielded results that were both surprising in some ways and predictable in others. Direct or indirect follow-ups on thirteen of my major subjects showed them all to be out of the drug business and involved in other ventures. When I originally described the scene, all of my subjects had been between 25 and 40. The people I returned to find were now well into their forties or fifties and retired. Although their level of involvement in the business (carrying with it a greater potential for insulation and profit), coupled with the exit barriers they encountered (the treadmill of the dealing lifestyle and the removal of their credentials for legitimate professional work), might have hypothetically enabled or induced them to remain with the activity longer, they burned out, bottomed out, busted out, grew out, and quit.[1] Some quit with the help of Narcotics Anonymous, some with the help of other detoxification programs. Some quit because they got arrested. Some quit because they had near-arrest escapes. Some got killed while involved in dangerous work. Many of the people I knew, however, just quit on their own.

They quit for many reasons that were intrinsic to the character and experience of their dealing careers. People's participation in every deviant activity follows a career trajectory, such that their later years of involvement differ significantly from their earlier years. Some aspects of the experience fade while others arise. Those that faded were most commonly associated with the novelty of the experience. My subjects quit, first, because the rewards of dealing, from the thrills, to the power, to the money, to the unending drugs, became less gratifying. These were no longer new or exciting; they became commonplace and taken for granted. The aspects of the deviant career that arose were most commonly those associated with aging, health, and increased vulnerability to law enforcement. These dealers also quit because, like Waldorf, Reinarman, and Murphy's (1991) cocaine users, their troubles, from the physical burnout, to the diminished excitement, to the paranoia and real risks associated with their activities, mounted. As they saw people around them getting killed, arrested, divorced, and becoming haggard, they finally decided, either at some major turning point, or over a gradual period of time, that they were tired of or unable to traffic in large quantities any longer. They had aged through the career and reached a point where they were ready to move out of it.

Their attempts at getting out were not all successful. Many factors continued to hold them to the drug world and undermined their success in the legitimate world (see chapter 7). Their exits, then, tended to be fragile and temporary, followed by periods of relapse into dealing. Reintegration formed the mirror image to the shifts and oscillations they made out of dealing: a series of forays into the legitimate world, many of them unsuccessful and temporary, that were often followed by subsequent re-endeavors. Each attempt at reintegration, however, brought them further back into society and away from the insulated world of the fast life. Yet even once made, their reattachment to conventional society was problematic due to their many years out of the mainstream economy.

FACTORS AFFECTING REINTEGRATION

What factors affected these people's lives and employment in society subsequent to their exit from the drug trade? Some were able to reintegrate more readily than others, finding a steady line of work. Others floundered, moving from activity to activity, unsuccessful and unsatisfied. Their final exit from the drug trade also saw them move into a variety of different venues characterized by distinct patterns. Factors affecting dealers' reintegration were rooted in the periods prior to, during, and subsequent to their dealing careers.

Pre-Dealing Factors. One element influencing dealers' ability to ultimately reintegrate themselves into legitimate society was their *age* at *onset* in illicit activities. Individuals who become active in drug trafficking or other aspects of the underground economy at a young age remove themselves from pathways to options of legitimate success. Like Williams's (1989) cocaine kids, they drop out of school and fail to accumulate years of experience toward work in a lawful occupation. Their attitudes are also shaped by their early drug world experiences, so that they lose patience for legitimate work and seek the immediate reward of the scam and quick fix. When they become disenchanted with drug trafficking or are scared enough to think about quitting, they have no reasonable alternatives to consider. In contrast, individuals who enter the drug world after they have completed more schooling and/or have established themselves in lawful occupations have more options to pursue.

Very few of the dealers I studied entered the drug world at an early age. In fact, out of my original sample, only five people went directly from high school into supporting themselves through drug money. None of the members of my follow-up sample followed the early onset pattern. Those I recontacted had all been in their late twenties or early thirties prior to entering into the drug world. Nearly all of them had been to college, and over half had graduated. Ten had been married and four had borne children. This introduced an element of stability and responsibility into their lives, and gave them some years of investment in the legitimate world that they could draw on in their future.

Related to this were the *prior interests and skills* individuals developed in the legitimate economy before they began to earn most of their income from dealing drugs. Very often maturation and growth involves an identity-forming process where individuals gradually narrow the range of career or occupational options to those in which they are interested. During this time they may begin to pursue one or more of these avenues and gain knowledge or experience in these areas. Such occupational experience is later helpful in aiding dealers' reintegration because it can offer them an area to which they can return, an educational foundation, or a base of legitimate working experience that provides some transferrable knowledge of and confidence about the legitimate world.

From my follow-up sample, Dave had worked as a real estate agent for the four years immediately prior to entering the drug business. He had previously held jobs as an auto mechanic, an appliance salesman, and the editor/publisher of a surfing magazine. Jean had been a housewife and mother for many years, with only sales experience in retail stores. Jim had pursued a career as a photographer, holding a job on the staff of a major national news magazine for several years. Barney and Jeff had been involved in aviation. Lou had worked as an auto mechanic and auto body technician. Marty had been a teacher in the secondary school system and Bobby and Sandy had owned a fish store. Later, a couple of them returned to these early roots. For instance, Bobby and Marty resumed their original jobs as a retail fish store owner and a teacher, respectively, while Dave spent several years operating surf shops on both coasts. Jeff and Barney returned to the aviation business, and Lou not only returned to auto maintenance and repairing, but went back to live on his family's property.

A third factor affecting dealers' later reintegration was the *social class* in which they are born and raised. When people grow up and become accustomed to a certain standard of living, they are reluctant to engage in downward social mobility. One of the noteworthy aspects of the members of my sample is their middle-class background. They are likely representative of a more widespread, hidden, middle-class population that is involved in the illicit drug trade on either a full- or part-time basis (cf. Morley 1989; Rice 1989). Such people move into drug trafficking to enhance their middle-class, materialist lifestyle, and when they leave the fast money world their ties to the middle-class lifestyle force them to reintegrate into legitimate society more quickly. All of my subjects had grown up in upper-middle, middle, or lower-middle class backgrounds, with parents engaged in a variety of occupations from educators, to researchers, to career military, to manufacturers, and sales.

Concurrent Factors. The manner and style in which individuals comported their lives during the active phase of their trafficking careers also affected their later efforts at reintegrating. One of the most salient features toward this end was the dealers' degree of *outside involvement.* A large number of drug dealers were engaged in other ventures in addition to trafficking. At both the upper and lower levels of the drug trade, individuals can participate in trafficking on either a part- or full-time basis. For example, Reuter et al. (1990) found that the majority of the arrested lower-level crack dealers they surveyed in their Washington, D.C. sample were employed in full-time legitimate jobs but "moonlighted" as dealers to supplement their incomes. Similarly, at the upper levels, a whole coterie of accountants, bankers, lawyers, pilots, and other legitimate businesspeople are involved part-time in the drug economy, arranging smuggling runs or providing illicit services to full-time traffickers (Morley 1989; Rice 1989). These individuals, who deal only part-time, are likely to have more interpersonal, occupational, and economic factors tying them to society. When they renounce their dealing they have fewer reintegration obstacles to face because they are already more fully integrated into the legitimate economy.

In contrast, those who deal full-time, like Williams's (1989) youthful Dominican-American dealers, Hamid's (1990) Caribbean-American dealers, and my Caucasian upper-level dealers and smugglers, have more likely renounced their investment in socially sanctioned means of surviving financially. Of the 65 subjects in my original study, nearly one-third remained involved in their previous jobs for a significant period of time while they were dealing in large amounts. This was the case for all but one member of my follow-up sample as well. Eventually, they all renounced these jobs, however, and withdrew to dealing or smuggling as their primary activity and main source of economic

support. Abandoning legitimate jobs or career tracks makes it significantly harder to reenter these lines after several years away, and only
Marty, the teacher, who remained in the classroom well into his
dealing career, was able to subsequently find another job in his profession.

Yet, even while engaged in full-time trafficking, individuals can
become involved with legitimate front businesses on the side. Because
they were making so much money, nearly two-thirds of my original
sample had pretensions of being involved in a legitimate business (for
the purpose of protecting themselves from the IRS) at one time or
another. This figure roughly applies to the follow-up group as well.
Jean, Jim, and Sandy worked in the catering business, Barney and Jeff
worked with airplanes, Ben owned an automobile dealership, and
Marsha ran an antique store. This kept these people partially tied to
the legitimate economy and made it subsequently easier for them to
reenter that economy on a serious basis once they left drug trafficking.
Maintaining some connection to the lawful world of work, as Meisenhelder (1977) has noted, also implies a lifestyle commitment to keep
some regular business hours. For these people, then, reintegration did
not require as much of a lifestyle transformation as it did for those
who had not worked at all. Thus, Jim eventually began his own
successful catering business and Sandy worked in a restaurant, skills
they had respectively acquired in their legitimate front businesses.

Knowledge and experience about legitimate work that was potentially useful to individuals' later reintegration could come not only
from outside involvements, but from *trafficking-related skills* as well. For
example, Dave used his connections in Mexico to find sources for
buying Mexican ponchos and sweatshirts so he could sell them to surf
stores all along the East Coast. He then parlayed this into a swap meet/
flea market business, where he owned enough goods to travel around
the country selling his products. His success in this venture enabled
him to buy enough merchandise to open a surf store of his own. At
the very least, the dealers and smugglers I studied became educated
and trained in handling money, working on credit, calculating profits
and expenses, and living with the uncertainty of entrepreneurship.
Those with the discipline and business acumen to become successful
in the drug world were often able to recreate some semblance of this

outside that arena. Others with less reputable and reliable approaches, who had survived in the drug business primarily on the selling strength of the product, did not usually fare as well.

Instrumental aspects of these dealers' lives were not the only significant factors affecting their later reintegration. The strength of these traffickers' *outside associations* were important as well. This included interpersonal relationships with their children, parents, siblings, close friends, and other family members. Such associations were important because they kept these dealers integrated, to some degree, into mainstream society. These upper-level dealers and smugglers trod a delicate line, as they lived inside of conventional society, yet insulated themselves within it. That is, they ate at the same restaurants, sent their children to the same schools, and lived in the same housing developments as other people, yet they kept their social contacts with those outside the drug world to a minimum. For protection they removed themselves from the inquisitive prying of people who would not accept their occupation and lifestyle. Some Southwest County smugglers and dealers went for long periods, then, without seeing former friends and relatives. Others, though, kept in touch with their most important associates, whether they lived locally or at a distance. Through these ties they remained connected to individuals and social worlds outside of dealing. These associations would be crucial for them to draw upon in their reentry to the legitimate world.

Such outside associates are not likely to "steer individuals away" from their deviance, as Braithwaite (1989) has suggested, nor are they likely to provide a ratio of definitions favorable to the law and thereby reorient dealers' and smugglers' normative attitudes, as Sutherland's differential association theory holds. Rather, they hold traffickers, to greater or lesser degree, from totally removing themselves from society and provide a bridge back into it when these individuals feel an internal push to reenter society.

Both outside involvements and associations served as the type of "bonds to society" described by Hirschi's control theory. While people diminished these bonds during their careers in trafficking, they did not cut them entirely. They then reached out to strengthen them during their attempts to move out of dealing and reintegrate. Other *de-insulating factors* served as bonds to society as well, maintaining these dealers' connections to the mainstream and easing them back. This included ties like sports and hobbies (cf. Irwin 1970), and could have included other such as religion. The dealers and smugglers in my sample all held onto some vestiges of their sport and hobby interests, rooting for their favorite teams, pursuing sports such as tennis or skiing, and indulging themselves in collecting things such as antiques or travel mementos. Religion, however, was not a significant part of their lives. Some individuals had come from religious backgrounds, attending parochial schools and church regularly, but this ended even before the onset of their dealing careers. While most of my follow-up subjects continued their sport and hobby interests after they quit dealing, none returned to religion.

A final factor characterizing dealers' active career behavior that affected their success and type of reintegration was the *degree of organizational sophistication* associated with their trafficking activity. Drug traffickers' involvement in deviant associations may follow a continuum of organizational sophistication, beginning with lone operators ensconced in a collegial subculture at the lowest end, and ascending to the loose associations of crack house crews, the more organized smuggling rings, the tighter and more serious delinquent gangs, and the deadly Colombian cartels or organized crime families at the highest end of the spectrum. We know from the broader study of deviance that individuals who are members of more organizationally sophisticated associations are more likely to be tied to those groups instead of integrated into society in a number of ways (see Best and Luckenbill 1982).

The drug traffickers in my follow-up group, much like those from my original sample, represented a mixture of both dealers and smugglers. As such, their involvement in criminal organizations ranged from the lone operator to the member or leader of a smuggling ring. While they were clearly drawn into serious criminal activity and formed identities based on this occupation and lifestyle, they made no lifetime commitment to the pursuit. Detaching and reintegrating into society required a major change of master status (Hughes 1945), but had fewer unbreakable side bets (Becker 1960).

Post-Dealing Factors. Drug traffickers' success at reintegrating into society was also affected by several factors they encountered subsequent to their involvement in dealing. As they oscillated back and forth between their phases of dealing and quitting, the availability of *legitimate opportunities* seriously affected the permanence of their retirement. As Shover (1985) has noted in his study of thieves, finding a satisfying job could tie an individual to a line of activity. A positive experience at a legitimate job can draw an individual back into more conventional peer associations, reinforce a nondeviant identity, occupy significant amounts of time, and diminish the motivation to return to dealing. While "straight jobs" were often looked down upon with disdain by Southwest County dealers in their younger days, they were more likely to view them favorably at this later age. This was reflected in Jean's comments about her changed attitudes toward her current life-style and work. People who came out of drug trafficking with some money, usually those who consumed less drugs and who trafficked at the highest levels (smugglers), were often better able to create satisfying legitimate opportunities for themselves. As Barney commented:

You spend the years from 25 to 35 in smuggling or dealing, you're too old to start a profession. But if you come out of it with some money you have a lot of options open to you. You can buy a job, buy a business, start your own business. You can lie on a resume. And you can do a lot of things when you're forced to that it would never occur to you that you can do. Like buy a passport, a birth certificate, a whole set of IDs. It's not as hard as you would think. And then you become someone else and you're free, the world opens up to you, once you have rid yourself of that financial restriction.

The importance of opportunity structures illustrates the value of Cloward and Ohlin's differential opportunity theory for reintegrating drug traffickers. Those who tried to oscillate out of dealing but could never find anything to support themselves in their hedonistic lifestyle returned to the drug world. Yet each time they attempted to quit it reflected a greater dissatisfaction with the dealing life. After a while, a less lucrative job opportunity, even Jean's bartending and waitressing job, appeared attractive.

Some drug traffickers were aided in their societal reintegration by *outside help*. As Braithwaite (1989:100–1) has noted, friends, associates, and acquaintances can aid former deviants' reintegration through "gestures of forgiveness" or "ceremonies to decertify offenders as deviant." Dealers may thus remove themselves from the scene, find a new life, make new friends, or meet a spouse (cf. Shover 1985) who may help them start over. This begins the process of rebuilding the social bonds that tie individuals to legitimate society. For instance, Marty was strongly influenced in his move to reintegrate back into society by his new wife who was opposed to his dealing activity, and Marsha was forcibly pulled from the dealing subculture by her boyfriend Vince, who had never liked her hanging around with the dealing crowd.

The extent and type of dealers' reintegration into society was ultimately affected by their *adaptability to the organizational world*. In my follow-up to Southwest County I observed a continuum between those whose experiences in the days of the wheeling and dealing and the big money had left them permanently unsuited for work as an employee in the organizational or bureaucratic world, and those who sought out and obtained jobs. Some of my subjects could never stoop to getting a job. They had entered the dealing world to secure freedom for their "brute being," and they would not endure the shackles of becoming an employee. Others were willing to get back into the working world, even if it meant taking a job at the bottom. Interestingly, finding oneself in "dire straights," as Dave and several others had, proved an insufficient inducement to an entrepreneurial, freedom-seeking person to get a job. They all had their limits, below which they would not stoop.

None of the wheeler-dealers, then, entered the confines of the straight "workaday" world they had either fled or disdained in the first place. Like many legitimate entrepreneurs, they could not imagine themselves punching a clock or working for someone else. Having tasted the excitement of the drug world, the straight world seemed boring. For them, staying within the world of independent business was associated with the potential for freedom and adventure. They could still dream of making the big killing and retiring. This also enabled them to avoid the awkwardness of trying to explain on a resume what they had been doing to earn a living during their dealing years. Like Dave and Barney, then, they became petty lawful entrepreneurs, leaving their glory days behind them.

In contrast, like Jean, some former dealers sought out a variety of jobs. Several of them had worked as employees prior to entering the drug world, while others tried to put together a legal front business that required them to work some regular hours during their dealing years. They did not feel uncomfortable, then, but rather enjoyed the assurance of a steady job and a predictable life. For them, quitting dealing and working legitimately became associated with security, domesticity, and freedom from paranoia. Their experiences with life as an employee, however, were never quite as predictable or as steady as the average worker.

Looking over the sum of their experiences, I found that my subjects were profoundly affected by their years spent in the illicit economy. Like other young people who failed, for various reasons, to enter career-tracking paths in the world of legitimate work, they found themselves having to make a mid-life career shift without any years of accumulation toward a secure future. Having earned significant sums of money early in their lives, they were also reluctant to later assume menial or entry-level jobs. Those who had earned credentials for legitimate careers often lost these, like Dave, due to arrest or imprisonment. They thus found themselves unemployable. Most reacted to this by eventually developing their own legitimate business ventures. Thus their years in trafficking were not wholly valueless, either financially or personally. The experience enabled them to see a side of life that might otherwise have remained blocked to them. They had lived with a passion and intensity known to few. They had traveled, met unusual people, and experimented with life in grand style. For those who survived, they were probably no worse off than many others who had lived for the present and let "mañana" take care of itself.

DISCUSSION

While scholars have addressed the issue of exiting deviant careers (cf. Faupel 1991; Frazier 1976; Harris 1973; Inciardi 1975; Irwin 1970; Meisenhelder 1977; Petersilia 1980; Ray 1964; Shover 1983; 1985), little has been written about the subsequent reintegration of former deviants into society. Brown (1991) has suggested that one way they do this is to capitalize on their former deviant status and become "professional ex-s," counseling and working to help others overcome their involvement in deviance. In Braithwaite's (1989) theory of crime, shame, and reintegration, he argues that individuals are steered away from their former deviant activities by caring others who accept them as essentially good, but reject their bad behavior. Rather than labeling and isolating them by casting the master status of deviant onto them, these friends, associates, and acquaintances aid former deviants' reintegration. Such reintegrative shaming, he argues, is only effective before individuals become ensconced in criminal subcultures, which support criminal behavior through their criminal opportunities, norms, values, and techniques of neutralization. At a more macro level, Braithwaite's theory suggests that "communitarian" cultures provide the most reintegrative form of shaming, by nurturing deviants within a network of attachments to conventional society.

While Braithwaite's theory of reintegration sheds light on the process by which individuals can be steered out of minor forms of deviance before they have significantly invested themselves in these behaviors and subcultures, it does not deal with the problem of reintegrating individuals who have already entered into criminal subcultures and seriously committed themselves to deviant or criminal activities, groups, and lifestyles.

Yet much crime is committed by individuals who begin criminal activities in their relative youth, much like drug traffickers, without intending to remain criminals all their lives. They go into these activities thinking they will make a lot of money and retire into some less dangerous line of work. Studies of deviant careers, in fact, show that large numbers of criminals and deviants (especially those who have never been incarcerated) naturally burn out, bottom out, grow out, and quit (Harris 1973; Irwin 1970; Waldorf 1983; Waldorf, Reinarman, and Murphy 1991). Once they have made the decision to exit deviance, their success depends largely on their ability to reintegrate into society. Braithwaite's theory, then, needs to be amended by a consideration of the reintegration of people who have passed the point at which he focuses.

My research suggests that shaming plays no role in these people's decisions to return to the more mainstream arena. Rather, they do it because they have evolved through the typical phases of their dealing careers and, like their peers, progress past the active into the inactive stage. With variations unique to each individual, dealers experience a progression through their early entry and involvement in the drug world, a middle period where they rise and experience shifts in their level and style of operation, an exit phase where they suddenly or gradually withdraw from the drug world, and the last phase, where they readapt themselves to the nondeviant world. Their eventual return to conventional society requires a process of reintegration, which is affected by the structural factors described here. They reintegrate, then, more because of "push" than "pull" factors, because the involvement in drug trafficking moves them past the point where they find it enjoyable, to the point where it is wearing and anxiety-provoking. Only once they have made the decision to leave the drug world, either temporarily or finally, do they reactivate their abandoned ties to the network of conventional society's attachments. This occurs, as Shover (1985) has noted, after they change their orientational (self-conceptions, goals, sense of time, tiredness) and interpersonal (ties to people or activities) foci, finding it preferable to detach from their deviant/criminal commitment and to reblend with the conventional society.

Their reintegration into this society is difficult, however. One of the hardest things is finding legitimate work. Years "derailed" from the mainstream in the career-building stage of their lives have blocked their entry into the professions and led to a failure to accrue connections and experience in legitimate occupational realms. They work, then, primarily in the entrepreneurial and secondarily in the employee (sales, unskilled, or semi-skilled labor) sector. Transferrable skills exist, but they are limited. Drug traffickers have gained experience working in an arena that functions more casually than most "straight" jobs. They could be irresponsible, be late, and be intoxicated for a drug deal, yet their connection would probably still wait for them because there was so much money to be made. Not many conventional jobs or deals are that profitable or forgiving. Former dealers then reenter the legitimate economy at an older age, where they are no longer the freshest and most attractive employees or trainees, bearing the stigma of unexplainable employment years. This limits their range of work opportunities. Yet compared to others who abandon youthful "compressed careers" (Gallmeier 1987) in such fields as sport, art, drama, or music, drug traffickers have at least had the benefit of working in a business arena. This brings with it useful, and transferrable, skills. After ten years most had made the adjustment and were well ensconced within the legitimate business world; they were earning decent money and living fairly well.

The second hardest component of reintegrating is making the adjustment to the diminished lifestyle of the straight world. While their new jobs do not pay as well, traffickers' ties to the drug world were never significantly to their work; relatively few individuals relished a deal well done or strove for intrinsic perfection in their operation. Rather, their satisfaction derived from the fast life and the easy money. They worked hard to play hard, not because they liked work. Many appreciate the mundane security of the everyday world, yet they never attain their former level of disposable income, excitement, flexibility, and the pleasure, spontaneity, and freedom they experienced during their halcyon days of drug trafficking. Some find a new identity and satisfaction in their post-dealing lifestyle, value system, and relationships, but this only occurs after a painful period of readjustment that includes feelings of relative deprivation and suffering.

Their post-dealing lives are thus profoundly affected by their years in the drug world. The attitudes, values, and lifestyle they adopted during the active phase of their dealing careers remain nascent within them. Most are straight for pragmatic rather than ideological or moral reasons. The quick buck and the "sweet" deal thus remain embedded within their vocabulary of motives. While they may be too old to keep up with their former drug-using pace or to return to the fast life, many still enjoy a touch of hedonism. In an era when the majority of middle-aged people are "former" marijuana smokers, party drinkers, and general revelers, these ex-drug traffickers still like to have adventures. It remains a part of their lifestyle and new identity, carried over from earlier times. Thus, while they have shed the dealing occupation, many retain some proclivity for deviant attitudes and lifestyles. They are post-dealers, but not completely reformed deviants. They live near the fringes of conventional society, trying to draw from both within and outside of it.

CHAPTER TEN

LAW ENFORCEMENT, DRUG TRAFFICKING, AND DRUG POLICY

The most recent wave of national concern over drug use and drug trafficking began in the late 1960s during the Nixon administration. Although such prohibitionist impulses have surged before, notably surrounding the passage of the Harrison Narcotics Act in 1914 and during the alcohol prohibition of the 1920s, the last three decades have seen us, as a nation, once again plunge into a puritanical fervor. Drugs have again become a major social and political problem and we have since witnessed the evolution and escalation of our national drug policy into a declared state of war. From Nixon to Reagan and Bush, these administrations have encouraged sensationalist media scares (Reinarman and Levine 1989), capitalizing on the political appeal of their hard-line moralist stance by generating an electoral base increasingly fearful of drugs. These policies have drawn us deeper into an intractable position with regard to federal spending, finances, and international relations. While several scholarly works have already drawn attention to various failures of the "War on Drugs" (Morley 1989; Nadelman 1988a, b; Reiss et al. 1990; Waller et al. 1990; Wisotsky 1990), in this chapter I draw attention to the sociological consequences of this drug policy for the social organization of drug distribution, particularly smuggling. I begin by reviewing changes in the social usage patterns of various drugs since the publication of the first edition of *Wheeling and Dealing*, and then discuss the history of recent drug enforcement and its relation to market economics and the sociological behavior surrounding drug trafficking. I conclude by drawing out the unintended consequences of America's drug policy.

SHIFTS IN DRUG USE

Since 1980, the National Institute of Drug Abuse's (NIDA) annual survey of high school seniors, conducted each year by the University of Michigan, has suggested that some drugs, most notably marijuana and (powder) cocaine, have undergone a decline in usage patterns (Bachman et al. 1987; Johnston et al. 1986). Estimates of the number of regular marijuana users have ranged from the conservative figure of 18 million in NIDA's National Household Survey, to the 50 million derived through surveys by NORML (National Organization for the Reform of Marijuana Laws) (Gettman 1989).

In contrast, methamphetamine, and one variant of it popularly known as "ice," has grown enormously in prevalence during this time. It moved through the country from the West, first being widely seen in Hawaii and now strongly entrenched on the West Coast. Methamphetamine has been consumed primarily by white, middle-class youth, and easily manufactured in clandestine chemical laboratories up and down the West Coast, especially in San Diego. Hallucinogens have also made a comeback recently through the introduction of MDMA (methylenedioxymethamphetamine), a "designer drug" originally developed in Germany that drew on and modified the properties of MDA. More commonly known as "ecstasy," MDMA has been used predominantly by middle-class white youth and middle-aged white professionals (Rosenbaum et al. 1989).

The greatest change in the drug scene has come from the introduction of crack cocaine, a transformation of the refined white powder cocaine into cohesive "rock" particles that are then smoked. Crack produces a more intense "high" and is more strongly addictive. Its cost per dose is inexpensive (around $5 a vial), making it the drug of choice among minority groups in the inner city . After its initial onset in these urban arenas, its popularity has diffused outward into the white suburban and exurban areas (Scandale 1991). Crack addiction, and the associated social consequences of violence, crime, neonatal addiction/abandonment, and deteriorating family structure, developed into a major social problem in the 1980s. Associated with the rise of crack has been a resurgence in the popularity of heroin, perhaps to temper the "speedy" effects of crack, and the two are sometimes used in conjunction (McDonnell et al. 1990; Treaster 1990). Both of these drugs have been directly and indirectly associated with the spread of the AIDS virus through such related behavior as needle-sharing, pipe-sharing, and promiscuous sexual activity.

Changes in the composition of the currently popular drugs has had a significant effect on dealing and, most especially, smuggling patterns, as popularity represents the force of demand. Since 1980 the production of drugs inside America's borders has flourished due to both illicit pharmaceutical manufacturing and domestic marijuana cultivation.[1] Domestic production bypasses existing smugglers and most upper-level dealing operators who rely on smugglers for their drug supply, utilizing newly formed middlemen to handle the products. At the same time, the growth of crack and heroin support the more traditional venues of importation and upper-level dealing.

EVOLVING LAW ENFORCEMENT AND DRUG TRAFFICKING

During the period from 1965 to 1990 significant changes occurred in the social attitudes and federal policies toward drug dealers and smugglers. These have had profound consequences for the social organization of trafficking.

Agencies. Prior to 1965, the Federal Bureau of Narcotics was responsible for the bulk of drug enforcement and was most renowned for its introduction of special agents known as "narcs" (cf. Manning 1980). With the swell of drug use in the 1960s, Congress passed the first of many drug statutes, the Drug Abuse Control Amendment of 1965. This act focused primarily on the control of pharmaceuticals diverted from legal channels. The government subsequently created several agencies designed to further challenge the drug problem, including the Bureau of Drug Abuse Control (1966), the Office for Drug Abuse and Law Enforcement (1972), the Office of National Narcotic Intelligence (1972), the Drug Enforcement Administration (1973), the Regional Information Sharing System (1980), the Organized Crime Drug Enforcement Task Force (1983), the National Narcotics Drug Policy Board (1984), and, most recently, the Office of National Drug Control Policy, directed by a high-level "drug czar" (1988).

Campaigns. These bureaucratic changes were accompanied by a series of law enforcement campaigns attacking drug dealing and smuggling. These began with Operation Intercept in the 1970s, which augmented the border patrol, increasing surveillance of individuals entering the country from Mexico, and was designed to apprehend people smuggling marijuana and cocaine on their bodies or vehicles (see Gooberman 1974). This sharply curtailed individual and small-scale smuggling operations, giving advantage to the rings or crews of smugglers described earlier in this book. Operation Intercept ended when the borders became so clogged that commerce was negatively affected, the Mexican government protested, and enforcement funds were curtailed. An herbal defoliation program followed, in which the chemical paraquat was sprayed over enormous sections of the Mexican countryside. This not only destroyed the Mexican marijuana crop (and damaged people's lungs who smoked the quickly harvested, partially grown crops), but also completely devastated the affected fields, making cultivation of any vegetation impossible for many years afterward. The consequence of this campaign was the temporary demise of Mexico as a source country for marijuana, sending U.S. smugglers deeper into the heartland of South America in search of drugs. As a result, Colombia escalated its marijuana production and became a more prominent player in the illicit drug trade. This enhanced smugglers' access to the other major Colombian export, cocaine.

During Nixon's presidency we witnessed the rise of the cocaine trade, stimulated in part by the government's policy of treating marijuana in the same category of danger as cocaine.[2] Many Southwest County smugglers subsequently turned to cocaine as a commodity because it was less bulky, less odorous, and more profitable.

With so much of the economy in both California and Florida, the major points of entry, stimulated by the drug industry, these states boomed financially and expanded rapidly. Currency surpluses began to appear at banks in both these states, as incoming cash exceeded the payouts at an increasing rate. In 1970 the discrepancy was $576 million; by 1976 it had risen to $1.5 billion (Nadelmann 1988b; Wisotsky 1990). This money-laundering was being done for drug smugglers and dealers by white, middle-class financial professionals. With only a slight deviation from legal practices, bankers could readily increase the fees earned by their banks and concomitantly their own salaries and commissions. A new campaign, Operation Greenback, was launched in 1979 to stem the flow of dirty money through American banks and to crack down on illicit businesses. This was, however, a short-lived operation that was quietly phased out of existence for two reasons. First, it met with strong resistance from members of the banking community, who often flatly refused to cooperate. Second, it was undercut by the deregulation during the Reagan era, with its cutbacks in regulation budgets and staff, and slackening in the monitoring of financial institutions. It became clear, once again, that enforcement was to be directed at visible and accessible vulnerable populations, not white, middle-class businessmen.

Upper-Level Dealing. The 1980s, then, were years when the drug trade flourished. Wall Street and Madison Avenue were rich with the heady profits of the fast-track mergers-and-acquisitions crowd, and cocaine was the drug of choice. The American ideal of entrepreneurship lay at the base of this drug trafficking model, with entrepreneurs drawn from the privileged classes of society. These were the part-time drug entrepreneurs, American businessmen employed in legitimate occupations who dabbled in importation and upper-level distribution or ancillary white-collar services for the drug crowd (Waldman et al. 1989). As one investigative journalist described them:

This class ranges from friends of Pete Rose (three of whom are doing time for coke deals) to friends of Oliver North (one of whom played a leading role in a scheme to import $10 million worth of cocaine into Florida). They are, in the words of one Treasury Department official, the "members of a wealthy, highly skilled, professional class, many of whom are highly respected members of their community. They are attorneys, accountants, bankers, and money brokers." (Morley 1989:346)

In contrast to these part-time drug entrepreneurs, individuals engaged in full-time upper-level importation and distribution were neither as likely to be white nor upper-class, being drawn more broadly from a mixture of white and minority groups and from the upper-middle, middle, and lower-middle classes. The only scholarly research on upper-level trafficking published since *Wheeling and Dealing* is Reuter and Haaga's (1989) study of high-level drug markets based on semi-structured interviews conducted in 1987 with 40 incarcerated dealers held in minimum-security prisons. Estimating that their respondents' careers peaked in the early 1980s, Reuter and Haaga offered a portrayal of high-level trafficking that confirmed my own. Entry into the business was relatively easy, requiring energy, discretion, and luck rather than money or skill. Dealing could be easily accomplished by individuals operating alone; larger crews were only required for the more specialized task of smuggling. These groups were loosely structured, resembling networks rather than formal organizations. Even though their population contained more minority group members than mine, they also found little recourse to violence (this contrasts markedly with the violence characterizing other segments of the drug market, especially the crack and heroin trades). Finally, they reported a fluidity to the national market, where entrepreneurial dealers could travel to different regions and do business, unencumbered by any monopolistic-style control over various territories. These entrepreneurs were not the only type of organization represented at the upper-levels of the business, however.

Internationalization of the Drug Trade. In the early years the majority of drug enforcement efforts had been confined to interdiction and domestic enforcement tactics such as the buy-bust and conspiracy charges. While law enforcement agencies had been successful in driving mom-and-pop operators out of business and were targeting American smuggling rings, they could do little to reach the international smuggling operations. Over a period of time, criminal syndicates arose in Colombia that organized, professionalized, and monopolistically controlled the cocaine trade. As one of the primary producing countries for marijuana and coca leaf, and the primary refining country for cocaine powder, Colombia has long supplied other countries with illicit substances. Colombians' initial contacts in the United States were Cubans expatriated during the Communist revolution who fled to Miami. After supplying organized groups of Cuban dealers for years and making relatively little profit compared to what the Cubans were earning through their domestic distribution networks, in the 1970s the Colombians began locating their own nationals inside the country to handle some of the upper-level dealing. At the same time this enabled them to more easily purchase the ether, acetone, and other chemicals needed for refining coca paste into powder domestically, as the DEA was making it difficult to obtain these in South America. The 1970s also saw the greatest rise in the organizational sophistication of Colombian dealing groups. Based in poverty areas, life was cheap and the lure of profit brought violent tactics to those who would control it. Groups forged together into larger organizations and muscled out independents. They evolved into crime "families" known as "narcotraficantes," often tied together by blood, marriage, or fictitious kinship. These cartels established power and monopolistic control through their reputation for violence (including torture and mutilation), their combined bribery and threatening of elected officials, and their beneficence to local villages whose members they then recruited to drug service. The largest and most powerful of these were based in the Medellin, Bogota, and Cali areas. Enforcers were then sent to the United States to eliminate rival dealing factions from among the vestiges of the Cuban organizations and other competitors in Miami.

By the 1980s, Colombian nationals in America began to grow more numerous and spread out to other parts of the country. The economic and political power of the cartels escalated as they became entwined with corrupt governments in Colombia, Cuba, Panama, and Honduras. This enabled them to extend their transportation system, money-laundering operations, and paramilitary arm. While the cartels were large and independent enough to handle all of their own functions (manufacturing, transportation, distribution, finance, and security) separately, they typically cooperated or shared members (especially at the lower levels, who were insulated from knowledge about upper-level commanders) and their services as well as facilities. They also drew on a common body of bankers, lawyers, and other professionals in the United States to assist them in their legal and financial dealing.

The cartels' vast outreach and escalated activities stimulated increased coca production in Peru and Bolivia (Morales 1989), enabling more widespread processing and international distribution. This resulted, in the early 1980s, in a vast increase in the availability of higher quality HCL (powder) cocaine accompanied by a sudden break in the price (Siegel 1982). While American smuggling crews were not driven out of the business entirely (increased consumption made drugs one of the major "growth industries" of the 1980s), their lower level of organizational sophistication dropped them to a secondary position in the international trade and made it more difficult for them to remain profitable.

When I returned to the field in 1991 I found kilos of cocaine selling in Colombia for $4,000, in contrast with the $35,000 of fifteen years earlier. At that time, Southwest county smugglers could buy a kilo for $35,000, bring it back to the United States and cut it in half. They could then sell the four pounds that resulted for $35,000 each, yielding a gross profit of $105,000 (per kilo bought) before drug use and other costs. At current prices, the same imported kilo would yield only $12,000 profit, requiring significantly larger loads to attain a reasonable level of return.

Lower-Level Dealing. During this time another coterie of drug entrepreneurs arose out of distinctly different roots. Americans of elite position had already discovered the more intense effects that could be generated by transforming refined cocaine into smokable "base," but the quality and price of the product in the 1970s had kept this form of use restricted primarily to high rollers such as entertainers and dealers. The advent of cheaper and purer raw materials swiftly enabled the widespread production of large quantities of crack, which could be sold in unit doses starting as low as $5 (Hunt 1987). With the innovation of this new product, crack took hold and began booming in the ghettos of the American inner city.

As at the upper end of the trade, not all lower-level traffickers devoted themselves exclusively to the drug business. In a survey of lower-level crack dealers in Washington, D.C. that drew on a population of primarily black, male, 18- to 40-year-olds charged with drug distribution offenses, Reuter et al. (1990) found that three-quarters of their subjects had held legitimate employment while dealing. These individuals regarded dealing as a form of "moonlighting" on their regular jobs, enabling them to earn a much higher hourly wage than their legitimate work for activities that were carried out primarily on weekends. The majority of these subjects also dealt to procure drugs for themselves at reduced cost or for free, rather than to earn vast sums of money. Their motivation was the hedonism and materialism of drugs and material possessions.

In contrast, Terry Williams's riveting ethnographic study of a teenage drug ring in the Washington Heights district of upper Manhattan, *The Cocaine Kids* (1989), provides a portrayal of full-time crack entrepreneurs. Williams followed the careers of eight Dominican-American youngsters who were organized into a lower-level selling crew by their mid-level supplier. Operating out of a crack house and selling on open-air street corners, these men and one woman had a loose confederation with each other. Their supplier served as their leader, spawning the group through his search for someone to serve as a reliable outlet and crack house manager. The manager, in turn, recruited street-level sellers who could move large numbers of $5 vials (as many as 100 to 150 in a given day). They were thus semi-independent agents in a loosely structured crew: they bought (under an informal quota system) from a common sponsor and sold for their own profit, enjoyed the benefits of his free cocaine (within reason), and had the advantage of the social support and limited mutual aid most commonly found among deviant "peer" groups (Best and Luckenbill 1982). These dealers came to the drug business seeking a means of upward mobility in an economically decimated area. Like the traffickers in *Wheeling and Dealing*, they did not intend to remain in the drug business all their lives; they shared the common entrepreneurial dream of amassing big money over a year or two and exiting into legitimate work. They were in it for the rewards of hedonism and materialism: the glamour, the excitement, the drugs, the fast life, the material possessions, the shot at the American dream. More than the people I studied, their work was dangerous and the likelihood of arrest, injury, or death great. As a result, their turnover was more rapid; they burned out, flaked out, or fell out in roughly three to five years.

Other recent research has yielded similarly structured portraits of the lower-level crack trade. Bourgois's (1989) study of a Spanish Harlem crack house described a comparable loosely tied group of lower-level dealers and other individuals held together by the relative safety of their indoor trafficking location (as opposed to the open-air street markets). Johnson et al. (1987) studied crack distribution throughout the greater New York City area and concluded that a "free-lance" system of operation was one of the major models of crack distribution. Hamid (1990) followed the careers of several lower-level drug entrepreneurs in Caribbean neighborhoods of Harlem and Brooklyn, suggesting that most of the crack dealers he observed operated either on their own (street selling) or in informal conjunction with their supplier and a small number of other sellers (crack house selling). Mieczkowski (1989, 1990) conducted a combined ethnography and survey of crack users and traffickers in Detroit, and concluded that the drug "appears to be distributed largely by multiple units of small entrepreneurs rather than any mega-organization that controls the crack trade" (Mieczkowski 1990:21). Thus, while previous studies of lower-level dealing have depicted either the lone independent dealer or the outlet of the criminal syndicate, the structure of lower-level crack dealing seems to be focused around small, informal crews or "posses" (Hamid 1990). These groups may be casually organized by suppliers who set the terms of pricing, availability, and formula for the manufacture of powdered (HCL) cocaine into crack (often done at the crack house level), with other members composed of sellers, a manager, steerers or touters (middlemen), lookouts, and enforcers (muscle, protection).

Yet at the same time, these and other studies have additionally suggested the presence of a slightly more organized format for lower-level crack dealing. The high volume of buying from repeat sales to relatively small numbers of users per seller or selling location in a given area (Hamid 1991) can foster an environment of greater market competition. The benefits to be derived from control of a given territory can yield violence over crews' ability to monopolize open selling in prime areas (Glick 1990). Groups able to physically overcome others have arisen and dominated entrepreneurial individuals and loosely tied sellers. In these situations we have seen the involvement of some urban youth gangs in crack dealing (Fagan 1989; Fagan and Chin 1989; Glick 1990; Klein et al. 1988). Glick (1990) has argued, based on his ethnographic study of Puerto Rican drug dealers in Chicago, that the gang structure and violence associated with crack dealing is particularly endemic to underclass and minority populations. Yet it is agreed by nearly all that the organizational range of these groups does not approach the centralization or tight control formerly found in the heroin market (Fagan and Chin 1989; Hamid 1990; Mieczkowski 1990). Only Johnson et al. (1987) have suggested that this market structure is leading to a "vertically organized crack business" model, which they see as eventually growing out of the freelance one, characterized by a formalized, multi-tiered, rational system of supervision and control.

Legislation. Legislation followed throughout the 1980s that further aimed at curtailing the business of drug dealers (both upper- and lower-level) and smugglers. The Comprehensive Crime Control Act of 1984 increased existing penalties for a variety of drug offenses, the Controlled Substance Registrant Act of 1984 outlawed stealing drugs from registered owners, the Aviation Drug Trafficking Control Act of 1984 enabled the Federal Aviation Administration to revoke licenses and registrations of pilots and/or planes tied to drug offenses, and the Comprehensive Forfeiture Act of 1984 made it easier for the government to seize personal assets. The Anti-Drug Act of 1986 then strengthened existing legislation by further increasing drug sanctions and facilitating governmental efforts. Yet with all this legislation, the drug business was booming, prices were falling, not rising, and enforcement agents were netting primarily low- and middle-level dealers, with minorities proportionately overrepresented.

The International War on Drugs. By the middle 1980s, the wealth and power of the Colombian cartels had grown enormously. An estimated 80 percent of the refined cocaine and 42 percent of the marijuana consumed in the United States was originating in Colombia (President's Commission on Organized Crime 1986). The leaders of the main cartels, Pablo Escobar, Jorge Ochoa, and Carlos Lehder-Rivas (followed after his death by Gonzalo Rodriguez Gacha), were worth an estimated combined $5 billion (Morganthau et al. 1989; *Newsweek* 1988). With this volume of business, not only local and national, but international law enforcement efforts began to descend on them. The United States began spending increasingly large sums on cooperation programs with South American countries designed to promote extradition, crop eradication and/or substitution, and destruction of processing operations. American paramilitary supplies were also given to these governments to pursue major drug cartels, with foreign aid made contingent on these governments' cooperation and support in the drug war.

Colombian drug kingpins could ignore domestic enforcement efforts, as corruption was so rampant they could bribe their way out of prosecution or imprisonment, but extradition treaties ratified with the United States in 1981 began to be enforced and Colombian traffickers were sent to jail in the United States. This led to a period of great bloodshed, where Supreme Court justices, drug enforcement agents, journalists, justice ministers, and hundreds of citizens were murdered by "narcomafia." Extraditions were suspended. In 1989, however, under pressure from the United States, Colombia's president declared a state of siege and resumed the extraditions. The cartels responded by joining forces and declaring a state of "war" on the government. Backed by U.S. support and equipment, the two sides threatened, shot at, and bombed each other in high gear. Ultimately, however, the traffickers outlasted the government. Popular support for the war, and the American government backing it, eroded, and politicians withdrew their unilateral support, leaving the cartels free to resume business as before. With this, the constant cries that the responsibility lay with the United States as the consumer country, not the producer countries, once again grew louder. As long as demand continued strong, they argued, it made no sense to curtail supply in any one country. This would merely cripple that country financially and result in the neighboring countries taking over their markets. Cutting off all of South America (a practical impossibility) would only increase the supply from the Far East. The problem had to be addressed at home.

Attacking Domestic Demand. In response, a 1986 bill brought a new target to the war on drugs: instead of pursuing traffickers, legislation targeted the demand side and the recreational user. This change of focus was further evident in Reagan's "zero-tolerance" initiative of 1988, making the complete elimination of controlled substance use the national goal and authorizing the fullest degree of enforcement for even minor amounts. This program was especially directed at drug users (through seizure sanctions) who were not otherwise accessible via criminal procedures. Consumers were further affected by the Drug-Free Workplace Act of 1988, which promoted drug testing of employees and enlisted employers in the federal fight against drugs. The mandatory sentencing program of 1989 then limited prosecutors' plea bargaining and restricted sentencing discretion among the judiciary.

The 1991 Persian Gulf War caused the war on drugs to recede into the background. Unlike the latter, the former was a war that could be won, a war against foreigners on foreign soil, a war that carried popular support both domestically and internationally. It siphoned money, political energy, and media attention from one arena to the other. No mention need be made of troublesome domestic issues as long as foreign ones prevail, enabling the United States to ease off its South American neighbors and pacify international tensions there. Once the military forces returned from the gulf and glory was no longer forthcoming from this arena, the presidency focused its attention once again on the drug front. Bush's new plan involved a major military commitment to interdiction and eradication. Yet here the Pentagon balked: they had learned from Vietnam to resist being drawn into another protracted, unwinnable military engagement that would put their people at risk to the lure of drugs. The president reached for his trump card but it would not be played. The war on drugs thus remains a continuing feature of the American political horizon, capable of temporarily ebbing away, only to rise up at any time to fill a media void, as long as the conservative, law-and-order pendulum swing begun in the 1970s and 1980s survives. It is an integral part of the "New Sobriety's" moral agenda, the campaign associated with "Just Saying No" to alcohol, tobacco, sex, and drugs. It fills a crucial role in the movement to assert greater governmental control into the lives of private citizens by serving as the crisis-raising arm: drugs cause work days lost to corporations, drains on employee and national health plans, rampant and wanton sexual behavior, atrophied lives and futures, violence and fear, loss of self-control. As long as the American public is willing to be convinced that these dangers of drugs far outweigh the costs of the drug war,[3] we will see no other political design.

MARKET DYNAMICS, ENFORCEMENT, AND
SOCIAL ORGANIZATION

Reviewing the last thirty years, we can see that the structure and social organization of drug trafficking has evolved in response to several factors. First, market dynamics have shaped its character. This includes such factors as price, availability, demand cycle (most drugs evolve through a natural cycle/career of popularity, booming early only to fade over time), and target population (predominant consumers). Drugs originating exclusively in foreign countries are more likely to pass through a restricted point of entry, making their distribution more easily controlled by small numbers of people. Drugs capable of being domestically manufactured have a more democratized base of distribution. Similarly, drugs whose use is concentrated in urban areas are likely to be influenced by competition over specific selling territories. Drugs that command a higher price are more apt to be handled by higher socioeconomic classes of dealers. And drugs evolve over the life of their popularity from being handled by more elite distributors to more common ones, from centralized sources of access to more widespread ones, or vice versa, from unfocused markets to more controlled ones.

Second, drug trafficking has been affected by the level and type of law enforcement. Each time the latter escalates, the former has to escalate to survive. Thus, when the U.S. government increased border vigilance against vehicular traffic, small, independent operators were eliminated from viability. Only operators organized into crews characterized by technologically advanced equipment, division of labor, and greater resources could negotiate the market. Likewise, when the government brought down greater strictures against entrepreneurial crews through a combination of legislation and concerted campaigns, these operators were disadvantaged. This created a market environment favorable to the organizational structure of the Colombian cartels and their greater manpower and resources, capacity for violence, strict enforcement of their rules and contracts, money-laundering, and paid political protection. The war on drugs has thus indirectly created a powerful, professional criminal syndicate, safely lodged outside the reach of its domestic law enforcement agents, that serves as its adversary. This antagonist, powerful enough to declare a state of war against an entire government and bring it to its knees, appears overwhelmingly insurmountable.

Thus, through a concerted policy based more on moral and political than on practical or social scientific grounds, our government has pursued a course that has yielded devastating unintended consequences. In attempting to diminish the flow of drugs and increase the costs to drug traffickers, we have created a climate favorable to large-scale illicit enterprise. In making our borders more difficult for amateur or entrepreneurial operators, we have fostered the rise of international criminal syndicates. By working to drive everyone we could defeat out of the smuggling business, we have encouraged a market situation that favored the drug operator beyond our grasp, one bigger and more powerful than our law enforcement resources could tackle. We have created the ideal climate for the ultimate, unbeatable antagonist.

NOTES

INTRODUCTION

1. The existing literature on drug trafficking can be divided into three categories. Academic portrayals of dealing and smuggling of "soft" drugs (i.e., marijuana, hashish, its various derivatives, psychedelics, and cocaine) include Anonymous 1969; Atkyns and Hanneman 1974; Blum et al. 1972; Carey 1968; Fields 1984; Flores 1981; Goode 1970; Johnson 1973; Langer 1976, 1977; Lieb and Olson 1976; Mandel 1967; Mouledoux 1972; Soref 1981; and Waldorf et al. 1977. Academic portrayals of "hard" drug dealing and smuggling (i.e., heroin, the opiates) include Gerstein 1976; McCoy 1972; Manning and Redlinger 1983; Moore 1977; Preble and Casey 1969; Redlinger 1969, 1975. Several good trade works have also been published that offer insights into marijuana and cocaine trafficking, such as Goddard 1978; Kamstra 1974; Olden 1973; Phillips and Wynne 1980; Sabbag 1976; and Woodley 1971.

2. Although I did not observe a great number of women dealers, several of my respondents reported dealing with quite a few women. Those who traveled to other parts of the country, especially the East Coast, to buy or sell there, claimed that Southwest County had many more women dealers than elsewhere. Smuggling, however, was a man's world. I therefore use the male pronoun when referring to smugglers.

1. RESEARCHING DEALERS AND SMUGGLERS

1. Gold (1958) discouraged this methodological strategy, cautioning against overly close friendship or intimacy with informants, lest they lose their ability to act as informants by becoming too much observers. Whyte (1955), in contrast, recommended the use of informants as research aides, not for helping in conceptualizing the data but for their assistance in locating data which supports, contradicts, or fills in the researcher's analysis of the setting.

2. See also Biernacki and Waldorf 1981; Douglas 1976; Henslin 1972; Hoffman 1980; McCall 1980; and West 1980 for discussions of "snowballing" through key informants.

3. See Kirby and Corzine 1981; Birenbaum 1970; and Henslin 1972 for more detailed discussions of the nature, problems, and strategies for dealing with courtesy stigmas.

4. We never considered secret tapings because, aside from the ethical problems involved, it always struck us as too dangerous.

5. See Douglas (1976) for a more detailed account of these procedures.

6. A recent court decision, where a federal judge ruled that a sociologist did not have to turn over his field notes to a grand jury investigating a suspicious fire at a restaurant where he worked, indicates that this situation may be changing (Fried 1984).

7. See Henslin 1972 and Douglas 1972, 1976 for further discussions of this dilemma and various solutions to it.

8. In some cases I resolved this by altering my descriptions of people and their actions as well as their names so that other members of the dealing and smuggling community would not recognize them. In doing this, however, I had to keep a primary concern for maintaining the sociological integrity of my data so that the generic conclusions I drew from them would be accurate. In places, then, where my attempts to conceal peoples' identities from people who know them have been inadequate, I hope that I caused them no embarrassment. See also Polsky 1969; Rainwater and Pittman 1967; and Humphreys 1970 for discussions of this problem.

2. SMUGGLING

1. For a more detailed discussion of the cultivation and distribution of marijuana in Mexico, see Kamstra 1974.

2. Coca-cola syrup, or even the mixed soda straight from the bottle, was often used to spray the marijuana. While the rationale used by growers for this treatment centered on its adhesive effects, most marijuana already had a naturally resinous quality which users associated with the drug's potency. Many smugglers were thus critical of the spraying process, claiming that the sugary additive did little beside adding weight to the substance, while damaging the quality of the marijuana.

3. For more detailed discussions of the cultivation and distribution of cocaine in South America, see Grinspoon and Bakalar 1976; Martin 1970; McNicoll 1983; Olden 1973; Rabaj and Campos 1980; Ramirez 1980; Waldorf et al. 1977; Yepez and Toledo 1980.

4. Marijuana, though, was not as limited at the point of importation as "harder" drugs, such as heroin. As documented by both my data and the President's Commission on Law Enforcement and Administration of Justice (1967), importation of marijuana was still often accomplished by independent entrepreneurs rather than by large criminal syndicates.

3. UPPER-LEVEL DEALING

1. Many middle-level, low-level, and ounce dealers also lived and operated within Southwest County. I included several people who dealt at these levels

and either moved up or stayed within the lower range in my sample to help me attain a fuller understanding of drug trafficking. But they fall outside my focus in this work, so I have chosen not to describe their operations in detail.

2. They also sold grams and quarter-ounces occasionally to a variety of upper-level marijuana and cocaine traffickers when these individuals ran out of personal stash.

3. Middle-level "cut-ounce" dealers and low-level gram dealers also populated Southwest County, but, as with their commercial marijuana counterparts, I will not offer a separate discussion of their activities.

4. I therefore make no attempt here to estimate the number of hands these drugs passed through between the smuggler and the ultimate consumer, especially since they could be middled countless times along the way.

5. THE DEALING LIFESTYLE

1. This fast life resembled, although it did not exactly correspond to, Rosenbaum's (1981:23) depiction of the ghetto heroin user's lifestyle.

2. Ironically, it seemed that in the 1980s the jet set began to emulate the dealing crowd. In an article entitled, "Drugs and the High Life," *Newsweek* (1983) discussed the cases of over a dozen "trend-setting jet-setters" who were arrested for allegedly smuggling large quantities of cocaine.

3. I sat down once with a commercial marijuana smuggler and we figured out that if he did one run per week (which was his average frequency) during the prime season of October to April and incurred no unexpected losses due to arrest, theft, or accidental mishap, he could clear a profit of $800,000 per year. This figure did not include a deduction for the expense of his personal drug consumption (and that of his crew or entourage), because most dealers and smugglers considered this a perquisite of the business rather than part of their net profit. This salary represented the upper end of the profit scale, since commercial marijuana smuggling was the most lucrative type of operation I witnessed. There was a vast difference between how much dealers and smugglers earned. When compared to legitimate work, dealers' profits were quite high, but the big money was always in smuggling.

4. Waldorf et al. (1977:32) referred to the feelings of affection people experienced that faded after the drug effect wore off as "cocaine friendships."

5. Elsewhere (Adler and Adler 1980), I have referred to this breaching of safety precautions to impress others, especially women, as "the irony of secrecy in the drug world."

6. In the dealer's vernacular, this term was not used in the clinical sense of an individual psychopathology rooted in early childhood traumas. Instead, it resembled Lemert's (1962) more sociological definition which focused on such behavioral dynamics as suspicion, hostility, aggressiveness, and even delusion. Not only Lemert, but also Waldorf et al. (1977) and Wedow (1979) have asserted that dealers' feelings of paranoia could have a sound basis in reality,

and were therefore readily comprehended and even empathized with by others.

7. See Miller 1978:232 for another discussion of the role of hedonism and materialism in motivating deviant work.

6. SUCCESS AND FAILURE

1. McAuliffe and Gordon (1974) have proposed the notion of a prestige hierarchy in the world of heroin dealing, suggesting that individuals who are highly ranked in this dimension gained not only the respect of other dealers but also access to better-quality heroin.

2. This disproves Reuter's (1983) speculation that upper-level dealers are fairly unconcerned with reputation and only rarely exchange information about each other's reputation. Redlinger (1975), however, has also cited variations in dealing styles and security practices as important contingencies of doing business.

3. In describing indices by which dealers were stratified, Blum et al. (1972) also mentioned reliability, competence in avoiding arrest, and money making success.

4. Hayano (1982:106) considered this one of the three pivotal factors affecting whether professional poker players became losers or winners.

5. Langer's (1977) respondents also shared the belief that due to police ineptitude, people generally only got busted when they broke the commonly known "rules."

7. DEALING CAREERS

1. This was similar to the type of relationship which existed between the call girls and pimps Bryan (1965) studied.

2. After five years, one former member of a smuggling crew still held in awe the smuggler who brought him into the drug world and taught him the business, doing favors for his old boss that no one else would, despite the fact that this man's reputation in the community had plummeted.

3. The exception to this was when lower-level dealers rose on the coattails of their suppliers: as dealers increased the volume of their purchases and sales, some of their customers followed suit.

4. While other studies of drug dealing have also noted that participants did not maintain an uninterrupted stream of career involvement (Blum et al. 1972; Carey 1968; Lieb and Olson 1976; Waldorf et al. 1977), none have isolated or described their career patterns as oscillating.

5. Other sociologists have also noted the difficulty in quitting deviance (Allen 1977; Carey 1968; Harris 1973; Irwin 1970; Livingston 1974; Lofland 1969; Ray 1961; Shover 1983; Stebbins 1971).

6. At this point, I must note a limitation to my data. Many of the dealers

and smugglers I observed simply "disappeared" from the scene and were never heard from again. I therefore have no way of knowing if they phased out (voluntarily or involuntarily), shifted to another scene, or were killed in some remote place. I cannot, therefore, attempt to estimate accurately the number of people who left the Southwest County drug scene via each of the routes I present here.

7. Blum et al. (1972) therefore refer to it as a "transitional" career, noting that most active dealers they interviewed had considered quitting, while most inactive dealers were considering resuming their involvement. Lieb and Olson (1976) noted the prevalence of periodic phase-outs at critical transition points throughout dealers' careers. The dealers they studied did this intentionally, so that they could get away to reassess the scene and then either drop out or reenter.

8. Thompson (1983) has described the "financial trap" which held assembly-line workers at a beef processing plant to their job despite its monotony, danger, and hard physical work. Because of its high pay scale and occupational culture of immediate material gratification, workers consistently fell into a pattern of buying expensive items on the installment plan. They then became trapped into remaining at this job because its high remuneration was the only way they could afford repayment. Drug traffickers represent an illicit variation of this pattern.

8. TOWARD AN EXISTENTIAL PERSPECTIVE ON DRUG TRAFFICKING

1. In this analysis, I draw on the typology of deviant organizations offered by Best and Luckenbill 1982.

2. For examples of this perspective, see Bryan 1965, 1966; Bryant 1974; Cressey 1953; Einstadter 1969; Heyl 1979; Hong and Duff 1977; Klockars 1974; Letkemann 1973; Maurer 1940, 1964; Miller 1978; Plate, 1975; Polsky 1969; Shaw 1930; Shover 1972; Skipper and McCaghy 1970; Sutherland 1937.

9. DEVIANT CAREERS AND REINTEGRATION

1. Previous studies of existing deviant careers have already identified age-related, structural, and social psychological variables as the prime factors driving most individuals to abandon their alternative lifestyles and careers (cf. Adler and Adler 1983; Frazier 1976; Inciardi 1975; Irwin 1970; Meisenhelder 1977; Petersilia 1980; Shover 1983).

10. LAW ENFORCEMENT, DRUG TRAFFICKING, AND DRUG POLICY

1. Nearly one-third of the marijuana consumed in this country is now grown domestically, despite well-publicized efforts to eradicate American cultivation.

2. In fact, cocaine is a Schedule II drug compared to the higher ranking of

marijuana, which falls into the category of Schedule I. This signifies that, according to governmental assessment, while both drugs have a high potential for abuse, cocaine has a more currently accepted medical use than marijuana.

3. This includes a heavy financial price tag, a problematic distinction between socially sanctioned and socially permitted drugs, a discrimination against minority groups, a funneling of inner-city youth into the illegitimate economy, an erosion of civil liberties and relations with foreign countries, and a futile struggle against the pursuit of pleasurable altered states.

REFERENCES

Adler, Patricia A., and Peter Adler. 1978. "Tinydopers: a case study of deviant socialization." *Symbolic Interaction* 1:90–105.
—— 1980. "The irony of secrecy in the drug world." *Urban Life* 8:447–65.
—— 1983. "Shifts and oscillations in deviant careers: the case of upper-level drug dealers and smugglers." *Social Problems* 31:195–207.
—— 1987. *Membership Roles in Field Research.* Beverly Hills, Calif.: Sage.
Anonymous. 1969. "On selling marijuana." In Erich Goode, ed., *Marijuana,* pp. 92–102. New York: Atherton.
Atkyns, Robert L., and Gerhard J. Hanneman. 1974. "Illicit drug distribution and dealer communication behavior." *Journal of Health and Social Behavior* 15:36–43.
Bachman, J. G., L. D. Johnston, and P. M. O'Malley. 1987. *Monitoring the Future: Questionnaire Responses from the Nation's High School Seniors.* Ann Arbor: University of Michigan Institute for Social Research.
Becker, Howard. 1960. "Notes on the concept of commitment." *American Journal of Sociology* 66:32–42.
—— 1963. *Outsiders.* New York: Free Press.
Becker, Howard, and James Carper. 1956. "The development of identification with an occupation." *American Journal of Sociology* 61:289–98.
Bell, Daniel. 1953. "Crime as an American way of life." *Antioch Review* 13:131–54.
Best, Joel, and David F. Luckenbill. 1982. *Organizing Deviance.* Englewood Cliffs, N.J.: Prentice-Hall.
Biernacki, Patrick, and Dan Waldorf. 1981. "Snowball sampling." *Sociological Methods and Research* 10:141–63.
Birenbaum, Arnold. 1970. "On managing a courtesy stigma." *Journal of Health and Social Behavior* 11:196–206.
Blau, Peter. 1964. *Exchange and Power in Social Life.* New York: Wiley.
Blum, Richard H., et al. 1972. *The Dream Sellers.* San Francisco: Jossey-Bass.
Blumer, Herbert. 1969. *Symbolic Interactionism.* Englewood Cliffs, N.J.: Prentice-Hall.
Bourgois, Phillipe. 1989. "In search of Horatio Alger: culture and ideology in the crack economy." *Contemporary Drug Problems* 16(4):619–49.
Braithwaite, John. 1989. *Crime, Shame and Reintegration.* Cambridge: Cambridge University Press.
Brown, J. David. 1991. "The professional ex-: an alternative for exiting the deviant career." *Sociological Quarterly* 32:219–30.
Bryan, James H. 1965. "Apprenticeships in prostitution." *Social Problems* 12:287–297.

—— 1966. "Occupational ideologies and individual attitudes of call girls." *Social Problems* 13:441–50.

Bryant, Clifton, ed. 1974. *Deviant Behavior.* Chicago: Rand McNally.

Burfoot, Jean. 1984. "The fun seeking movement in California." In Eileen Barker, ed., *Of Gods and Men: New Religious Movements in the West,* pp. 147–64. Macon, Ga.: Mercer University Press.

Cameron, Mary Owen. 1964. *The Booster and the Snitch.* New York: Free Press.

Carey, James T. 1968. *The College Drug Scene.* Englewood Cliffs, N.J.: Prentice-Hall.

Carey, James T. 1972. "Problems of access and risk in observing drug scenes." In Jack D. Douglas, ed., *Research on Deviance,* pp. 71–92. New York: Random House.

Cavan, Sherri. 1970. "The hippie ethic and the spirit of drug use." In Jack D. Douglas, ed., *Observations of Deviance,* pp. 314–26. New York: Random House.

Chambliss, William J. 1984. *Harry King: A Professional Thief's Journey.* New York: Wiley.

Cloward, Richard A., and Lloyd E. Ohlin. 1960. *Delinquency and Opportunity.* New York: Free Press.

Cohen, Albert K. 1955. *Delinquent Boys.* Glencoe, Ill.: Free Press.

Cressey, Donald R. 1953. *Other People's Money.* Glencoe, Ill.: Free Press.

—— 1969. *Theft of the Nation.* New York: Harper and Row.

Cummins, Marvin, et al. 1972. *Report of the Student Task Force on Heroin Use in Metropolitan Saint Louis.* Saint Louis: Washington University Social Science Institute.

Della Cava, F. A. 1975. "Becoming an ex-priest: the process of leaving a high commitment status." *Sociological Inquiry* 45:41–49.

Douglas, Jack D. 1971. *American Social Order.* New York: Free Press.

—— 1972. "Observing deviance." In Jack D. Douglas, ed., *Research on Deviance,* pp. 3–34. New York: Random House.

—— 1976. *Investigative Social Research.* Beverly Hills, Calif.: Sage.

—— 1977a. "Existential sociology." In Jack D. Douglas and John M. Johnson, eds., *Existential Sociology,* pp. 3–73. New York: Cambridge University Press.

—— 1977b. "Shame and deceit in creative deviance." In Edward Sagarin, ed., *Deviance and Social Change,* pp. 59–86. Beverly Hills, Calif.: Sage.

Douglas, Jack D., and John M. Johnson, eds., 1977. *Existential Sociology.* New York: Cambridge University Press.

Douglas, Jack D., and Frances Waksler. 1982. *The Sociology of Deviance.* Boston: Little, Brown.

Ebaugh, Helen R. 1988. *Becoming an Ex.* Chicago: University of Chicago Press.

Einstadter, Werner J. 1969. "The social organization of armed robbery." *Social Problems* 17:64–83.

Fagan, Jeffrey. 1989. "The social organization of drug use and drug dealing among urban gangs." *Criminology* 27(4):633–67.

Fagan, Jeffrey, and Ko-Lin Chin. 1989. "Initiation into crack and cocaine: a tale of two epidemics." *Contemporary Drug Problems* 16(4):579–615.

Faupel, Charles E. 1991. *Shooting Dope: Career Patterns of Hard-Core Heroin Users.* Gainesville: University of Florida Press.

Fields, Allen. 1984. "Weedslingers: a study of young black marijuana dealers." *Urban Life* 13:247–70.

Flores, Estevan T. 1981. "Dealing in marijuana: an exploratory study." *Hispanic Journal of Behavioral Sciences* 3:199–211.

Frazier, Charles. 1976. *Theoretical Approaches to Deviance.* Columbus: Charles Merrill.

Fried, Joseph P. 1984. "Judge protects waiter's notes on fire inquiry." *New York Times*, April 8:47.

Gallmeier, Charles P. 1987. "Dinosaurs and prospects: toward a sociology of the compressed career." In K. M. Mahmoudi, B. W. Parlin, and M. E. Zusman, eds., *Sociological Inquiry: A Humanistic Perspective*, 4th ed., pp. 95–103. Dubuque, Ia.: Kendall-Hunt.

Geller, Allen, and Maxwell Boas. 1969. *The Drug Beat.* New York: McGraw-Hill.

Gerstein, Dean Robert. 1976. "The structure of heroin communities (in relation to methadone maintenance)." *American Journal of Drug and Alcohol Abuse* 3:571–87.

Gerth, H. H., and C. W. Mills, eds. 1946. *From Max Weber.* New York: Oxford University Press.

Gettman, J. 1989. "Decriminalizing marijuana." *American Behavioral Scientist* 32:243–48.

Ginsburg, Kenneth N. 1967. "The meat-rack." *American Journal of Psychotherapy* 2:170–85.

Glick, Ronald. 1990. "Survival, income, and status: drug dealing in the Chicago Puerto Rican community." In Ronald Glick and Joan Moore, eds., *Drugs in Hispanic Communities*, pp. 77–101. New Brunswick: Rutgers University Press.

Goddard, Donald. 1978. *Easy Money.* New York: Popular Library.

Goffman, Erving. 1963. *Stigma.* Englewood Cliffs, N.J.: Prentice-Hall.

Gold, Raymond. 1958. "Roles in sociological field observations." *Social Forces* 36:217–23.

Gooberman, Lawrence A. 1974. *Operation Intercept: The Multiple Consequences of Public Policy.* New York: Pergamon.

Goode, Erich. 1970. *The Marijuana Smokers.* New York: Basic.

—— 1972. *Drugs in American Society.* New York: Knopf.

Gouldner, Helen P. 1960. "Dimensions of organizational commitment." *Administrative Science Quarterly* 4:468–90.

Grinspoon, Lester, and James B. Bakalar. 1976. *Cocaine.* New York: Basic.

Hall, Jerome. 1952. *Theft, Law and Society.* 2d ed. Indianapolis: Bobbs-Merrill.

Hamid, Ansley. 1990. "The political economy of crack-related violence." *Contemporary Drug Problems* 17(1):31–78.

—— 1991. "From ganja to crack: Caribbean participation in the underground economy in Brooklyn." *International Journal of the Addictions* 26(6):615–28.

Harris, Mervyn. 1974. *The Dilly Boys.* Rockville, Md.: New Perspectives.

Hayano, David. 1982. *Poker Faces.* Berkeley: University of California Press.

Henslin, James M. 1972. "Studying deviances in four settings: research experiences with cabbies, suicides, drug users and abortionees." In Jack D. Douglas, ed., *Research on Deviance,* pp. 35–70. New York: Random House.

Heyl, Barbara Sherman. 1979. *The Madam as Entrepreneur.* New Brunswick, N.J.: Transaction.

Higgins, Paul C., and Richard R. Butler. 1982. *Understanding Deviance.* New York: McGraw-Hill.

Hindelang, Michael J. 1971. "Bookies and bookmaking." *Crime and Delinquency* 17:245–55.

Hoffman, Joan E. 1980. "Problems of access in the study of social elites and boards of directors." In William B. Shaffir, Robert A. Stebbins, and Allan Turowetz, eds., *Fieldwork Experience,* pp. 45–56. New York: St. Martin's.

Homans, George. 1950. *The Human Group.* New York: Harcourt.

Hong, Lawrence K., and Robert W. Duff. 1977. "Becoming a taxi-dancer: the significance of neutralization in a semi-deviant occupation." *Sociology of Work and Occupations* 4:327–42.

Hughes, Everett C. 1945. "Dilemmas and Contradictions in Status." *American Journal of Sociology* 50:353–59.

Humphreys, Laud. 1970. *Tearoom Trade.* Chicago: Aldine.

Hunt, Dana. 1987. *Crack.* New York: Narcotic and Drug Research, Inc.

Huntington, Mary Jean. 1957. "The development of a professional self-image." In Robert Merton, George Reader, and Patricia Kendall, eds., *The Student Physician,* pp. 179–88. Cambridge: Harvard University Press.

Ianni, Frances A. 1972. *A Family Business.* New York: Russell Sage.

Inciardi, James A. 1975. *Careers in Crime.* Chicago: Rand McNally.

Irwin, John. 1970. *The Felon.* Englewood Cliffs, N.J.: Prentice-Hall.

Jackson, Bruce. 1972. *Outside the Law.* New Brunswick, N.J.: Transaction.

Johnson, Bruce D. 1973. *Marijuana Users and Drug Subcultures.* New York: Wiley.

Johnson, Bruce, Ansley Manid, Edmundo Morales, and Harry Sanabria. 1987. "Critical dimensions of crack distribution." Paper presented at the 1987 annual meeting of the American Society of Criminology, Montreal, Quebec.

Johnson, John M. 1975. *Doing Field Research.* New York: Free Press.

Johnston, L. D., P. M. O'Malley, and J. G. Bachman. 1986. *Drug Use Among American High School Students, College Students, and Other Young Adults, Na-*

tional Trends Through 1985. Rockville, Md.: National Institute on Drug Abuse.

Kamstra, John. 1974. *Weed*. New York: Bantam.

Kaplan, Howard. 1980. *Deviance in Defense of Self*. New York: Academic Press.

Karp, David A. 1973. "Hiding in pornographic bookstores." *Urban Life and Culture* 1:427–51.

Kelman, H. C. 1958. "Compliance, identification and internalization: three processes of attitude change." *Journal of Conflict Resolution* 2:51–60.

Kirby, Richard, and Jay Corzine. 1981. "The contagion of stigma." *Qualitative Sociology* 4:3–20.

Klein, Malcolm, Cheryl Maxson, and Lea Cunningham. 1988. "Gang involvement in cocaine rock trafficking." Paper presented at the annual meeting of the American Society of Criminology, Chicago.

Klockars, Carl B. 1974. *The Professional Fence*. New York: Free Press.

—— 1977. "Field ethics for the life history." In Robert Weppner, ed., *Street Ethnography*, pp. 201–26. Beverly Hills, Calif.: Sage.

—— 1979. "Dirty hands and deviant subjects." In Carl B. Klockars and Finnbarr W. O'Connor, eds., *Deviance and Decency*, pp. 261–82. Beverly Hills, Calif.: Sage.

Kotarba, Joseph A., and Andrea Fontana, eds. 1984. *The Existential Self in Society*. Chicago: University of Chicago Press.

Lang, John. 1981. "Marijuana: a U.S. farm crop that's booming." *U.S. News and World Report*, October 12:63–64.

Langer, John. 1976. "Dealing culture: the rationalization of the 'hang-loose' ethic." *Australian and New Zealand Journal of Sociology* 12:82–90.

—— 1977. "Drug entrepreneurs and dealing culture." *Social Problems* 24:377–85.

Lemert, Edwin. 1962. "Paranoia and the dynamics of exclusion." *Sociometry* 25:2–20.

Lesieur, Henry R. 1977. *The Chase*. Garden City, N.Y.: Anchor.

Letkemann, Peter. 1973. *Crime as Work*. Englewood Cliffs, N.J.: Prentice-Hall.

Lieb, John, and Sheldon Olson. 1976. "Prestige, paranoia and profit: on becoming a dealer of illicit drugs in a university community." *Journal of Drug Issues*, 6:356–69.

Liebow, Elliot. 1967. *Tally's Corner*. Boston: Little, Brown.

Livingston, Jay. 1974. *Compulsive Gamblers*. New York: Harper and Row.

Lloyd, Robin. 1976. *For Money or Love*. New York: Vanguard.

Lofland, John. 1969. *Deviance and Identity*. Englewood Cliffs, N.J.: Prentice-Hall.

Luckenbill, David F., and Joel Best. 1981. "Careers in deviance and respectability: the analogy's limitations." *Social Problems* 29:197–206.

Lyman, Stanford. 1978. *The Seven Deadly Sins*. New York: St. Martin's.

McAuliffe, W., and R. A. Gordon. 1974. "A test of Lindesmith's theory of addiction: the frequency of euphoria among long-term addicts." *American Journal of Sociology* 79:795–840.

McCall, Michal. 1980. "Who and where are the artists?" In William B. Shaffir, Robert A. Stebbins, and Allan Turowetz, eds., *Fieldwork Experience*, pp. 145–158. New York: St. Martin's.

McCoy, Alfred W. 1972. *The Politics of Heroin in Southeast Asia*. New York: Harper and Row.

McDonnell, Douglas, Jeanette Irwin, and Marsha Rosenbaum. 1990. "Hop and Hubbas." *Contemporary Drug Problems* 17(1):145–56.

McIntosh, Mary. 1973. "The growth of racketeering." *Economy and Society* 2:35–60.

McNicoll, Andrew. 1983. *Drug Trafficking: A North-South Perspective*. Ottawa, Canada: The North-South Institute.

Mandel, Jerry. 1967. "Myths and realities of marijuana pushing." In Jerry L. Simmons, ed., *Marijuana: Myths and Realities*, pp. 58–110. North Hollywood, Calif.: Brandon.

Manning, Peter K. 1977. *Police Work*. Cambridge, Mass.: MIT Press.

—— 1980. *Narc's Game*. Cambridge, Mass.: MIT Press.

Manning, Peter K., and Lawrence J. Redlinger. 1983. "Drugs as work." In Ida H. Simpson and Richard L. Simpson, eds., *Research in the Sociology of Work*, 2:275–301. Greenwich, Conn.: JAI Press.

Martin, Richard T. 1970. "The role of coca in the history, religion, and medicine of South American Indians." *Economic Botany* 24:422–38.

Matza, David. 1964. *Delinquency and Drift*. New York: Wiley.

Maurer, David W. 1940. *The Big Con*. Indianapolis: Bobbs-Merrill.

—— 1964. *Whiz Mob*. New Haven: College and University Press. [First published in 1955].

—— 1974. *The American Confidence Man*. Springfield, Ill.: Charles Thomas.

Meisenhelder, Thomas. 1977. "An exploratory study of exiting from criminal careers." *Criminology* 15:319–34.

Merton, Robert K. 1938. "Social structure and anomie." *American Sociological Review* 3:672–82.

Mieczkowski, Tom. 1989. *The Detroit Crack Ethnography Project*. Report to the Bureau of Justice Assistance, Contract OJP-88-M-39J.

—— 1990. "Crack distribution in Detroit." *Contemporary Drug Problems* 17(1):9–30.

Miller, Gale. 1978. *Odd Jobs*. Englewood Cliffs, N.J.: Prentice-Hall.

Miller, Gale, and George Ritzer. 1977. "Informal socialization: deviant occupations." In George Ritzer, *Working*, 2d ed., pp. 83–94. Englewood Cliffs, N.J.: Prentice-Hall.

Miller, Walter B. 1958. "Lower class culture as a generating milieu of gang delinquency." *Journal of Social Issues* 14:5–19.

Moore, Mark H. 1977. *Buy and Bust*. Lexington, Mass.: Lexington Books.

Morales, Edmundo. 1989. *Cocaine: White Gold Rush in Peru.* Tucson: University of Arizona Press.

Morganthau, Tom, with Erik Calonius, Shawn Doherty, David L. Gonzalez, Michael Lerner, Peter McKillop, Mark Miller, Patrick Rogers, and Richard Sandza. 1989. "Cocaine's dirty 300: how the Colombian drug cartels operate their sophisticated, $5 billion drug business in America." *Newsweek* November 13:36–40.

Morley, Jefferson. 1989. "Contradictions of cocaine capitalism." *The Nation* October 2:341–47.

Mouledoux, James. 1972. "Ideological aspects of drug dealership." In Ken Westhues, ed., *Society's Shadow,* pp. 110–22. Toronto: McGraw-Hill, Ryerson.

Nadelmann, Ethan. 1988a. "U.S. drug policy: a bad export." *Foreign Policy* 70:83–108.

—— 1988b. "The case for legalization." *The Public Interest* 92:3–65.

National Commission on Marijuana and Drug Abuse. 1972. *Marijuana: A Signal of Misunderstanding.* Washington, D.C.: U.S. Government Printing Office.

National Narcotics Intelligence Consumers Committee. 1981. *Narcotics Intelligence Estimate, 1978.* Washington, D.C.: U.S. Government Printing Office.

Newsweek. 1983. "Drugs and the high life." May 30:48.

Newsweek. 1988. "The drug gangs." March 28.

Nieves, Alvar L. 1978. "Some further notes on the concept of commitment." Paper presented at the annual meeting of the Pacific Sociological Association.

Olden, Mark. 1973. *Cocaine.* New York: New American Library.

Petersilia, Joan. 1980. "Criminal career research: a review of recent evidence." In N. Morris and M. Tonry, eds., *Crime and Justice: An Annual Review of Research,* vol. 2, pp. 321–79. Chicago: University of Chicago Press.

Phillips, J., and R. Wayne. 1980. *Cocaine: The Mystique and the Reality.* New York: Avon.

Plate, Thomas. 1975. *Crime Pays!* New York: Simon and Schuster.

Polsky, Ned. 1969. *Hustlers, Beats, and Others.* New York: Doubleday.

Preble, Edward, and John J. Casey. 1969. "Taking care of business: the heroin user's life on the street." *International Journal of the Addictions* 4:1–24.

President's Commission on Law Enforcement and Administration of Justice. 1967. *Task Force Report: Organized Crime.* Washington, D.C.: U.S. Government Printing Office.

President's Commission on Organized Crime. 1986. *America's Habit: Drug Abuse, Drug Trafficking, and Organized Crime.* Washington, D.C.: U.S. Government Printing Office.

Prus, Robert C., and C. R. D. Sharper. 1977. *Road Hustler.* Lexington: Lexington Books.

Rabaj, Seraffin, and Victor Campos. 1980. "Profiles of the problems of coca in Bolivia." In F. R. Jeri, ed., *Cocaine 1980. Proceedings of the Interamerican Seminar on Medical and Sociological Aspects of Coca and Cocaine*, pp. 154–58. Lima, Peru: Pacific Press.

Rains, Prue. 1982. "Deviant careers." In Michael Rosenberg, Robert A. Stebbins, and Allan Turowetz, eds., *The Sociology of Deviance*, pp. 21–41. New York: St. Martin's.

Rainwater, Lee R., and David J. Pittman. 1967. "Ethical problems in studying a politically sensitive and deviant community." *Social Problems* 14:357–66.

Ramirez, Rubin H. 1980. "Coca production in Peru." In F. R. Jeri, ed., *Cocaine 1980. Proceedings of the Interamerican Seminar on Medical and Sociological Aspects of Coca and Cocaine*, pp. 191–95. Lima, Peru: Pacific Press.

Ray, Marsh. 1961. "The cycle of abstinence and relapse among heroin addicts." *Social Problems* 9:132–40.

Redlinger, Lawrence J. 1969. "Dealing in dope: market mechanisms and distribution patterns of illicit narcotics." Ph.D. diss., Northwestern University.

—— 1975. "Marketing and distributing heroin." *Journal of Psychedelic Drugs* 7:331–53.

Reinarman, C., and G. Levine. 1989. "Crack in context: politics and media in the making of a drug scare." *Contemporary Drug Problems* 16:535–77.

Reiss, S., with M. Miller, D. Farah, and M. Smith. 1990. "Adios to the Andean strategy?" *Newsweek* September 10:32.

Reuter, Peter. 1983. *Disorganized Crime*. Cambridge, Mass.: MIT Press.

Reuter, Peter, and John Haaga. 1989. *The Organization of High-Level Drug Markets: An Exploratory Study*. Santa Monica, Calif.: Rand Corporation.

Reuter, Peter, Robert MacCoun, and Patrick Murphy. 1990. *Money From Crime*. Santa Monica, Calif.: Rand Corporation.

Rice, Berkeley. 1989. *Trafficking*. New York; St. Martin's.

Riemer, Jeffrey W. 1977. "Varieties of opportunistic research." *Urban life* 5:467–77.

—— 1979. *Hard Hats*. Beverly Hills, Calif.: Sage.

Rochford, E. Burke Jr., 1985. *Hare Krishna in America*. New Brunswick, N.J.: Rutgers University Press.

Roebuck, Julian, and Wolfgang Frese. 1976. *The Rendezvous*. New York: Free Press.

Rosenbaum, Marsha. 1981. *Women on Heroin*. New Brunswick, N.J.: Rutgers University Press.

Rosenbaum, M., P. Morgan, J. Beck, D. Harlow, D. McDonnell, and L. Watson. 1989. "Exploring ecstasy: a descriptive study of MDMA users." Final Report to the National Institute of Drug Abuse.

Sabbag, Robert. 1976. *Snow Blind*. New York: Avon.

Scandale, Frank. 1991. "Cocaine quietly finds fresh turf." *Denver Post* May 20:1A, 10A.

Schutz, Alfred. 1962. *Collected Papers I and II.* The Hague, The Netherlands: Martinus Nijhoff.

Scott, Marvin B., and Stanford Lyman. 1968. "Accounts." *American Sociological Review* 33:46–62.

Shaw, Clifford. 1930. *The Jack-Roller.* Chicago: University of Chicago Press.

Sheldon, Mary. 1970. "Investments and involvements as mechanisms producing commitment to the organization." *Administrative Science Quarterly* 15:473–81.

Shover, Neal. 1972. "Structures and careers in burglary." *The Journal of Criminal Law, Criminology, and Police Science* 63:540–49.

—— 1983. "The later stages of ordinary property offender careers." *Social Problems* 31:208–18.

—— 1985. *Aging Criminals.* Newbury Park, Calif.: Sage.

Siegel, Ronald K. 1982. "History of cocaine smoking." *Journal of Psychoactive Drugs* 14:277–99.

Skipper, James K., and Charles H. McCaghy. 1970. "Stripteasers: the anatomy and career contingencies of a deviant occupation." *Social Problems* 17:391–405.

Smith, Adam. 1937. *The Wealth of Nations.* New York: Modern Library.

Snodgrass, John. 1982. *The Jack-Roller at Seventy: A Fifty-Year Follow-Up.* Lexington, Mass.: Lexington Books.

Soref, Michael J. 1981. "The structure of illicit drug markets." *Urban Life* 10:329–52.

Stebbins, Robert A. 1970. "Career: the subjective approach." *Sociological Quarterly* 11:32–49.

Suchman, Edward A. 1968. "The 'hang-loose' ethic and the spirit of drug use." *Journal of Health and Social Behavior* 9:146–55.

Sundholm, Charles A. 1973. "The pornographic arcade." *Urban Life and Culture* 2:85–104.

Sutherland, Edwin H. 1937. *The Professional Thief.* Chicago: University of Chicago Press.

Sykes, Gresham. 1972. "The future of criminality." *American Behavioral Scientist* 15:403–19.

Sykes, Gresham, and David Matza. 1957. "Techniques of neutralization: a theory of delinquency." *American Sociological Review* 22:664–70.

Tannenbaum, Frank. 1938. *Crime and the Community.* Boston: Ginn.

Thompson, William E. 1983. "Hanging tongues: a sociological encounter with the assembly line." *Qualitative Sociology* 6:215–37.

Thrasher, Frederic M. 1963. *The Gang.* Abridged ed. Chicago: University of Chicago Press.

Treaster, J. B. 1990. "Cocaine users adding heroin to their menus." *New York Times* July 21:1, 26.

Turner, Ralph H. 1976. "The real self: from institution to impulse." *American Journal of Sociology* 81:989–1016.

U.S. Congress. Senate. 1951. *Crime Committee Report.* Special Committee to Investigate Organized Crime in Interstate Commerce. 82d Congress, 1st sess., Senate Report no. 307. Washington, D.C.: U.S. Government Printing Office.

—— 1965. *Report of the Committee on Government Operations.* Permanent Subcommittee on Investigations. Washington, D.C.: U.S. Government Printing Office.

Waldman, Steven, and Mark Miller, with Michael A. Lerner, and Peter McKillop. 1989. "The drug lawyers." *Newsweek* November 13:41–44.

Waldorf, Dan. 1993. "Natural recovery from opiate addiction: some social-psychological processes of untreated recovery." *Journal of Drug Issues* 13(2):237–80.

Waldorf, Dan, et al. 1977. *Doing Coke: An Ethnography of Cocaine Users and Sellers.* Washington, D.C.: Drug Abuse Council.

Waldorf, Dan, Craig Renarman and Sheigla Murphy. 1991. *Cocaine Changes.* Philadelphia: Temple University Press.

Waller, D., with M. Miller, J. Barry, and S. Reiss. 1900. "Risky business." *Newsweek* July 16:16–19.

Walsh, Marilyn E. 1977. *The Fence.* Westport, Conn.: Greenwood.

Warren, Carol A. B., and Paul K. Rasmussen. 1977. "Sex and gender in field research." *Urban Life* 6:349–69.

Wax, Rosalie. 1952. "Reciprocity as a field technique." *Human Organization* 11:34–37.

—— 1957. "Twelve years later: an analysis of a field experience." *American Journal of Sociology* 63:133–42.

Wedow, Suzanne. 1979. "Feeling paranoia: the organization of an ideology." *Urban Life* 8:72–93.

West, W. Gordon. 1980. "Access to adolescent deviants and deviance." In William B. Shaffir, Robert A. Stebbins, and Allan Turowetz, eds., *Fieldwork Experience* pp. 31–44. New York: St. Martin's.

Whyte, William F. 1955. *Street Corner Society.* Chicago: University of Chicago Press.

Williams, Terry. 1989. *The Cocaine Kids.* Reading, Mass.: Addison-Wesley.

Wilson, James Q. 1975. *Thinking About Crime.* New York: Basic.

Wisotsky, Steven. 1990. *Beyond the War on Drugs.* Buffalo, N.Y.: Prometheus Books.

Woodley, Richard A. 1971. *Dealer: Portrait of a Cocaine Merchant.* New York: Holt, Rinehart, and Winston.

Yepez, Samuel, and Luis Toledo. 1980. "Police experience in the scope of prevention and education (Peru)." In F. R. Jeri, ed., *Cocaine 1980. Proceedings of the Interamerican Seminar on Medical and Sociological Aspects of Coca and Cocaine,* pp. 191–95. Lima, Peru: Pacific Press.

INDEX